CLASS PORN

Molly Hite

In her statements – at least where she dares to speak out –
woman retouches herself constantly.

Luce Irigaray

I figure this is one of those things you have to ease into very slowly. No rush, take your time, move around a little, no sense *forcing* things. Feel out the terrain, as it were.

Beginning with the tits, for instance, which is where they generally begin. They're very, ah, *into* tits, grab her there she'll follow you anywhere. Erogenous zones.

Except that tits isn't quite it, not the word I want, too pointy, like those Barbie Dolls that come preshaped for the kind of bra my mother always got me, cone-chested. Nipples like bullets if they had any nipples which of course they don't. Actually it must be frustrating to have a doll with tits but no nipples, the lure presumably being surrogate cleavage but I you eliminate the nipples there's no point in taking the bra *off*, which is in turn the point of cleavage. Also, you'd probably figure that the doll had it right and you were the one with abnormal knobs on your front like a mutant TV. I can imagine growing up believing you're not supposed to have nipples. It wouldn't be all that strange considering the other things you're not supposed to have. God only knows what will come of bringing hard plastic paradigms into the picture.

At any rate, tits is the wrong word and probably accounts for a great deal of the confusion you encounter when you try to make erotic chat in a mixed gathering. What we have here are breasts. Pliant, spongy even, faintly reminiscent of water balloons. Breasts. Gleaming whitely in the, ah, sunlight. Alabaster. *Her alabaster breasts, right.*

Um, bounced. No. Nope nope nope: no bouncing. Her stately alabaster breasts. No. Her firm alabaster breasts, her firm but not at all hard ditto, not as hard as you might imagine despite their being alabaster.

I have researched this topic, standing by the newsstand reading *Playboy* and eating M and M's at eight in the morning, before classes start. I can claim some acquaintance with the conventions. Conventions only take you so far, of course, but at least they're there: I'm not just winging it. I like to feel I'm working in a tradition.

So. *Her alabaster breasts*, all right, sometimes they have faint blue veins like Carrara marble. Mine don't, they have freckles, write about what you know. Her attractively freckled alabaster breasts, no, *her alabaster breasts*.

Sprang – *no* they didn't, flopped, no, tensed, no, yearned skyward. No.

Not a lot of *action* in these, ah, breasts, really more sedentary decorous placid inert. Like water balloons. But important nonetheless, make no mistake, given the conventions. I have been given the conventions, up to a point. For example, Mr. Errol Flynn in his autobiography provocatively titled *My Wicked, Wicked Ways* reports that his ladies, *his* ladies, always removed the bra last. After the panties. I was sixteen when I read this in the back room of the downtown library in Salina and it confused me. It still confuses me. The priorities.

Her alabaster breasts reached out and grabbed his gun. His rapier. His nail file. They turned their nipples in his direction. They just sat there looking smug. They hummed a little tune. He was overwhelmed.

Yes, well, there it is or there you are or she is, breasts exposed, man watching. He looks, she exposes. Then he exposes. No. He doesn't, he can't, they won't let him; she's in charge here and no one else gets to exhibit without permission. Funny how they spend all that time looking and then at the crucial moment what they want to do is *show* you something. Zip it up, that's right. So here she is: dauntlessly she faced him, breasts alert, eyes aglow, dauntlessly alert breasts, smoldering eyes. He's crazy for her, you can see that even zipped up. She could care less. Sans souci or insouciant, depending on how, ah, *cosmopolitan* you want to make this, insouciantly wiggling her breasts at him, flexing them athletically in his direction, blowing little kisses with them, come *on* arching her back lithely supplely willowy in such a way that her insouciant breasts were thrust in the direction of his questing fingers. Which were about twenty feet from her insouciant breasts actually because there was a deep chasm separating the two of them what you might call a chasm of unfulfilled desire. Metaphor. Or moat. No matter how his questing fingers yearned for her insouciant breasts there was this terrible chasm, or moat, between them. It was very deep, over his head, and he couldn't swim and anyway there were alligators. She could swim but didn't want to. Also they were her alligators.

The telephone is ringing in the bedroom.

I pick it up in the middle of the second ring. I could have picked it up on the first ring, skidding down the hall and around the corner in Frank's yellowing sweatsocks, but that might have seemed too eager. On the other hand, after the second ring the Pakistani graduate student will pick it up. He always gives me first refusal but if I don't get there in two rings he co-opts the conversation and it's hard getting him off the line. I keep telling myself it's a language things or a culture thing, and of course he's incredibly lonely which doesn't make me any more comfortable, but still I get upset when he invites people over. My students usually; they're the only ones that call. Jo Michaelson a couple of times. She likes to talk with him about culture shock.

"Hello," I say, having timed it right.

"Miss, ah, Missus Nyland?"

"Yes," I say, not wanting to choose between them.

"Ah. I trust I haven't gotten you at an, ah, *inconvenient hour.*"

"No," I say. There is a little space here that I decide I'm supposed to fill, so I say, "I was just doing some writing." It sounds like Norford but I'm not absolutely certain, and Norford is the kind of person whose name you can't ask after a certain point.

"Writing!" he booms back at me so loudly that I get tinny echoes out of the receiver. "Well, then this *is* a bad time, isn't it?"

"No," I assure him. "I was just stopping. Taking a break."

"A break!" he booms again, echo effect. "Then perhaps if I'm very *brief*—"

"I'm in no hurry," I say after the silence has gone on too

long.

"I'd like to set up a file on you in the main office. So that the contract committee can review your, ah, record," Norford says while I nod vigorously and make little assenting noises with my lips pressed together. "Will that be all right?"

"Mm," I say.

"Fine then. Shall we go ahead and set up an appointment to discuss your status?"

"Status," I say.

"Your status in the department. We can wait till later to schedule it if you like, although I wouldn't advise—"

"Fine!" I cry. "Now will be fine."

"Aaaaah," says Norford, and there is a little flutter that probably means he is holding his memo book up against the receiver so I can get the full sensuous experience of how busy he is. Norford is always riffling through is memo book to find a time when he might be free for an hour or so, especially at depart-men-tal meetings when he's got everyone trapped in the conference room while he figures out when we can have our next depart-mental meeting. "Mm," he says now. "How about ten-thirty a week from Wednesday?"

One of my classes meets in that time slot. "I'm teaching," I say.

"Ah," says Norford. "Well." More shuffling. "How about eleven, then?"

"Eleven when?"

"A week from Wednesday."

Classes are an hour long. I figure he must be pushing on purpose, although god knows everyone is waiting for him to fall apart completely, go emeritus before he goes gaga, and maybe he's losing it right now, Sunday night, in the midst of my status. "Eleven-thirty?" I suggest, daring.

It's evident that I've seized too much initiative. "Mm," says Norford finally, "no, I'm afraid I'm not exactly, ah, *available* at eleven-thirty." This sounds like a reproach. Am I supposed to know about something going on at eleven-thirty a week from Wednesday? Another departmental meeting? Some guest lecturer? His *birthday*? "Friday," says Norford. "Friday afternoon might be just possible."

"Friday would be fine," I say. I don't teach on Fridays. Nobody in the English department teaches on Fridays except the graduate students who serve as teaching assistants, and since I tend to resemble them I'm very careful not to be around at that time. It's a matter of status, actually. Also I like to sleep in and then go to the IGA in the late afternoon on Fridays. It's generally the high point of my week.

"Fine," says Norford. "Well then, we'll just make it Friday, then, about one? One-*ish*?"

"Fine," I say.

"Well then, I shall see you." This has to be conclusive evidence that it's Norford. He always gets that shall business straight.

"I shall look forward to it," I say.

"Goodbye then. Ah."

"Yes," I say.

"Goodbye, then, *Mrs.* Nyland." He's decided on my title. I'm grateful, although I hadn't been wondering.

"Goodbye, Professor Norford," I say, managing finally to speak his name. I have trouble with names generally, even more trouble when they're names I ought to know for my own good. I don't know the names of any of my students except for the behavior problems. But Norford has already hung up, being a very busy man with doubtless a great deal of status to manipulate. Anyway he never lets you get the last word, even if it's a perfectly innocuous word.

I put down the receiver and turn up the radio that sits on the bureau next to the phone. I hardly ever turn it off these days, just down, so that something is going on under the silence. Right now Cher is singing *All I really want to do Is baby be friends with you.* Sometimes the DJ announces it as Sonny and Cher but as far as I know Cher is the only one singing on this cut. It's a little hard to tell because they sound a lot alike, although Sonny is usually raspier. I have the original, although I don't have a record player any more, Bob Dylan singing it himself or rather howling it, and sniggering helplessly on the lines *I ain't lookin' for you to see like me, Feel like me or be like me*. It's that *be like me* that cracks him up. Some girl probably yelled at him once, "You just want me to be like you," and now she's getting hers on the airwaves all over the country. I can imagine yelling something like that.

I listen to Cher making *doooo* into some sort of baroque turn where Dylan just yodeled. Frank used to say we were in the era of the non-singer, that it was part of our cultural neurosis. By non-singer he meant people like Dylan and Barry McGuire singing "Eve of Destruction" and Mick Jagger. He also had a category of people who sang but when they did it wasn't music. He wasn't down on all of it of course, he really *respected* Joan Baez and he was reserving judgment about Peter, Paul and Mary, but on the other hand he didn't have much sympathy for rock and roll, which he said was a watered-down sterilized version of the real stuff, you know by guys who've paid their *dues*? Like Howlin' Wolf and Muddy Waters and Blind Lemon Jefferson and oh, Bird and Trane and Ornette ad like that. "Little prick," I say out loud, having dis-covered from my two years in New York that while talking to yourself isn't exactly okay it's certainly done. The referent is amorphous. I actually have a couple of people in mind: it's an incantation of sorts. Cher fades out and gets supplanted by my favorite version of the Pepsi Generation song, the soul version, *Come ali-yi-yive*. I like it. I like almost everything on the radio these days, even the commercials. What are you, regressing to your adolescent, he's shouted at me, but I'm not regressing really, I never had an adolescence, I'm a late bloomer. If I am a bloomer.

Actually I was never the type to be an adolescent. My mother told me I was the classic type, so I wore pageboys, which never go out of style, and saddle oxfords with crew socks, which never go out of style, and pink lipstick and clear nail polish and maybe a little Vaseline on my eyelids when I had a date, which was never. The truth was that all these things went out of style shortly after my mother left college. My mother would look at the girls my own age wearing jeans in public, rolled up to show off the shape of their calves, of shirts so tight you could see the crack between their buttocks, and French-heeled shoes with sling backs and cut-outs, their hair rising into improbably smooth, glistening helmets with little fringe bangs and a bow where the bangs met the helmets, and my mother would shake her head and say she felt so sorry for those girls, they made themselves so unattractive. "Whereas you, Eleanor, have a perennial charm," she would say, rasping the back of my skirt to steer me past the windows of the Oriental Café were Juli and Teri and Marlene and Earline and Joni and Shari sat ruining their appetites and giggling with crowds of desirable boys. I hated my mother for this, but my hatred was complicated by the fact that I knew who it was they were all giggling at. I could take it, but she didn't have the wit to erect defenses. I also knew, although I didn't particularly want to think about it, that my mother was always hoping we would be taken for sisters. We probably did get taken for sisters, too: sisters my mother's age.

So I never knew any of the things you're supposed to pick up during adolescence, how you rat your hair to make it bulbous, what happens to your feet when you put them in those anti-orthopedic shoes, how you giggle with boys. With Frank I was always watching, checking: have I got it right, is this the way we do it? It never failed to surprise me that he thought I was a girl. I knew perfectly well I didn't have the training.

Sonny and Cher, both of them now, are singing, "I Got You, Babe," a cut currently getting a lot of air play, chorus done over an oboe, which somehow makes everything infinitely pathetic, as if without each other they'd have nobody, babe. Oboe notwithstanding, it's waltz time, fairly upbeat, so I skate sock-footed down the linoleum of the hall and into the study, also linoleum, thinking I don't got anybody, babe, or is it I don't got nobody: I'm always fighting the tight-assed logic of those double negatives. It doesn't help that during working hours I'm the tight-ass, that's what I'm for: now think about it Kevin, if you say you don't got no money you're saying you do have *some* money, you see?, Kevin, sullen, not having none of it. The problem is that I don't have the primary sources. I get my nonstandard dialect from the radio. I read books for experience. Write about what you know: alabaster breasts, lips slack with desire, mystic recesses, protuberant members. I read them all as the Supreme Court passes them down: *Lady Chatterley, Lolita, Tropic of Cancer,* even *Ulysses*, one of the truly unrewarding dirty books, when I was volunteer assistant at the downtown library in Salina. At home I read *Anne of Green Gables* and *Girl of the Limberlost* in copies that belonged to my mother. When Frank finally did it to me I said you just kept going in and out. I thought he would keep going further and further in and we'd get closer and closer in increasing increments of rapture and when he worked all the way in we'd both come: that was what I had figured out from my reading and, I supposed, from an overly literalistic construction of the word "screw." Luckily he wasn't paying much attention when I said that. I reworked my premises and when he speeded up I breathed yes, oh harder, oh my God, phrases also derived from books. It wasn't what I'd expected.

The finished papers are stacked at the upper left-hand corner of my desk, which used to be Frank's desk but wasn't worth moving. I mark them in green ink because according to the guide-lines for instructors in the Basic program red marks make students feel they're being judged. They *are* being judged, of course, but the general idea seems to be that if you use some other color they won't notice. As all my papers for this week are graded, there is no pile of papers in the lower right-hand corner, ready to hand so to speak as I am right-handed. Frank is left-handed, a sign of genius. He hardly ever writes anything on the papers he gets; once he said he was going to get a rubber stamp that said *BULLSHIT*, but he never got around to it. One of the things he really liked about me was the way I work through my essays, moving a page at a time from the pile on my lower right through the center of the desk, where I work it over – festooning the margins with minuscule green exclamations (*Your spelling is slipping, Kathi! Be sure to use that dictionary!*) – to my upper left, where it rests. He told me shortly after we started living together that I was the most anal retentive person he had ever met, which was as it turned out good, because he is anal expulsive and really fond of his own shit. Or maybe anal explosive. I tend to get these things wrong. I say sub-conscious, for instance, when Frank says I mean unconscious. He's strong on terms for what I mean. As the papers are all graded I can finally do something else. What I want to do, of course, is deal with the topless alabaster woman and the man who is watching.

This is more difficult than it sounds. Although what I have here is the basic *Playboy* situation, there really isn't a lot left to do with it since it's essentially a situation, not a plot: a tableau quivering with erotic promise but resisting development. While the accretive successes of *Playboy* have established that the well-dressed young man and the topless, billowing woman constitute a virtually archetypal painting (the man gazing and turning pages, the women on these pages expressing various degrees of wholesome lasciviousness) there is very little that can be added once the balance is achieved. Eros seems to lie in the tension rather than in its sweaty dissolution, which may be why he was always asking "Was it good for you?" as if there were some object that we held between us. I decided after a while that he was just using a formula, like How are you? Which used to baffle me: I'd stop everything and think oh, neurotic, paranoid, having difficulty getting out of bed, various ways that I in fact was. But then I worked out that the only answer to How are you? is Fine. Just as the only answer to Was it good for you? is Yes. I never felt it was appropriate to ask if it was good for him.

I consider briefly the possibility of having the man unzip his fly ad take out his, ah, thing while the woman puts her blouse back on and looks at him, but you can't fool around with the conventions like that, it's not titillating and too much like real life. Obviously the thing is to be looked *at*, otherwise it wouldn't mean anything my research in *Playboy* all those early mornings. I've thought about it and I'm not at all sure that I'd get out of the house that early to go look at pictures of naked men, much less men with their things out. Simple role-reversal doesn't do it. To be desired, that's the point. But not taken. Which was, of course, what Julie and Teri and Di and the rest of them were doing while I was being steered: they were holding out.

I never got to hold out on Frank, and he called me a cock-tease before I could explore the ramifications. Once he had indicated there were names for girls like me I gave in. I think I was a little comforted by the fact that I had finally fallen into a recognizable sexual category. But I suppose I've always wanted to

any question. Louise and I can dialogue for pretty much the whole class period while the others examine their fingers and nourish their resentment of Louise, who gets them off the hook.

Louise is in the uncomfortable position of actually being a Louise in an era when acceptable girls are named Julene and Marlene and Earline and Joan and Susan and Judy and Nancy and Diane, or more recently Joni, Suzi, Judi, Nanci, and Di, the Italianate i's in each case being dotted with a circle, a star, or even a little flower, which slows down penmanship considerably. Louise, who will never shorten her name to anything, wears harlequin glasses that glitter as she turns her head to watch me. She also wears skirts like no one else's, gathered bunchily at the waist but in some odd way tapered so as to be quite tight at the hemline. Her legs are bumpy, white and unstockinged. She wears brown orthopedic oxfords with white nylon ankle socks. The ankle socks are the final appalling touch, as far as I'm concerned, since even if somebody is making Louise dress this way I know that if she really wanted to she could ditch the socks somewhere on campus.

I've written on the board:
Brazil is best known for the following products:
There are three reasons for the delay:
I can tell you one thing and one thing only:
I have a question:
John knows what is holding up the committee:

The class is very quiet. Louise's glasses are opaque reflectors. Heads drop as my gaze sweeps over the room, as if royalty were passing.

"All right," I say, "can anyone tell me what these examples have in common?"

Louise is sitting very straight, almost smiling. It's early, the questions are still safe and can be farmed out to the less prepared. Louise comes in at the kill.

"Mark?"

"Ah," says Mark. He squints at the board. "Ahem," he says. He is sitting back in his chair with his legs out in front of him, crossed at the ankles. The back row is always boys and they always adopt a semi-reclining position, even when it isn't eight-thirty in the morning. "They all end with those two little dots," says Mark.

"Good!" I say, much too violently. Several students jerk awake. "Can you remember what those two little dots are called?" Mark is looking at his fingers.

"Joe?" I say

"Ahm," says Joe, who sits next to Mark.

"Anyone?" I cry gaily, my smile so broad it's pushing my ears back. Louise is smiling too, trying to catch my eye.

"It was your reading assignment for today," I say, knowing full well that they resent such reminders, consider them bad form. Louise is making little chickenlike movements with her head to attract my attention. "It's in Chapter Four," I say, concentrating on keeping my face unanguished as both shoulder muscles go into spasm. I don't know how to get around these occasions when they haven't done something they're supposed to have done. I've thought about it a lot. There were times when I asked other people how they handled such situations but they were always either scornful or incredulous, so now I only admit I have problems to Jo Michaelson, who also teaches Basic and collects disaster stories. I hadn't really anticipated so much unreceptiveness from my peers, but then we have a lot of charismatic teachers around her and you can only be so charismatic about colons. I didn't think I'd be blamed for that, but even Frank used to get cold and disapproving when I narrated some new mortification to him over dinner, and Frank used to be proud of being a lousy teacher. I think what changed was that he started getting students who couldn't charge him with statutory rape. Of course he stopped coming home for dinner at all shortly after that, so I never did get to put my finger on what it was he disapproved of.

"On page 52 in your book," I say. "How many of you have your books today?" There is a spotty show of hands, none of them from the back row, where they're getting slitty-eyed and restless. "Well, let's turn to page 52," I say, smiling maniacally now that I've gone and antagonized them. Love me, my face is pleading, I do it for your own good. "Those of you that haven't brought your

books   can   look   on   with   someone   else," I   say,
provoking a great scraping of chairs. I give them several minutes
to complete their various maneuvers and then say, "Okay, now
everybody tell me what those two little dots are called."

"Colons," drone three or four voices in unison. There is
an abrupt, startled snicker on my right. Nursing student, I decide.

"And what do colons do?"

There is a long silence. According to the book colons do
several different things. No one here is a speed reader.

Louise is fairly trembling. Now she has raised her hand,
straight up, not the languid, drooping raised hand of the more
adjusted students. Louise requires recognition, has earned it by
remembering something that isn't in the book.

"They   set   up   a   sense   of   expectation," she   says
breathlessly.

"That's right," I say, horribly relieved. I told them this last
Thursday, but that was four days ago and anyway no one ever
remembers what I say. I once overheard one of my students
telling another, "Oh, nothing happened today, she just talked."

Now I write on the board, *Colons set up a sense of
expectation*. As I write I can hear them pulling out notebooks,
fumbling for pens and pencils, borrowing from each other. When
I write it on the board you're supposed to copy it down: that's
another one of those behaviors, innate or learned. According to
the clock above the board I still have forty-five minutes to go.

"Now," I say, "can anyone tell me *how* in each of these
examples the colon sets up a sense of expectation?" They all look
at their hands again.

Louise waits for me after class. What Louise really wants
is to sit with me in the student union where everyone can see us
together, and to explain that while she's a terrible writer, really
terrible, she's actually very intelligent and sensitive. I know all
this because it has become the burden of Louise's weekly essays.
"It is my true belief that people put to much on outer appearance,"
Louise wrote last week. So far I've been able to get out of going to
the student union with Louise. What I really want to do now is go
to   the   student   union   by   myself,   buy   three   cardboard

containers of coffee, and take them back to my office in Schwindemann where I can drink them with my door closed and mull over what Norford called about last night. I've only begun to imagine the possibilities for humiliation that a meeting on the subject of my status in the department might entail. "I have just one question," says Louise, setting up a sense of expectation.

"Yes," I say, looking over Louise's shoulder. Like my students, I have a hard time looking directly at people who embarrass me. I have an uneasy sense of Louise lying awake nights thinking up questions complex enough to lure me into the student union.

"Which way are you going?" says Louise, too casually. "I was just going over to the Pub myself."

The Pub is the Putnam Union Building, strictly nonalcoholic. "I'm going in the other direction," I say, hoping I won't be held to it. In the other direction is University Boulevard, with its overpriced hamburger and doughnut shops catering to students.

"Well, I was wondering about how if colons set up a sense of expectation how that works with Dear Sir," says Louise. "Like in a business letter? Dear Sir. Colon."

"Yes," I say.

"Well, I was just wondering how that sets up a sense of expectation. I mean, do you expect the rest of the letter? Also times."

"Times," I say.

"Like in eight colon thirty," says Louise, looking miserable. "I was just wondering."

"Yes," I say, feeling suddenly guilty. "Yes, well those are very good questions. Very good questions. I haven't really thought about those things but I *think* maybe those are just conventions that don't have much to do with what I was saying about setting up a sense of expectation but don't hold me to that, I'll have to do some research before I can answer you one hundred per cent accurately." I'm still looking shiftily over her shoulder, partly because I think eye contact with Louise might be fatal and partly because I want to be sure no one in my department comes upon me in the middle of this disquisition.

Louise is radiant. "It's really neat to know somebody who

knows things like that," she says.

"That's what I'm for," I mumble, looking at my hands. "I mean professors, that's what professors are for. We're resource persons. People."

"That's a beautiful thing to say," says Louise.

"Yes," I say. "Well, I've got work to do. I'll let you know tomorrow." I execute a neat right turn on one hell and realize I'm striding off in the direction of the Pub after all. When I stop, Louise walks into me. "Forgot what I was doing," I mutter and then feel outraged that I'm explaining myself to my most craven student.

"Well, thanks for the help," Louise chirps. "It really helped."

"Mm," I say, turning down a corridor that leads to a fire door. I lean against the wall and practice variant accents for "*merde*," a word that my mother for some reason thought was a ladylike expletive, for several minutes until I'm reasonably sure she is out of the building, and then I backtrack so that I come out a side door. Since I can't go for coffee now that I've made all those elaborate excuses to Louise I work out a devious route to the rear entrance of Schwindemann, and get there just as Ralph Hamilton comes bursting through the weedy hedge that screens the faculty parking lot.

"Short cut," he explains. "What?"

"Nothing," I say. I wasn't, in fact, saying anything. I was doing cat fight noises. I do some throat clearing now to suggest an obscurely sinal source for whatever he heard. Ralph is a full professor, one of those red, beefy men who are described as "a helluva nice guy" by other men, in Ralph's case by other full professors.

"Eleanor," he says.

He isn't leading up to anything, he's just placing me. "Right," I say.

"You like your classes, Eleanor?"

"Yes," I say. There is no other answer.

"Good, good." We're on the little porch in front of the door, but he isn't making any move to go in and I feel vaguely that

I shouldn't initiate any action. I stare at his tie, which has maroon and yellow stripes that probably mean something. Frank was the one who told me about ties, how they're like semaphores. I'd always thought they kept collars shut or something.

"Eleanor," he ruminates. "Eleanor."

I'm finding this unnerving, as it is already the longest conversation I've ever had with him. "Yes," I say.

"Eleanora," he says.

"Pardon?" My other taught me never to say "What?"

"Eleanora is better," he says. "I'm going to call you Eleanora. What do you think?"

"Huh," I say.

"It's prettier," he says.

"Ah," I say. I find I'm making a little bow, maybe because I've just remembered that Ralph is a medievalist. I feel gauche about this but I'm already bowed over when it hits me what I'm doing. I straighten up. "I was named after Eleanor Roosevelt."

"Looks like a camel," says Ralph. "Her *cunt* looks like a camel. I'm going to call you Eleanora."

I know it's important to let him know I'm not a prude, so I give him my tight classroom smile.

"Whatcha teaching this semester, Eleanora?"

"Bonehead," I say. It's called English 100: Review and Practice in the catalogue. Largely because it's always been called Bonehead we've been encouraged lately to call it Basic.

"Good for you," says Ralph. He transfers his briefcase, one of those monumental buckled leather things, into his left hand and pulls open the door. "Eleanora," he says, gesturing me in. I find I'm bowing again, this time in motion. "What else?" he prompts me. "All Bonehead?"

"I've got one section of World Masterpieces," I say.

"World Masturbators," he corrects me. "That's what we call it. World Masturbators, you get it?" This time I manage only to dip my head, trying to play along. I want to learn how to play along. I haven't had a lot of practice.

"I'm teaching a graduate seminar on the lyric and my Chaucer course," he tells me as we lumber down the hall, his pace. I'm grateful he's said that: I wasn't sure when I should ask, or how, for that matter. I know I should get them to talk about themselves. "My famous Chaucer course, they all know about it," he continues as if I'd asked. "They talk about it in the dorms. I tell them right off the bat it's going to be dirty and if they think they're going to be offended they should get out right away. I tell them right off the bat what words they're going to be hearing, twat, cunt, quim, fuck." He's checking out my expression. I work on looking receptive and tolerant. "I say, you think that's new stuff? You think I'm going to be *shocked* or something? And you'd be surprised, there's always someone who thinks those are new words, like they just got invented. I tell *them*. Sometimes I get letters from their parents."

"Oh?" I say. I'm pleased with this: it seems to be the right response in the right place.

"Yeah, complaints. I tell them, come and talk to me, but you better know what you're talking about. You can't believe the ignorance of some of these people."

I can't think of anything safe to say here so I smile again to show him I'm on his side.

"Huh," he says, as if he's running down. "You wouldn't believe it," he says again.

"I guess not," I say. "I just get complaints that what we're reading is too hard. Parents seem to think World Masterpieces is too hard for their kids."

"World Masturbators," says Ralph.

"Yes," I say. It occurs to me that what I should have been doing is giggling and now it's too late, this is the third time he's said it. I should have been giggling all along.

"Well, have a good one," he says. We're not at the stairs yet, but he takes off down the hall leaving me in the middle of my first giggle, which comes out metallic and twanging. He hasn't even remembered to call me Eleanora.

I follow him, keeping my pace slower and watching the floor, which is old linoleum, that institutional brown with white and yellow streaks, highly polished and running in waves so that the surface is a pattern of ripples that change as you move. I like the sense of being under water, although I'm less inclined to feel immersed in it since last week when I slipped and went skidding on the side of one stacked heel into a garter-baring split and had to be helped up by a little pack of senior faculty who had been walking behind me. Among them Ralph Hamilton, I'm pretty sure.

I'm settled in my office with the door open just a crack, my minimal concession to the fact that this is officially my office hour, when a voice behind me says, "I've been thinking about your problem with *Hamlet.*"

I go on writing a marginal comment in tiny green capitals. After a pause a hand clasps the back of my neck, then slides to my left shoulder, massages it briefly, and slides away. Tom Lippman, I decide, considering the ambivalence of the gesture. I could do with some more massage, but that would probably commit me to too much so I continue writing.

"I've thought of some secondary sources you might find useful," the voice continues. Definitely Tom: he needs very little encouragement. Without turning around I flap at the air with my free hand, a dismissive or placating gesture depending on how you want to read it.

Tom chooses to be placated, which is like him. "I mean, things that might be valuable on a rather more basic level," he says to my back. "Or you might say a beginning level. I mean, if you happen to be teaching students who have a lack of I don't want to say sophistication really because even my students—"

"Freshmen," I say. "Nonmajors."

"Like that," says Tom. "It's a question of experience, really," he adds.

"And age," I say. "Also interest. Nonmajors are usually less interested."

"That's true," says Tom. There is a long pause while he reflects on this. "You have a good head, Eleanor," he says finally.

"Thank you," I say. I'm remembering Louise's comment: *"it's really neat to know somebody who knows things like that."* "It's why I went to graduate school," I say. Through all this I'm writing in the right-hand margin of the paper in front of me, *and perhaps if you spent more time PREPARING to compose your essays you would find the actual writing process easier.* I'm pleased that I am doing both of these things at the same time. Perhaps I'm finally approaching the point where I will be able to mark essays automatically, without paying any attention to them at all. This will be an enormous relief and will give me time to wonder what has happened to my article on Wordsworth and Buber.

"Speaking of that," says Tom. "There's been a certain amount of, ah, question."

I twitch and decide the chances for torpor are over for good today, despite my relatively caffeine-free morning. "Question about what?"

"Oh, you know. Your credentials. Your dedication." I have to turn around to look at him now: it's as if he's won this round. He smiles at me. He has a great smile. "You went to Columbia, then?" He means did I go to Columbia too. "You're doing romantics or something?"

"Wordsworth," I say.

"Interesting." Wordsworth is very much out of favor, especially in the circles I was traveling in when I first got here. "You see yourself as a scholar, then. Not a, ah, pedagogue."

"Both," I say. "How do you think of yourself?"

"That's different," he says. "I mean, are you a teacher first and foremost. That's where there's some, ah, question."

I don't like the way this is going, but I don't have the nerve to ask who is raising the questions. I'm not even sure I want to know. "Do I have to choose?" I ask.

"Well." He is, my God, looking at his hands. "I mean, there's a new thing, a new specialty, maybe you hadn't heard. Very much in demand. Composition." He looks up at me helplessly. "I thought maybe you'd heard."

"I've heard." That's where they were trying to channel the iffy women in graduate school. It was a good specialization for academic couples, they said. Halves of academic couples, they meant. I look at my own hands, which look chewed.

"I know how dedicated you are to teaching," he says. "And there are so few really dedicated teachers these days, when we need them most." I've never been called dedicated before. I'm not sure I like it. I feel as if I'm losing something. "I'm just thinking of the students," he adds. "Especially the students who aren't, shall we say, sophisticated—"

"Freshmen," I prompt him. "Nonmajors."

"That's the wave of the future," says Tom. "I mean, you can look at it this way, who really needs a class in Wordsworth? I mean, so there are daffodils, so okay, but this is the real world, we've got to make them think for themselves. Daffodils are on their way out."

I'm trying to translate this as he goes but I'm still missing the point. "That's not his best poem," I say.

"*Any* poem," he says. "You know, knowing what a dedicated teacher you are I feel it would be just terrible if you were, you know, misunderstood." This is the threat, then. Under other circumstances, say two-thirty in the morning circumstances, it would probably scare me silly. Right now I'm feeling oddly excited. It's a specific feeling, locatable in fact, starting just north of my abdomen and covering a patch that includes my left breast. My attractively freckled left breast. I concentrate on the sensation, trying to deal with it clinically and to remember that Tom can produce analogous effects at will, and on students, colleagues, faculty wives, and the occasional faculty husband. Still, there's some-thing appealing about his moist, brown-eyed sincerity. Young man on his way up, I remind myself. Although not as young as I am.

"We haven't really *talked* in quite a while," Tom is saying, which is an interesting way to put it because last year he never spoke to me at all. These periods of heightened intimacy, where he appears in my doorway and condescends to me, began exactly four weeks ago with the onset of Fall semester. I suppose by that time even the densest observer could gather that Frank wasn't coming back.

"What makes you think I'm having a problem with *Hamlet*?" I feint.

Tom shifts gears without discernible effort. "That's one of the things we have to talk about," he says. "One of the many things." He gives me what I suppose is a meaningful look. "The subject came up, as you may recall, at Norford's party. As a matter of fact you may not recall, since you were pretty loaded at the time."

I close my eyes. I do remember the party, but not how far I went.

"You were telling Norford how much you admired his last book—you stressed 'admired,' I noticed, because it became clear you didn't *like* it very much—not," here Tom raises a hand in protest, "that this was the message Norford himself not, although he's a pretty sharp old guy. You know what he said to me?"

I can only shake my head.

"He said that I was an extraordinarily forward-looking young man." Tom shakes his own head in amazement. "He's a great guy, you know? He knows a lot about people, what makes them tick, that sort of thing. So I told him I couldn't go too far wrong if I just studied him and followed his example." He has been looking at the floor during this recital but now he raises his eyes to mine. "You know, there are people who think he's been chairman long enough and he ought to step down or even retire, but I—" he takes a deep breath here, "I really *respect* that guy. And we're very close, you know?"

"Mm," I say, wondering how much more of this I can take before I get hysterical. "All this happened at Norford's party?"

"Oh, not the part about me and Norford, our—" Tom feels for the word. "Our *closeness*, you know, that's been what you might call ongoing. But the stuff about Norford's book, you said all that at the party. And that's also when you said you were having problems with *Hamlet*," he concludes triumphantly. "Norford asked me about it last week. He was quite concerned, said the things he was telling you about light imagery and animal imagery seemed to be going right by you. He thought maybe you were one of those new people, the kind that sneer at close-readings, but I said you weren't like that."

"No," I agree. People are always telling me what kind of person I'm not and I'm always falling in with them. I'd like someone to tell me what sort of person I am. I want to be grouped.

"But like I said, he knows people. The reason he called me

was he felt maybe junior faculty have a hard time paying attention to old fogeys like him—that was the way he put it, personally I think he's way ahead of most of us. But I can see the other side too." He smiles engagingly. "I'm really a very open-minded kind of a guy," he says.

"Oh yes," I say, as clearly I have to say something. Evidently he likes this. I try to think of other encouraging things to say to him, but all I can manage is to look impressed.

"Well," he says, "the long and the short of it is that I said I'd give you a hand."

"With *Hamlet*," I say.

"With *Hamlet*." He smiles, and after a moment I manage to smile back, feeling like a conspirator. I'm not sure I can cope with the idea of Norford's concern, dear Lord what did I say? The party was Norford's annual gesture toward the faculty or perhaps opening shot. It took place, as always, on the Saturday before school started and no one was allowed to beg off because that was the weekend you were supposed to be writing detailed, witty syllabi or, in my case, mustering all your resources for still another band of recruits who don't what a gerund is. As a gesture it was pretty minimal: Ritz crackers, potato chips, a bowl of mixed Rice Chex, Wheat Chex, and Cheerios soaked in salad oil and then toasted by Mrs. Norford, who kept urging them on people, a graying cheese ball provided by one of the wives, and too many half-gallons of cheap Scotch, bourbon and gin. I don't like any of them so it was something of an achievement that I managed to get hideously drunk.

I can remember only patches of that evening, little clearings in the general fog. I remember, for example, leaning with Jo Michaelson, who is titular head of the Basic program and my titular boss, against the back door in the kitchen and watching Lois Lafferty trying to interest the Boys' Club in her striptease. Lois is the only woman on the regular faculty and she's always trying to make up for it. Jo was chanting "Put it on, put it on," fake *sotto voce*, while Lois threw her dirty looks and fumbled with her zipper. After a while the Boys' Club got bored and trooped out of the kitchen with Lois following them hobbling pathetically on one high heel because Bill Brewster managed to get the other shoe down the garbage disposal. "See?" Jo was saying. "*She* got tenure." Then the fog closed in again. I'm not sure whether this happened before or after the incident with Norford.

Tom has pulled my other chair, my student chair, toward him, turned it around, and straddled it boyishly with his arms folded across the top so he can rest his chin on them and gaze intently at me. "Mind if I sit down?" he asks when I'm finally looking at him again, and we both laugh, although my laugh is a little out of control.

"So you're going to teach me about *Hamlet*," I say.

"I'm going to teach you about *Hamlet*," he says.

I've been teaching *Hamlet* since I was a teaching assistant at Columbia. It's practically the only work I can say I know well. It's practically the only work I can say I know well. Course development committees have been figuring lately that *Hamlet* speaks to alienated youth. Alienated youth, of course, believe that *Hamlet* is written in Old English, but ten that type never stays in college anyway. I've never been able to convince anybody that students don't identify with Hamlet even if he is a student too. Occasionally they identify with Horatio, who has a kind of class president quality and, of course, survives. Sometimes they say Hamlet ought to go back to school and get an engineering degree or some-thing.

"Now *Hamlet*," Tom is saying, "is what you might call a problem play—by that, "hand up warding off an incipient objection, "I don't mean you have a problem with it or I have a problem with it. No. But Hamlet, *he* has a problem. And your students, they have problem with *him*. Isn't that what you're trying to say?"

"No," I say, having reached my limit with "trying to say." "I mean, not exactly but pretty much," I add, chickening out. He narrows his eyes at me. I'll bet he narrows his eyes at himself in the mirror while he's shaving. He has that look, as if he knows exactly what effect he's producing. It's a pretty good effect, too, I have to admit it turns me on.

"I don't have to do this," he says. "I'm just trying to help you out is all. Do you want me to help you or not?"

"Of course I do," I say. "I was just joking."

He's kept his eyes narrowed. "That's a pretty strange kind of *joke* I'd say," he shoots back at me. I'm charmed: it's the same stupide repartee the boys in high school used when they stood by a girl's locker and led up to what she was doing Saturday. Not my locker, of course. I lower my eyes and try to imagine the effect of feathery lashes against alabaster cheeks. No. Not alabaster.

"I'm sorry," I say.

"Well, if you really mean it," he says back.

"I really do," I'm trying for a subdued coo. I've heard this sort of thing run on and on, niggling little variations on the same theme until the boy figures he's safe: this girl is absolutely predictable.

"Well, just as long as you're really sorry," says Tom rakishly. I decide not to risk a giggle. During this exchange he has reared back in the chair and thrown his legs in front of him like brakes. Now he resumes his intent posture, chin on arms, arms folded on chair back. "As I was saying, *Hamlet* is what you might call a problem play. But look at it this way, problems are what make this play the immortal work of literature that it is. I mean, *life's* a problem play, am I right? I get a lot of psych majors in my Shakespeare class."

"Really," I say, as a response seems to be called for.

"No lie. They hear about my approach, you know? I have what you might call a modified psych approach to Shakespeare, although it's well within the bounds of literary scholarship. Nothing flaky, you know what I mean. So a lot of psych majors take my class as an elective." He pauses to savor the effect. "That is, they elect to take my class. They don't have to take it. They don't need it for their major. Although I'm not sure it shouldn't be required for their major, seeing as it deepens their grasp of human nature."

"It does," I ask, again on cue, although I'm wondering about a deepened grasp.

"Well, I didn't say so," Tom admits. "It was one of my students, actually. She was an English major, but she understood that *Hamlet* addresses the human condition." He smiles reminiscently. "Marvelous girl."

"So you take a modified psych approach," I say to get him back on track.

"Right. I used to have them do interpretive readings, but I had to give that up pretty quickly." He wrinkles his nose at me. "They had just amazing problems with the blank verse, they'd stop at the end of every line if you can imagine. So I thought hey, that's not the way you get them into the characters."

My turn again. "So what did you do?"

"I started reading the stuff myself. The soliloquies. And Claudius's scene when he's trying to pray, *that* one really gets them. I start out with Hamlet's 'Now I am alone,' and then, without even explaining what I'm doing, I maybe put on a different jacket and put on this *crown* I have, I've been hiding in my desk so it's a big surprise, and then I go right into old Claudius. And they love it, it really opens up the characters for them. You can't imagine the insights I get out of them after I do that number."

I can't imagine. "What kind of insights?"

"Strong insights," he says evasively. "You can't really do that, though, I mean because of, ah, gender distinctions. I mean, you couldn't play Hamlet for instance."

"Sara Bernhardt did," I say. Suddenly I have a vision of myself in black with tights. I look good in tights.

"Yes, well." Sara Bernhardt isn't what he had in mind, which I could have guessed. Now he's thinking. "You could do Ophelia, though, or what her name, the mother," he says. "Or—" and her he gazes at me exactly like Mickey Rooney when it hits him that he and Judy Garland can get the whole gang together and put on a *show*—"hey, get this, *I* come to *your* class and *we* do a scene together, like that Hie thee to a nunnery—"

"Get," I say. "Get thee to a nunnery."

"Get, hie," says Tom. "Same thing. Maybe I'm thinking of the Bad Quarto. Anyway, we could do that, and then I could do O, that this too too sullied flesh should melt, which really gets them into Hamlet's problem." He squints at me. "I'll bet you're thinking it's O that this too too *solid* flesh should melt, aren't you?"

"No," I say, "it's would melt, not should melt. Would."

"That's the sort of thing you shouldn't carp on with your students," he says. "It turns them off." He gets up, turns the chair around to face forward, and sits down again. "Do you want to do this or do you want to sit around picking at my quotes?"

Quotations, I think, but I don't say it. "Tom," I say instead, "I don't have any problems with *Hamlet*."

"You said you did," says Tom, not looking at me.

"I don't even remember what I said."

"Obviously," says Tom.

This is unanswerable, so I swivel around in my chair and start writing in the margins of the paper I've been working on. It's a technique that always drove Frank crazy when he came stumbling home eager to confess something. As my remarks are basically simpleminded expressions of good will it's easy to keep writing them. I write: *You've really been aiming HIGH, haven't you Ronnie?* Ronnie is a girl, a large, pudgy girl with tiny eyes, otherwise she would be Roni.

Tom has decided to take pity on me. "What you said," he says now, "is that for all the years you've been teaching *Hamlet* you've never really understood it."

I'm relieved to hear this is all. I've been worried that I sank to new lows in drunken self-denigration at that party. "Tom," I say, "there are degrees of not understanding, just as there are degrees of understanding. I didn't mean I didn't know anything about *Hamlet*, I only meant I have no—" But here I make the mistake of looking at him. He doesn't have any idea what I'm talking about.

"What you *said*—" he begins sulkily.

"Right," I say, "right, I don't really understand *Hamlet*. Nobody really understands *Hamlet*."

"I do," says Tom.

I find I'm simply poised there with my mouth open, so after a minute I close it and lean back in my chair. Finally I say, "Okay. I don't understand *Hamlet*, I just *thought* I—"

"It's okay, Eleanor," he's saying over this, and now he leans forward and actually pats me on the shoulder. "You're not in the Renaissance," he says. "No one expects you to have a solid grasp of a complex, deeply psychological play like this one."

I take a deep breath. "No," I say.

"No what?"

"We're not talking about the same thing."

"That's a very *mature* observation, Eleanor. That's why I offered to help you. We come out of very different backgrounds but that's what a department like ours is for, people helping each other."

Even while I'm enraged I have to admire the authority with which he takes over my words and makes them his own. "You still aren't getting what I'm saying," I tell him, although I can already see this is why he's going to win.

He's miffed now. "No, Eleanor, it's you who don't get what I'm saying. I'm saying it's all right."

Give it up, I think. He's looking at me expectantly, or perhaps accusingly. Tom's face expresses only a limited range of emotions, owing perhaps to the fact that his eyes are so prominent and dark that they distract from anything the rest of his face might be doing. Bedroom eyes, I suppose. They look rather like olives, I decide, and find myself considering idly the possibility of impaling them on my fingers, the way I always wore the olives off those hors d'oeuvre trays everybody made up for parties when I was little. The idea is vaguely sensual: olives always felt cool and protective over the tips of my fingers. Tom's wouldn't be pitted, of course.

But this isn't addressing the business at hand, which is to say something soothing that will be the equivalent of lying on my back with all four paws in the air. I've never been good at pacifying; it's one of a great number of things I've never been good at. I know intellectually what's called for, but I'm weak on applications. Now as the silence stretches out between us I formulate a sentence. "Do you think we really could do some of those scenes together?" It's a deceptively simple sentence, I decide, and requires a completely ingenuous delivery. I know I'm not up to it, but clearly I have to say something.

Tom looks blank, or perhaps embarrassed. More, I tell

myself: the only thing to do now is go on. "I've always been scared about performing," I lie. If he were actually paying attention, he'd realize that this is my fourth year of teaching. "Since you've got experience, maybe I won't panic though," I add. This is better. He's seized on the invitation and is now eyeing me as if from a great height, one eyebrow raised. The eyebrow is a nice touch. He has some good facial tics, I have to grant him that. I resolve to pull out all the stops. "Maybe if I had a costume," I confide. "If I did Ophelia I could maybe wear this robe I have, it's satin, very nice, and kind of innocent without being, you know, sexless." The robe is a spontaneous invention. If not Bernhardt then Jean Harlow.

It thaws him. "Robe?" he queries, still with the eyebrow up. The effort seems to be getting to him; he's now lifting one side of his mouth as well. "A robe," he muses. "It isn't a *bath*robe, is it?"

"Oh no," I assure him. "It's quite slinky. But good for Ophelia. Virginal." My robe is blue chenille, bald at the elbows. I don't even know where you'd get a white satin one.

He drops the eyebrow, which relieves me as one whole side of my own face is getting tense from the strain of watching him. "Slinky," he echoes. He's treating the word as if I'd inadvertently let it slip. "A slinky robe that's also virginal," he says. "Quite a *robe* you must have there."

I'm out of lines. The conversation has reached a level of generalized innuendo that I recognize but can't quite participate in: it's not in my training. Also, I'm not at all sure how I feel about this role I'm falling into. On the one hand it's irritating to have him presuming that I'm saying more than I intend, falling loose-lipped into perilous intimacy. On the other hand, it's nice not to be responsible for your own statements, to be valued precisely be-cause you're not responsible. "It's a *nice* robe," I insist demurely. Boys like nice girls. They like overcoming them. I can tell that Tom is pulling himself together for further devastations, so I clasp my hands in my lap and look at them.

"Better to wear your *nightgown*," he says finally, "or whatever you wear to *bed*." This surpasses even my lowest expectations, but I can also feel my face getting hot. I keep my eyes lowered. Now it comes to me, a beautiful flatfooted response. I can be provoked into revealing that I never wear anything to bed.

"I never—" I begin, then catch sight of the audience, Ralph Hamilton's head in my doorway. Just the head: Ralph is peering around from the hall in a large-scale pantomime of I was just passing by and couldn't help but. I open my eyes very wide. It's wonderful how all this minor muscle behavior *comes* to me: maybe it's innate and emerges on the appropriate occasion. I can think of nothing to say. I realize that it's entirely appropriate for me to have nothing to say. Ralph appears to be thrilled with me.

"Tom!" he roars. "What are you doing to this woman?"

"Me?" Tom is playing pained, using a two-tone syllable that goes up maybe half an octave. "I'm not doing anything," he yelps. "*She's* the one telling me all about her nighties."

"I am not," I whine. I didn't know I had that whine in me. They both turn toward me. "He's trying to find out about my *underwear*, Ralph," I say in the voice of Juli Kirkpatrick, cheerleading captain of my high school: Oh you *guys*. "Make him *stop*," I drone, with exactly the same intonations.

"My motives are entirely pure," says Tom.

"Oh, I know about your motives," says Ralph. He drapes a brown corduroy arm across Tom's shoulders: they're always touching him, I remember, and find I'm a little jealous. "Preying on innocent women. Innocent schoolteachers. You cad."

It's high praise they're handing back and forth. "Honestly," says Tom, "I came in to talk to Eleanor here about her teaching. *You* know." And here he elbows Ralph, who is still draped over him like an outsize Tweedledum. Ralph drops the arm and elbows back.

"Her teaching," says Ralph. "And what is he teaching *you*, Eleanora?"

"I'm a slow learner," I say.

"Aw, come on, Ralph," Tome says over me.

"Next thing, he'll be asking you to serve on a committee," says Ralph, winking hugely at Tom. "Committee" sounds like a euphemism.

"It hasn't gone that far yet," says Tom. They both collapse in suppressed hysterics. They're discussing me in my presence as if they're setting me up for a gang bang, something I'll presumably enjoy if I just relax and let them have their way with me. "She'll be good, don't you think?" Tom is saying. Ralph laugh, shaking his head. Oh you guys.

"I don't understand," I say helpfully. They roll their eyes at each other.

"She doesn't understand," says Tom.

"Better that way," says Ralph.

"What are you guys talking about?" Actually, I have no idea what they're talking about but I don't mind terribly being the center of attention.

"I like them intellectual," says Ralph. "They never catch on."

"What Ralph here is trying to say," Tom explains, "is that we foresee a, ah, a situation in which you might be able to be of service—"

"Service!"

"Come on, Ralph. Academic service."

"Is that different from what you do for Patsy?"

No fair, I think, leave wives out of it, but the atmosphere has chilled just slightly. Once you mention wives it's a short step to husbands, virtually unavoidable, and yes, I can see it hitting them: they're thinking about Frank. It's like him to intervene just when I'm beginning to have fun.

"Is it really five of eleven?" Tom again, he has impeccable reflexes.

"I've got to *teach*," I wail, residue of my cheerleader persona, but they start whuffling together again like a pair of old horses as I edge them out ahead of me. We're all leaving my office together, as if I'm part of something, as if I've been chosen. That's what they've been saying, isn't it, that I'm part of something, I've been chosen? That's why they're teasing me. Teasing is another thing I'm not used to.

We go different ways at the head of the stairs. The light outside is dazzling after the subterranean shadows of Schwindemann. I find I'm squinting to make things out, baffled

by radiance. Then a song starts, somebody's transistor radio
going by.

I can't get no-o
Sat-is-fac-tion
I can't get no-o
Girl-ie ac-tion—

The voice is dangerously repressed, it blows my mind that he's
named Mick Jagger, a dangerous, beautiful name. Listen to Muddy
Waters, Howlin' Wolf, Little Richard even, Frank used to tell me,
go to the roots, Frank was big on roots. I like the roots okay, but
I especially like the flowers. *Look* at him, he shouted once, they're
all the age of your students and that boy, that boy especially is
skinny, spastic, nothing but ungainly poking elbows and knees.
All this from Frank, who is short, stocky, and—he taught me the
word—hirsute. I've noticed. It's true, too: Mick Jagger is all bones
and sinew. I can imagine him leaving permanent marks on my
body.

The volume is building as I go down the stairs being
careful not to slip because it's much too easy to slip.

Well I try
An' I try
An' I try
An' I try
I can't GET NO—

It faces away after I cross the street. Another session on
colons is coming up. Suddenly it strikes me as terribly funny that
I'm teaching colons—teaching colons *twice.* "*Up* your colon!" I
say, English rock-star accent. No one seems to have noticed.
Everyone is hurrying to class. A little undercurrent of drums
blows back at me: *Hey-hey-hey.* No satisfaction, I tell myself, and
for some reason feel just fine.

*H*e kept his eyes closed, tried to keep any untoward movements of his face or body from revealing his state of consciousness. his conscious state. that he was conscious had regained consciousness, right. Right: He had almost certainly been drugged and didn't know had no notion no idea how long he had been asleep sleep had claimed his body his heavy limbs his angular sinewy muscular thin What was prompting him to pretend play-act act as if as though to counterfeit sleep no somnolence right was something that had never happened to him an unusual state of affairs a situation unheard of unprecedented in his experience. This is going to be harder than I thought.

I mean, he's lying there in the middle distance, exposes, as it were, though not physically, not yet, and the thing that is throwing him is he doesn't know where he is. Right. *He did not know where he was.* Which is unsettling for him, because he's the type that doesn't get lost and denies it if he does, the type that insists on finding a parking place on the street even if it means driving all night and missing the movie, even though everybody else is yelling oh come on Frank just pull into a garage, we'll pay for it. *Not to know was counter to all his breeding and all his training. In-deed, for him not to know was a virtual contradiction in terms, for did he not make the truth himself by fiat, forcing the world to reflect back his own image?* You can't tell him anything. It's like he wrote the map.

When he reached a new land his first act was to name it, and thus he always knew where he was before anyone else did. He named bays, inlets, and coves, mountains and valleys, hamlets, villages, towns, and cities, and he named inhabitants, in general and in particular. The women he possessed were born anew from his touch, rechristened with his own appellation so that his seed would bear his mark and would grow in time to represent the scope and strength of his will. It was his nature to manufacture reality out of his own substance by broking no argument. His conviction was strongest, his voice loudest. Consequently, he knew most: he insisted, and fought anyone who thought differently.

I'm currently trying to stop smoking. The brand I'm trying not to smoke is Marlboros. I've chosen Marlboros for reasons that have nothing to do with not smoking, which is probably why I'm having so much trouble. I associate Marlboros with integrity. The reason I associate Marlboros with integrity is that whenever I think of that leathery cowboy I feel ignoble worrying about lung cancer.

But here was something wrong: for the first time some alien force was invading his mind and obscuring his instinctive and overweening sense that what he cared to call true was, in fact, the truth. How could he not know where he was? Was he not where he had planned to be? Even if his ship were sunk, his men dispersed, was he not

I don't normally chain-smoke but I'm out of matches and once I let the flame go out that's it. Actually, I could light a cigarette on the stove even though it's an electric stove; I've done that; it's not impossible, although it smells funny and sometimes little clumps of tobacco get stuck to the burner and just sit there smoldering and smelling strange, not at all like tobacco. It's odd too that of all the brands I've kept coming back to Marlboros. It's not that I identify with the Marlboro man exactly, although I do find him attractive, I'll admit that. Not sexy, really, just attractive.

Was he not Joe not likely *Bob Roy Dave Rod Bruce.* Rougher. More rugged. Untamed. *Tex.* No. *Biff.* Barbaric really, untamed power, a hint of the Neanderthal. Massive. *Big.* Well, a little obvious. *Bik.* Possible. But razory, dangerous, cutting. Jagged. Chaggard. God, sometimes it just comes to me.

was he not Bik Chaggard, warrior prince and hero, master of fates, captain of souls?

That I associate Marlboros with the Marlboro Man is one of those advertising triumphs, of course. There's nothing intrinsic about Marlboros that I like—I mean, I doubt I could pass a taste test on them.

He was not, he realized, sure. He could not, he realized, arrive at hard and fast conclusions. And so in desperation he opened his eyes and looked around him. And then closed them and smiled, doubts dispelled. He knew exactly where he was.

He could be nowhere else but in the heaven reserved for heroes, for surrounding him were hundreds of women, achingly beautiful, endlessly diverse. He could not discern immediately whether the regal figure with the disquieting green eyes whom he had encountered earlier on the barren no blasted oh what the hell that barren, blasted heath was among them, but here were women of every shape and color, every race and nationality, their black, blue, brown, hazel and green eyes fixed upon the skirt of his tunic, which was rising and spreading under their gaze like a circus tent.

There were fourteen butts in my ashtray and I'm not getting anywhere.

"Holy shit," he breathed. No one moved.

I'm supposed to string this out for two hundred and fifty pages, and already I'm thinking about giving up, but then I'm easy, I already know that.

Their very stillness arouses him. As they watched, his member began to throb rhythmically as if in anticipation of the havoc it would soon wreak among these opulently endowed bodies among many of these opulently endowed bodies among a few two or three of those opulently endowed bodies. There is such a thing as verisimilitude, after all. That was another thing my reading didn't prepare me for. I thought it was men who were insatiable, women who dropped off to sleep smiling Gioconda fulfillment.

Still no movement among them. But they could surely grasp his needs so to speak understand his predict see that he had something that needed doing But he had needs, surely they knew that; he trembled with lust: let them assuage it, they who had aroused him beyond endurance. "Who's first?" he shouted.

Still no one moved. Their beauty was provocative, maddening, an enticement to his ravaging organ. "You," he breathed, pointing a trembling finger, "black girl. Come ficky-fick. Comprenday?"

Suddenly, astonishingly, the Nubian turned to the woman on her right, a proud beauty with black hair to her magnificent but-tocks, a warm golden complexion, and great legs, and kissed her on the mouth. The two bodies met and intertwined; his instrument twitched uncontrollably in frustration and despair. "Not that way," he cried, enraged. "Here. Look, right here." He attempted to fling himself on their moist, quivering, very dark brown and beige flesh, but his legs were heavy and unresponsive, his flesh lax and inert.

As he watched, helpless, the whole circle became inflamed until he was at the center of a writhing mass of pulchritudinous bodies. The spectacle in itself was an affront to his manhood; what made it intolerable was the time these women were taking. Someone would start moaning and jerking around and that would catch on until they were all screaming and sobbing and fastening onto each other in ways that thoroughly offended his sensibilities, and after an interminable period of this they would subside and then start all over again. He, who could come within fifteen seconds of entering a woman, found their inefficiency appalling.

"Someone at least suck me off," he cried piteously, and came, finally, all over his tunic. They ignored him. He swore horrible vengeance and fell asleep, leaving them to it. When he woke again it was dark and his legs were crusted with dried semen. The women were nowhere to be seen. Wearily he dragged himself upright and began to walk inland.

I may not be up to this. Oh, so to speak. I shy away from the details, even though it's the details that turn me on. That's how I got started with Janet, in fact. We'd be lying there, late, in the dark, in our twin beds, and then Janet would start this raspy muttering about what she'd like to do to me. For a long time I thought she just quietly went crazy every night: no one had ever told me women could do things to each other: it wasn't in any of the books I'd read, and given my understanding of the mechanics of sex it wasn't likely I'd figure anything out for myself. I'd lie very still, pretending to be asleep, keeping my breathing steady, and eventually Janet would go to sleep leaving me awake all night and wondering what would happen to me, the possibilities getting more bizarre the more sleep I lost. I never told anybody, though. I was also getting very excited: you have to remember that I had been lying around in a state of arousal for something like four years, convinced my horniness wouldn't go away unless some guy actually stuck it in me, and stymied by the knowledge that if some guy did stick it in me my life would be ruined. Finally one night in the middle of one of those hoarse fantasies I sat up and said "Yes, please." I thought everything would change then, but it didn't. Janet and I shared a bed, Janet's bed, for a while, and after that I'd start out in Janet's bed and moved to my own when Janet complained she couldn't like straight. Our daytime life wasn't much affected except that Janet borrowed more of my clothes and, being larger, stretched them.

I couldn't get over thinking there should have been more to it. Loyalty. Affection. I was carrying out my project of becoming brilliant then, so I spent a lot of time on my stomach with four or five different books around me, writing running commentaries in the margins, all the margins. I'd figured out that the important thing was not to let my attention lapse. She resented that, but not because I wasn't spending time with her. She was never around evenings anyway. Once I said that she of all people should be glad I was becoming brilliant but all she said was "Don't say you of all people, that's a dumb thing to say" and kicked me out of her bed again. I started biting my nails about then, probably because Janet was always going over hers with an emery board: she had *boxes* of emery boards. My mother was appalled when I came home for Thanksgiving. She kept grabbing my hands and staring at them mournfully, thinking no doubt of all the Pond's Lotion we'd rubbed in together over the years. I burned a lot of bridges around then.

That was the reason I took up smoking, in fact, so I'd stop biting my nails. Now I do both. There are twenty-two butts in my ashtray and I can't go on like this. I empty the ashtray and come back to where I'm sitting staring at the wall, which just shows how far downhill I've gone. Once I'd have seen that wall as an opportunity, a place to post twenty lines of poetry per day to memorize, twenty Latin irregular verbs, twenty words no one ever spells right, beginning with *accommodate*. Once I viewed blank surfaces as a challenge. But I'm not brilliant any more, just prematurely old.

It isn't helping my erotic imagination either that I'm trying to decide whether to get rid of the Pakistani graduate student in the basement. If I decide I ought to get rid of him then I'll have to decide how. How is a harder question than whether. He's becoming quite forward in his behavior. For a while he was coming up the steps and waiting in the kitchen for me to come downstairs. He never went any further than the kitchen, but I'm used to bouncing around my own house in my underwear, and last week I bounced in wearing the push-up bra I'd bought to see if I'd look like a *Playboy* cover girl in it. On the cover they still wear bras. From hi reaction I gathered that I looked better than I'd thought, not that he'd be the world's best judge. Jo Michaelson, who counseled me the day after that episode, said that for someone brought up the way he was, the entire American continent must seem like one big brothel. I said yes, but that a push-up bra was taking things at least a step beyond the provocation of bare legs or an unveiled face and that I didn't want to go home again ever. Jo said throw him out. I compromised by buying and installing furtively a simple bolt, the kind you find on the inside of doors to toilets in public bathrooms. I was quite proud of my handiwork. That night I sat at my desk and listened as he hurled his body against the door. At least it sounded as if that was what he was doing. He's quite slight; also, he'd have to hurl in an upward direction because the door is at the top of the basement stairs. I didn't say anything to him. I don't ever want to see him again: he has his own little kitchen and his own outside entrance. He's another of Frank's legacies. Frank liked the house especially because it had a mother-in-law apartment he could rent out to some Third World suppliant: for all his mannerisms, Frank was tight with money. After I put in the bolt I threw away the push-up bra. It brought responsibilities.

Last night, however, when I was grading essays on the subject of City Life and Small Town Life: A Comparison or Dorm

Life and Sorority/Fraternity Life: A Comparison or Living With Your Parents and Living On Your Own: A Comparison, there was a brisk knock on the front door and when I opened it he was standing under the porch light holding up a bottle of Sauterne. "Night-cap?" he asked. I shut the door and locked it, then strode into the kitchen and checked the bolt on the door to the basement. He was still banging on the front door ten minutes later, when I called Jo Michaelson.

"Alcohol's a bad sign," said Jo, who knows these things. "They're not supposed to drink, period. They go to hell."

"Nightcap?" the Pakistani graduate student was shouting outside.

"I'd throw him out," said Jo. "Tell him you're calling the police. Tell him you want him out of there in an hour."

"He just paid me this month's rent," I said.

"Give it back to him," said Jo.

"I've already deposited it."

"Write him a check."

"Oh," I said. After I hung up I went over to the door and called through it, "I want you out of here."

"What?" he shouted back.

"Go away," I said.

"I live here," he shouted.

"I'm calling the police," I said.

"I am a visitor to your country," he shouted. "I do not understand."

"I want you to move," I said, articulating very clearly. "I want you to leave this house. I do not want you to live in this house any more. I will give you your rent back."

"Open the door," he shouted.

I opened the door. He'd put the bottle of Sauterne on the porch, in front of his feet. "You too cannot tolerate my color," he said.

"It's not your *color*," I begin.

"It is my color," he said. "With all American girls it is my color. They say it does not matter. But do they be friends with me? No."

Not *all* American girls," I pointed out. There have been

noises downstairs plenty of times.

"You say you be different," he said. "What really this means is you be my landlady who take my money. But join me in a friendly nightcap? No."

It seemed to me that his command of the language was deteriorating, but maybe he was just upset. He seemed far more fluent when Frank was around. I wish I could be sure one way or the other.

"I am busy," I said very clearly. "I am working. I do not car for a nightcap."

"You tell me when you want to go to bed," he said.

"No," I said. "No."

"You American girls."

"No," I said. I shut the door and locked it. I wished I'd called the police, but the time for that had passed somehow.

Now I'm waiting for him to do something. He probably won't do anything just because I'm waiting. This could go on for months, years. I know that if I do call the police they'll throw him out, no questions asked. Because of his color, naturally. I wonder how far I have to go to make up to him for that.

I'm on my fifth cigarette since I emptied the ashtray. Eros is dead for the evening, I decide, and sweep the pages of porn narrative into my desk drawer. The top paper in the pile at the lower right-hand corner of my desk reads *Dorm Life and Sority/Fraternty life: a Comprason*. I move it to the center and read.

I live in a dorm so I dont have any comparsion with Sority/Fraternty life Dorm Life is Okay I geuss. My roommate is named Jeff hes from the East. Were on the 4th fl. This is all I have to write because, I don't have any comparson with Sorrirty/Frternaty life but next yr. hopefully a friends getting me in.

I write in green ballpoint,

Joe, I've told you that you can't get out of assignments this way. If you don't know anything about fraternity life you should ask somebody who does – or write on another topic! Note that you need not address the question of sorority life: sororities are for girls! Please note my spellings.

I stare at the wall for a while and then write in somewhat larger letters,

I cannot accept this paper.

The first thing he'll ask me is what grade he got. I haven't given him a grade yet; he hasn't fulfilled one assignment yet. I know perfectly well that he hasn't comprehended this fact and will not comprehend this fact. As long as I haven't given him a grade he'll assume he's doing just fine. I'm giving him the benefit of a doubt, I tell myself. I'm not sure why. He'll never understand the benefit of a doubt and will feel betrayed when I finally do have to give him a grade. What it amounts to is I hate to be the bearer of bad news. I pass Joe's paper on to the upper left-hand corner of my desk. The Pakistani graduate student still hasn't made his move. The Pakistani graduate student. I don't even know his name. For a long time I thought his name was Abou, but then I began to wonder about creeping influences from third grade, where we all memorized a nice poem about a gentleman of color, my only acquaintance until college with gentlemen of color:

Abou Ben Adhem, may his tribe increase!
Awoke one night from a deep dream of peace,
And saw, within the moonlight in his room,
Making it rich, and like a lily in bloom,

It didn't scan. Mrs. Rath, my third grade teacher, loved it. When I recited it I tried hard to make it scan, just for Mrs. Rath:

Making it RICH and like LIly in BLOOM.

"You're going too fast, dear," said Mrs. Rath.

I unstaple the pages of the next essay and pull the opening page to the center of my desk.

The telephone is ringing in the bedroom.

I run for it, get I in the middle of the first ring. There is a pause and then a click. Then nothing.

If it's the Pakistani graduate student he's calling from outside. And I can't imagine that he wouldn't say something.

It's more likely to be *for* the Pakistani graduate student. Someone who doesn't want to speak to me, who doesn't even want me to know who's calling. One of those American girls he's brought home, maybe.

Well good for him then. Let her drink his Sauterne. Or make noises in the basement. And it hits me suddenly that those noises are reason enough to evict him. But I know I'll never be able to mention them to him.

On the radio someone is singing in a mincing falsetto to the accompaniment of a virile series of piano chords: *Come on now, baby* (plunk plunk, plunk plunk, plunk plunk, plunk plunk, plunk) *You know you really turn me o-on.* It's a very dirty song if you listen to it. In the chorus he makes sounds like coming, like a *woman* coming. The falsetto seems to keep them from figuring out what the song is about. I love it when they get away with things like that on the radio.

I go back into the study and look at the paper now in the center of my desk.

Dorm Life and Sorority Life: A Comparison

I noticed the name on the first day, Kimi Kelly. This girl has a lot going for her. For one thing, the name itself is very desirable, and when you put the Italianate I on the end you get something so cute you know the girl is already busy all weekend, and when you add the alliteration you've got a cheerleader at the very least. But the final touch is that although Kimi types her papers, she very carefully dots her i's with big circles. And inside the circles are little smiley faces, two of them. Kimi takes the pains to fill in the smiley faces on every one of her papers.

Kimi's paper begins characteristically.

Let's face it, there is a lot to be said for dorm life and sorority life. There are plus's on both sides. Well I am in a sorority and I love it! This does'nt mean dorms are'nt nice places to live in, too!

Kimi, one of the better students in Basic, has paragraphs.

Let me tell you what is nice about sorority's. First of all the girls are nice. They are nice in the dorm, too, but these girls are special. They are my sister's! (I don't mean they are my real sister's but, in some ways even more then my real sister's no offense Jill and Kath!) They take care of me and show me how they do things in the House. An example is: when I became a Pledge. It was the happiest day of my life! But some of the girl's said: "You

should role you're socks down, that way you're ankles look nicer."
Well was I embarrassed! I come from a town that is nice but it is
Hicksville USA! Then they told me about wearing you're stockings
UNDER you're socks. I never would have thought of that but their
right you're legs look smoother that way. I've put down my pen
somewhere in the middle of the second paragraph. I can mark the
paper later. I'm avid for this kind of information.

Later on, when I'm convinced the Pakistani graduate student
won't be dropping by the front door tonight, I peel off my jeans
and Frank's sweat socks and put on a garter belt and a pair of
stockings, Cinnamon. I haven't yet had the nerve to wear the
stockings to school. They're very noticeable: not many people
have orange legs. I stand sideways to the mirror and suck in my
stomach. My mother would say I should be wearing a girdle. I
started wearing a girdle to church when I was ten. My mother lied
to me, and I didn't know until I left home that there was any other
way to keep stockings up. A lady always wears a girdle in public,
my mother told me, walking slightly behind me as we went down
the aisle, gripping the back of my navy blue good wool dress,
steering. Then I'd feel faint in church and have to ease off my
knees and slide back into the pew, keeping my head down, an object of solicitude for all my mother's friends who would hiss, "Are
you having your period, dear?" and "Put your head between your
knees," which was impossible when you were wearing a
girdle.

After a while I take off my sweater. My bra is padded,
although not very much. Lightly Shaped, it said on the package.
Sideways to the mirror with my stomach sucked in I look pretty
good. The stockings are shiny, the way you'd think whores' stockings would be, or the stockings of expensive Follies girls or hard
women from another era with their cigarettes. I've let my cigarette go out. I think about wearing little angora ankle socks over
the stockings and rolling the cuffs of the ankle socks down over
my sexy, pointy-toed shoes, which I still don't own. I don't have
any ankle socks either, unless you count Frank's, which I've left
lying in a little urine-colored lump on the linoleum. I'm a
grownup. The uniforms are different.

Before I go to bed I do sit-ups to Eric Burden and the Animals singing "House of the Rising Sun." It doesn't make a whole lot of sense to have a man sing that song. I'd sing it so you were sure what it was about. I'd be raw, gutsy, Honey I *been* there. If I stopped smoking maybe I could sing. The woman singing it ought to smoke, though. She ought to be just a wreck. Ravaged, shiny stockings and everything.

I lie awake, as usual thinking about the possible combinations of clothing I can put on tomorrow, how far I might push things, although when it comes to morning and the business of dressing I find I never push anything at all. Despite my escape from Kansas I still dress a lot like my mother. I also think about what I should wear when I have my meeting with Norford next week. I've almost forgotten tonight's telephone call.

*D*ear Ellie,
         So here is the stuff about the female porn. It is not a lot because they are not sure whether it's going to go or not and don't want to invest much in it or even a little in it frankly. You will notice this is pretty pathetic. Pussy books for pussies is what I call it, all genteel and probing, you know? Except for maybe a little queer fore play among the girls for openers as it were. They think it's fore play. I did go to lunch with the porn lady, since it was on her what the hell? She was wearing one of those little Jackie Kennedy pillboxes and a little pink mohair suit, which is a lot of pink all at once, and drinking stingers, a whole lot of them. I said you were a lady pornographer with a run of bad luck which she seemed to like except I think she also thought it was all really me, like I was chicken shit and couldn't admit I wrote dirty. So be prepared for innuendoes, you know?

         You asked what I was doing. Like I said you really have to be here but I am painting stripes around corners, pastel stripes mostly. I have a show right before Christmas too which is doing pretty well if you know anything about galleries which you don't. I hope you get out of Middle America. If you do you are welcome to stay with me but no funny stuff. I was sorry about your husband leaving although if he left you you just have to say he was an asshole and it was all for the rest. God I can not believe I am writing to an English teacher. You are probably making red marks all over this.

         Well best of luck and if you want me to pretend to be you or get you some dirty books or something to help you figure out what dirty is let me know. If you do write a pussy book for pussies I want to read it.

                         Yours truly,
                         Janet

I'm standing over my one saucepan, which I got at the Congregational Rummage last spring after I told Frank to take all the cooking stuff because I wasn't making any more goddamned meals boiling water for coffee. Vapor is beginning to rise, and the letter is getting damp as I hold it in front of me. It was in the mailbox, along with an issue of *Newsweek*, a bank statement, a copy of something called *Aesthetic Inquiry* that I'll have to forward to Frank, and another letter, typed, with no return address, when I finally tied myself into the blue chenille bathrobe with balding elbows that I lied to Tom Lippman about and came limping down-stairs making wounded bobcat noises, pathetic but with an under-tone of snarl. It's afternoon, possibly late afternoon. My watch and my alarm clock have both stopped. Premier Ky is on the cover of *Newsweek*, and the caption above his head reads *Who Rules Vietnam?*

The sheet of paper that Janet enclosed with her letter is the pale peach color of dime store underwear. I unfold it now as I stand swaying above the coffee water, vaguely preoccupied with getting the steam up into my sinuses.

For Immediate Release
Corona Announces Women's Erotica Line

"Erotic literature has long been a field dominated by the male," claimed Albert Bliss, Managing Editor of Corona Publishing, Inc., today upon announcing the creation of a new paperback line, AUREOLA BOOKS. "We feel this is inequitable," Mr. Bliss continues. "Today's woman is a sexual being, too!" he divulged. "We here at Corona are very excited about this new line, which will offer accounts of the feminine sexual experience sensitively and honestly rendered by women themselves or men who have a special insight in-to women's unique sexuality: NO HOLDS BARRED!"*

According to Mr. Bliss, AUREOLA's first release, scheduled for October of this year, is "Till I Faint" by Olivia La Barr, the shattering, provocative account of one woman's quest for true fulfillment. "It is a rare, courageous and exciting story," Bliss observed. "We are very 'turned on' about it here at Corona," he added.

AUREOLA invites authors who believe their material is "right" for the discriminating female reader to contact Miss Aurora Madden-Pryce above. Discretion is, of course, assured.

The bit about discretion strikes me as sleazy. Unused as I am to the world of publishing, I'm still fairly sure that Aureola isn't a heavily funded operation. Corona seems to expect it to pay its own way until it has proved itself out here on the barricades of the sexual revolution, so to speak. I'm currently leaning over the saucepan full of water, which is taking forever to come to a boil, shaking my head slowly from side to side as if I don't know what the world is coming to, although that's not it at all. I'm just trying to get my whole face into the steam. Steam not only clears the sinuses but plumps out wrinkles, or so I read yesterday in *Good Housekeeping* while I was standing in line at the checkout counter looking for articles that weren't on menopause or Carol Burnett. I'm getting too sedate. Or sedated maybe.

Little bubbles are rising to the surface of the water now. I inhale noisily, wondering how long it will be before the steam starts burning my face. I'm considering burning my face on purpose so as to be able to peel off the top layer and reveal the moist, baby-soft layer underneath. You don't get ideas like that from *Good Housekeeping*, I learned about flaying faces from Vogue, on the Pub newsstand right beside *Playboy*. *Vogue* wants you to go to this clinic on East 64th Street to have your face burned, but I'm in Middle America and anyway a do-it-yourselfer. I find I'm playing Chicken in the steam now, pulling away at just about the time I could be developing some interesting blisters, plunging back when I could have escaped with just a healthy pink glow, currently un-desirable in *Vogue* but allowed, in an understated way, by *Mademoiselle*. In *Vogue* they want you to be white, with maybe some gray shadows under your cheekbones. Big eyes. White, but vulnerable.

Aurora Madden-Pryce is some name. It would never have occurred to me to call myself Aurora Madden-Pryce. I've considered other names, mainly Stephanie or, daringly, Gabrielle, names I associate with long lashes, long legs, but nothing so *thorough* as Aurora Madden-Pryce. It's one of those names you can't get at, an invulnerable name, but here I find I've gone into my reflexive sneer and have to pull away from the steam to do mouth relaxation exercises. I have a book that tells you how to do those: you're never too young to work on sneer lines, I figure. What scares me most of all is that I'll develop one of those dissatisfied mouths. My mother has one of those.

It's hard not to be dissatisfied, of course. If you don't get those lines it's a real triumph, as I see it. I find myself thinking that Aurora Madden-Pryce wouldn't be plumping out her wrinkles in the afternoon over an old Revere Ware saucepan; she's use the night cream, probably the kind that used to be made with Royal Jelly until they found out it gives you raging hormones, and a separate cream for her eyes and her hands and what they call a feeding lotion, which is so mysterious I can only imagine spooning it into wrinkles. She'd have a dewy-moist youthful complexion. She'd have firm, contoured breasts, for that matter, unlike me because I never sent for that cream that produced alarming cleavage in thirty days or your money back, although I fantasized about it night after night. Discretion was, of course, assured with the cream to, but at fourteen I was afraid that if my bosom started to herniate, everything would be traceable to the plain brown wrapper, the ad-dress in Beverly Hills, the blurry advertisement at the back of *Modern Screen*, which I never admitted to reading, officially pledged at the time to sincerity and Library Science. I suppose I'm still afraid to send for it. I have the same problem with the idea of buying makeup: what if someone I know sees me? Frank was al-ways looking me over, on the alert for a blob on my lashes, an alien color.

Aurora Madden-Pryce at Aureola, the porn lady. I try it out into the steam: "Hello this is Aurora Madden-Pryce at Aureola, the porn lady?" Once more, this time with a generic Southern accent: "The *pone* lady?" I'm thinking of lacquered fingernails, crossed legs, sumptuous pre-Raphaelite hair. It's a great name. It can't be her real name: no one gets a name like that from her parents. Anyway, even if the porn were incredibly tasteful, aimed at the very discriminating female reader, you wouldn't go around let-ting everyone know you were the porn lady, would you? Not even if you were a dedicated agent of the sexual revolution. You can't take the sexual revolution home with you, that's the point: you'd get heavy breathers hanging around your garbage chute looking for sanitary napkins and God knows what else, you'd attract the less discriminating kind of reader, the kind that arranges to come into his hand right when you're breezing self-sufficiently around the corner and through the turnstile, who goes yaaaaaagh and throws it in your face: you couldn't take that kind of risk. You have to draw the line between public and private. So Aurora Madden-Pryce has to be a pseudonym, that's all. Plucky girl, invading new territory, unleashing new perils. I should stop inhaling the steam before my nose hairs dissolve.

Of course they'll be my perils too if I come through, so to speak, with my own pussy book for pussies, tentatively entitled *Revenge of the Lenoreans*. And I intend to come through, although only now am I beginning to consider the implications. Granted, my Wordsworth and Buber piece has come boomeranging back from all the major journals and is at present looking for a home among the flakier publications, but perhaps this is the price you pay when you take a seminar on Existential Theology and the Literary Imagination. There's always, "Wordsworth and the Neoclassical Tradition Once Again," which will be Chapter One of my dissertation once I have another chapter in the works, and is surely stodgy enough for my intended audience, my intended peers. The point is, can I realistically do both, write Amazon exploitation fantasies while establishing myself as a Wordsworthian? Stupid question: you keep them separate, ergo Aurora Madden-Pryce, who may be Queenie Leavis for all I know. In the classroom, in the conference registration, in scholarly journals, I'll be Eleanor Nyland, flushed with integrity, spare, excitable, like Katharine Hepburn in *The Rainmaker* before Burt Lancaster takes down her hair. But outside. Outside the ivory tower, the groves of academe, Middle America or, face it, Hicksville USA I'll be. Well, who? Someone quite different obviously. Someone growing out her luxuriant, glossy, *chestnut* brown hair until it cascades down her back. Katharine Hepburn in *The Rainmaker* after Burt Lancaster, etc. Down to her waist. Down to her ass, damn it. Eyes of a startled faun. You wouldn't think to look at her.

I'm getting bored with steaming my face, so I spoon instant coffee out of the jar into my mug, the one that says, disgustingly, *MRS. MR.* went, needless to say: Frank was nothing if not thorough. I'm using too much, knowing the coffee will be opaque and bitter. It's medicine more than anything else: I drink it to wake up, not for pleasure. There's very little I do for pleasure, actually. Since I left my mother's house I've devoted myself to get-ting through school, getting the right degree, the right job, perhaps not incidentally the wrong husband but that's explicable, almost inevitable: choosing means to ends. But for a moment here I stand swaying above my mug, head in the steam again, thinking about what name I should choose for my pornographic persona, inventing myself. Then I stir the coffee again and carry it over to the breakfast nook in the corner along with the rest of my mail. Frank never liked the idea we had a breakfast nook and called it different things, usually "the corner where we keep the little table," to avoid the *Good Housekeeping* connotations. It has yellow and white checked café curtains with two rows of yellow rick-rack across the bottom of each tier, a legacy of the previous tenants. Frank was always after me to make new curtains that didn't look so goddamned cozy, but I like the way light comes through these, especially now in the afternoon. It was almost an omen when I discovered that the breakfast nook faced west, as if I'd stumbled on the only house in town that cherished late risers. Frank of course got up at five every morning to write. He said you did that if you were serious about the profession.

There is no return address on the letter. *Miss Elinor Nyland.* This is wrong: I'm Mrs. Nyland, it's Frank's name. And the misspelling, *Elinor.* It makes me just a little uneasy.

Inside is a single sheet of paper with a single typewritten sentence, neatly centered.

You have an admirer, Elinor.

I stare at it for a while, trying to see the joke. Something to do with Frank, probably; they like to get you where you're weakest. Although Frank left last spring and it's almost October.

But then a lot of people didn't know for sure he was gone until the school year started. When I was in high school the phone would ring and it would be some boy, with other boys moaning and cracking up in the background, saying he'd been watching me and found me unbelievably sexy, especially in those saddle shoes with those ankle socks. I'd hang up and turn around to find my mother hovering anxiously, brightly, waiting for news that her daughter the classic type had finally been asked out. I'd say the boy wanted a homework assignment.

So. *You have an admirer, Elinor.* Presumably to indicate how little there is to admire about me. I sit with my coffee, looking out the window at the writhing apple tree in the back yard. On the wall to the left of the window, over the kitchen counter, are two eighteenth-century floral prints, framed and behind glass. The names of the flowers appear in italics below the pictures. The flowers are proper to months: April, September, the months of our birthdays. I bought the prints because I believed they would create an atmosphere conducive to scholarship. An orderly period, the eighteenth century. Flowers popped up in season, hard-edged, minutely detailed. Frank on the Augustans: they knew how to live, had a damn good time, raconteurs and old port, he could respect that. Someone has sent me a letter: *You have an admirer, Elinor.* Why go to the trouble? Why rub it in?

I feel peeled. Yellow light slants from the curtains across the table top picking out tiny bubbles in the acrylic finish. An oily scum has formed over the surface of my coffee, too cold to drink now. There's no way to protect myself. No matter how well I guard against them they get in anyway, I can't anticipate them, never understood why it makes sense to hurt me. I mentioned this to my mother only once. My mother said, "I cried because I had no shoes and then I met a child who had no feet." From this I gathered that my mother couldn't cope with my inadequacy and that there was a vaguely therapeutic motive behind her insistence that I make a career out of helping children who had no feet, so to speak. My mother had many similar pieces of wisdom– "You're only unhappy when you're thinking of yourself," for instance, which had as an implied corollary that you might be happy if you'd just think of somebody else, preferably somebody without feet, of "Hard work chases those blues away," which didn't work for her either. My mother said I had a bad attitude.

I'm moaning without moving my lips right now, which takes a certain amount of concentration. Moaning actually helps, although I had to leave home to find that out. I experiment with little aggrieved coyote yips as I carry my mug to the sink and pour the coffee into the drain. It's an uncharacteristically wasteful gesture; normally I'd add more hot water to the current mixture. But at this moment a new and unprecedented possibility is occurring to me.

I'm suddenly thinking that the letter could be taken at face value, that I really might have an admirer. There's no overwhelming reason why not, after all. Until recently I had a husband, and once I had him there were other men who spoke to me in corners at parties, more or less admiringly. I'm not all that bad, after all. I'm not one of those people with no feet, whatever else my mother was intimating. I rinse out my coffee mug and take another look at the letter. It's nicely typed, although this is probably not a clue, as it's fairly easy to type a sentence the length of *You have an admirer, Elinor*. I hold up the paper to look for a water mark. I'm not sure what a water mark is, but I do discern the words *Eaton's Corrasable Bond* when I squint, and this is satisfying, although I use Eaton's Corrasable Bond myself and so do all my students. Who among us doesn't anticipate erasing something? You can get it at the campus bookstore.

The water is boiling. I lay the letter on top of the *Newsweek* so that General Ky's eyes peer over the top like Kilroy's. This time I shake even more coffee into the cup—it's high time I woke up. I'm beginning to get excited about the prospect of an admirer. It could be anybody, of course, not necessarily someone I'd want to have admiring me. On the other hand, whoever it is can spell *admirer*, which is a start. And punctuate: I'm so excited that I leave my mug on the stove beside the boiling water and bend over the letter. You have an admirer. Comma. Elinor. Forget the way my name is spelled: this is a very sophisticated comma; not one of my Bonehead students would put a comma there, or not on purpose. For a moment I'm stopped by the thought of an inadvertent comma, but that would be too much, too cruel, and also too unlikely. It's a competent comma, almost professorial, although a professor would presumably find my address by consulting the faculty roster and thus could be expected to spell my name as it appears there, which is to say correctly. Damn. I want it to be a professor. Most of the grownups I know are professors.

A student, then? I can't imagine a student admiring me, at least not in a way that would provoke an anonymous letter. If I were a male professor it would be a different story, of course, be-cause male authority figures are almost by definition attractive. What is attractive is the authority. Female authority figures are almost by definition repulsive. What is attractive in a woman, as far as I can see, is a kind of manipulative weakness: look up into his eyes while twisting him around your little finger and other anatomical impossibilities, see *Seventeen*, *Cosmopolitan*, *Glamour* and my high school Home Economics teacher who tried to teach me charm. My mother never got over my flunking charm. All of this suggests that if the male professor is an ideal crush-object, the female professor is at best sexless and at worst some sort of horrible distillation of (check as many as apply) your mother, the librarian who wouldn't let you chew gum, your first grade teacher who favored girls, the lady down the block who said she was going to tell your parents. Female teachers are there to be overcome. Whereas male professors embody a more benign power that you generally want to, ah, participate in. Frank always had a few *good* young men hanging around, also a number of young women who wanted to hear the real truth about Vorticism or Dadaism or Imagism or Symbolism, hoping, I suppose to elicit similarly exciting insights into their own dark psyches. By this line of reasoning I ought to be able to conclude that my admirer isn't a student. Not a male student anyway. It could always be someone like Louise Feitelson.

The idea sends me back to the stove to tip the remains of the boiling water into my coffee mug. Of course it's very likely to be Louise Feitelson, just her kind of thing in fact, and at this point I slop boiling water on my hand and drop the mug on the kitchen floor.

As I stare at the beige splatter on the white linoleum floor I have what amounts to a vision of Louis's glasses, perkily tilted at the corners, inset with small rhinestones. Then I tell myself that Louise can't have written the letter. Louise isn't advanced enough to have come up with that comma on her own, and I haven't yet given my lecture on The Comma in Direct Address. Louise is at least consistent in her ignorance. It's even a point of pride for her, I suspect, not to know anything about punctuation that I haven't told her.

As I put the mug in the sink and squat down with the dish-rag to work on the splatter I find myself thinking once again that coffee can leave permanent stains, although you might not notice anything at the time. It can turn your teeth yellow by degrees, for instance. My mother told me that if I was going to start drinking coffee I'd have to start brushing twice as often, coffee having this invisible dirtying power, very suggestive. My mother never drank coffee. It acted on her nerves. I drink coffee *because* it acts on my nerves and also, of course, to spite my mother, although I brush twice as often too: even as I'm doing all sorts of things my mother doesn't sanction I've never stopped believing her. Right now, for example, I'm so uneasy about possible coffee stains on the linoleum that I've decided to break out the serious scouring powder, sold only to janitors and marked *For Institutional Use Only*, which I scored last week from the weirdly young-old man who cleans my office. Furthermore, I'm planning to wash the dishrag in a mixture of Fab, baking soda and Twenty Mule Team Borax that I evolved last summer when I began seriously examining the effects of various products and combinations of products on my laundry. At this point I'll also wash all my towels and wash-rags and sheets and pillowcases. In the meantime there are the floors of the kitchen and the breakfast nook, inseparable from the kitchen floor really because all are the same white marbled linoleum, then the stairs with their tricky cracks, and then the entire upstairs, also done entirely in white linoleum. It's a question of drawing lines. Once I've started there doesn't seem to be any reasonable place to stop. I'm aware that this is probably insane. There was a time when I could think of myself as an agent of order, working tirelessly to sort and tidy the paraphernalia of our life together, but now my neatness is only compulsive, a reflexive wince at possible squalor, another legacy of my mother.

He moved out last May, during finals week. He wasn't giving any finals, as he was only teaching upper-division courses. As I was only teaching lower-division courses I was giving four finals, one for each class. When he left I was very, very busy.

My initial response was that I hated him and had always hated him and had always known he was going to walk out on me. This lasted about two weeks. Then I turned on myself and snarled at my own passivity. Other than a brief period when I was mostly drunk and elated that he couldn't see me being drunk, I spent most of the summer feeling, in an inevitable progression, hateful, passive, snarling, and then hateful again. I never really considered taking another job or moving to another city or even out of the rental house we had shared, which is to say that I periodically considered these alternatives and dismissed them as beyond my powers of coping. I was actually quite surprised when he told me he was leaving. In the vacuum afterwards I told myself that I had known it all along, that it was only a question of time, that we had come to regard each other with weary tolerance at best. Each of these observations was the product of hindsight. I couldn't shake off the shock, or the suspicion that of all the people around him only I hadn't expected him to go.

He was already famous by the time I started graduate school, partly for having started a dissertation that would be (growly throat-clearings from the senior faculty here) a real contribution, and partly for being outrageous. I've always been around people who are famous for being outrageous, presumably because I put up with them, but Frank was the first person I'd ever met who was famous for being outrageous and also succeeding, which meant that he was the one outrageous person I've ever been associated with whose intelligence didn't require lengthy explanation. I heard about him immediately, the second day I was in residence, and by the end of the week I was dying to meet him.

Rather strangely, I thought, he was also dying to meet me.

Three weeks into the semester I went to a party in a labyrinthine apartment owned by the university and rented by several graduate students, and he sidled up to me and grabbed my elbow while I was taking off my coat. "They were right, you are jailbait," he said.

I checked him out. He was dark, broad and hairy, "What do you mean?" I asked, although of course I knew.

"You look young," he said. Just once I wish someone would say, "You look good."

"I'm from Kansas," I said. In New York this constitutes an explanation.

"Kansas!" he cried. Closing his eyes and pursing his lips he intoned rapturously, "There's no place like home. There's *no* place like home!" Then he opened his eyes and shouted, "Judy Garland, my first love! Hey, have you ever noticed how they were always shooting her from angles where you couldn't see her *tits*?" Frank was a fast mover.

He was the only man I'd ever spent any time with who had nothing obviously wrong with him. He got along with people. He had a future. Other people thought he was smart. He didn't suspect too many people of being out to get him. The things that actually were wrong with him were also in a funny way the things that were right with him. For instance, he often talked to me about other women as if he were talking to another man. "Look at the ass on that one," he'd drone into my ear as we walked hand in hand down Broadway. Or "I wouldn't kick that one out of bed." I usually tried to act as if he hadn't said anything, although some-times I wondered if he wanted me to say something like "Wow, yeah, I'd love to get between *those* legs"; he seemed to expect some response and I know I usually disappointed him. At first I tried to turn the whole thing into a joke, but that was a mistake. Frank was supposed to be the one with the sense of humor. I was supposed to suffer him. I couldn't pinpoint how I'd figured this out, since he'd never specifically addressed me on the subject of my behavior around him, but it was definitely his idea: even the expression "suffer him" was his idea, although I'm not sure he actually ever said those exact words. In his company I progressed rapidly from being jailbait to being the mature one, then one who fed him lines, led him away from parties, nursed his hangovers, made him coffee, proofread his chapters, and generally suffered him. He called me jailbait in bed sometimes. Once he called his secret Lolita, meaning it was my age that was a secret I suppose. I smiled inscrutably, the way he liked, and suffered that too.

It was all so easy and so fated, somehow, that I was merely relieved when he proposed. We took the subway downtown one day and that was that. I was Mrs. Frank, adjunct to brilliance and of course a fine little scholar in her own right—how, um, *interesting* to be working on the romantics, due for a comeback any day doubtless, doubtless. He was writing the definitive work on the *Cantos*. I learned about putting wine right in there with the pot toast and gave dinners at which Frank expounded and I waited for people to say everything was fine, really, the food was delicious, no they'd had enough but it was delicious, really. That summer Frank finished the first draft of his dissertation and I taught two classes of incoming freshmen how to write introductions and conclusions. Then Frank's star shot out of sight so rapidly that I was still writing labored, *caring* little comments at the end of papers I was failing when he was already embroiled in significant literary feuds.

The occasion was "Haiku and Icon: The Integrity of the Aesthetic Artifact Once Again"—he was going in for colons in a big way, and in more ways than one as it turned out—delivered in the sort of room where you'd have expected to get a pitch for encyclopedias of Positive Thinking, packed with paternal gentlemen who seemed to be deciding whether he was the prodigal son. The Indian summer heat came pulsing through the floor-to-ceiling orange fiberglass drapes as he read, and I tried not to go to sleep and counted words I wouldn't dare use: *polyvalent, equivocity, dithyrambic, iconography*. It seemed futile to continue pretending I was too pure to use them. And then in the question and answer session a Yale gray eminence had risen, courteously, to ask, courteously and ironically, one deadly question that was really a statement, and Frank had faced him squarely, looked him square in the eye, and said, "Well, you caught me with my finger up my ass, didn't you?" Total consternation. Instant acceptance. So *New York* of Frank. After that I lost track of everything: we were seized and stuffed into cars and ended up at someone's house where I lost him in a sea of natural shoulders. Much later I threw up, discreetly, in an upstairs bathroom. I cleaned it up, too. It was unpleasant, but it beat trying to stand up in a hot living room filled with people saying nice things about Frank.

The week after that happened I came home carrying a pork loin roast from Gristede's, what the hell, and two sets of student papers, to find Frank lying on his back on the rippling floor we'd sanded ourselves at the end of the summer, talking international long distance to some luminary at Cambridge—England this time. "We-ll," he was saying, a descending scale new to me and redolent of Flatbush, "you know I'm an asshole." Public-school neighing rattled the receiver. "Yeah, well, I'm not sure I *see* it that way," said Frank. I stood there with my arms full thinking about the papers that would occupy me that night and the following night and the next night, once again preempting my projected study of place names in Wordsworth, while Frank, who had guilelessly told both his classes the minute he got back from the conference, "I'm really a lousy teacher, you guys are getting screwed," talked shamelessly about people who were only names on book jackets to me. I took the pork roast into the kitchen, hacked off a slab of it, and was cutting it into niggling little strips when he came in and leaned on the counter. "Hey," he said finally. "You don't need to do that. We can go out or something."

I said, "You're from Indiana. Your father is in corporate law. You don't talk like that."

"I been here a long time," he said, which was the end of that argument. I continued to reduce the pork loin roast to filaments. I intended to make something complicated involving ginger and garlic. I wouldn't have gone to the trouble normally, but I'd figured out he really didn't like exotic food all that much.

By the time he got his first real job, real albeit in Middle America, he had the beginnings of an ulcer and a full-fledged drinking problem. Perhaps to keep me out of the kitchen he negotiated a job for me too. You could call it that. As he explained, they couldn't very well put me on a tenure track when I hadn't even finished my degree. I pointed out that he hadn't finished his degree either, but he said that was a whole other thing. I was, explicably, the lesser light, his trapping. I taught remedial classes to rooms full of students who had been told there was something wrong with the way they were writing and I would fix them. He taught a graduate seminar on Pound and Eliot that adjourned to a bar and broke up so late sometimes that I would be lying on the bed in my slip trying to defer panic by concentrating of a map of Grasmere and Environs when he rolled in, full of expostulatory verse and emptied of semen. Sometimes we'd try to screw, sweatily. More often we'd exchange hostile remarks: "Have fun?" "I'm sorry, I had fun. What can I tell you?" "You're still from Indiana. Nobody from Indiana says What can I tell you." We were very banal in our hostility. When I told him I wanted to take a walking tour of the Lake District he was so supportive I canceled the trip, telling myself bitchily that if I couldn't stop him at least I wasn't about to give him carte blanche to screw all his students. I didn't even know he was negotiating for the next job up the ladder until he announced in late May that he would be leaving in the company of the willowy graduate student who had called once in early May to accuse me of being a Non-Life-Affirmer.

I got to keep the rental house, most of the furniture, and the job he had arranged for me. My contract had just been renewed, so legally I was in the clear. Actually the university had wanted Frank and got stuck with me, the booby prize. After he left, I found myself simply occupying the rental house while the town heated up and emptied and no one called to invite me to the lake or the mountains, or only Jo Michaelson, to report brusquely that she was off to Greece with some other boring old ladies and that Frank was a little shit. I wasn't comforted. Frank had been saying he was a shit for the last three months. It was characteristic of him, his charm, his false modesty.

I disliked the way I was taking it, but my dislike didn't change anything. Instead of launching into my dissertation I was spending whole days playing solitaire, dealing out one hand after another, scooping the cards up as soon as I had laid them out, quick to sense futility. I drank brightly colored sticky liqueurs that I bought in little airplane-size bottles and poured over ice in a wine glass: Kirsch, Pernod, Cherry Heering, apricot brandy, crème de menthe. Sometime during the middle of August I started making long distance phone calls to acquaintances of several years past. I called Janet only after I'd exhausted my resources, and after fifteen minutes of listening to Pinky Hatch, briefly of the graduate school and the Existential theology seminar, now assistant to somebody who had something to do with copy at Doyle Dane, describe the probably course of her engagement, marriage, and subsequent life with someone named Buzz if Buzz turned out not to be married already. "I won't go out to dinner with Frank," Pinky promised moistly and several times. "I won't even have a drink with him. Anyway, Baltimore's a long way off and if he was going to call he *would* have by now." After concluding this conversation I drank off the three airline-size bottles of Drambuie I'd been saving for something really big, like Frank's death or return, and called a girl named Allie who used to live down the hall and still kept in touch with Janet.

"Huh" Janet said when I finally got through to her. "You're up late in Podunk." It was in fact, two-thirty, and I was lying on the wall-to-wall carpeting in the living room balancing a wine glass full of melting ice on my diaphragm. "S'all right though," she allowed. "I work late."

"I hear you're a painter," I said, having heard it from Allie five minutes earlier. I'm still trying to figure out how that happened. Janet was a Home Economics major in college.

"Funny thing," said Janet cryptically. "I got married, you know," she continued. "It didn't work out. He was always putting *moves* on me."

"I'm sorry," I said.

"I'm not," said Janet. "Not my thing. Hey, what's happening in Podunk?"

"Not much," I said, feeling that I ought to resent hearing it called Podunk. "My husband left me two months ago."

"Good deal," said Janet.

"No," I said, and began to cry.

"Shit," said Janet.

I sobbed for a while across the wires.

"You like that action, huh," she said.

"What?"

"Men."

"Yes." It felt wonderful just letting the tears ooze out and down my cheeks like sticky liqueur.

"You going to stay there or what?"

"Oh, I don't know." Amazing how many tears I could produce. The wine glass lay on its side and cool water was seeping into the carpet beneath me.

"Can you write dirty?"

"What?"

Janet, as it turned out, had run into someone from a dirty book press who was looking for dirty books by women. "*For* women too, but about men," Janet said. "Not my thing."

"No," I said, discovering I had stopped crying. After she hung up I lay on the damp carpet and thought about writing dirty. It didn't seem beyond the realm of possibility.

Shortly after this conversation I got my first letter from Frank. It was a graceful, apologetic letter; I didn't think he had it in him. The air was more rarefied in the big leagues, what with the genuine superstars in residence. He liked the give and take but Lynda had pretty much decided she didn't want to finish up her degree after all, and you could hardly blame her when you hung around some of these guys who pretty much ate and drank literary theory, so she was taking a potting course, getting into the non-intellective. I probably knew exactly how she felt, having lived so long with a workaholic intellectual like him. By the way, would I mind claiming Mental Cruelty?

I took me several days to compose a reply. It took me that long to come to grips with the fact that Frank couldn't recognize his own irony. After that I started trying to write dirty. It was harder than I'd imagined. I spent a lot of time starting at sheets of typing paper waiting for inspiration to strike, to just, you know, *take* me. As far as I know it never showed up. Maybe I wasn't relaxed enough. I have a lot of hangups, I decided.

In the process of trying to write dirty I became, if possible, cleaner. The liqueurs moved to the breakfast nook and I shampooed the living room carpet with a machine I rented from the hardware store and some incredible foaming stuff you sort of massage in and then *suck* out, on the model of deep cleansing cream but demonstratively more effective since with the cream you only wipe. I embarked on a project to put a tough, long-lasting finish on the linoleum floors. I began doing controlled experiments on various washday products.

All this meant putting Wordsworth on the back burner, so to speak, but I knew he was the type who would forgive me. I think of him always as the rheumy laureate, extruding sticky gobs of *The Recluse* into senility, soggy and tolerant. I sympathized with him instantly when I learned he was out of fashion, and always felt that in return for my sympathy he would stand up for me. I clung to him while Frank was raging back and forth through the *Cantos* summoning the gaunt and inflexible spirit of an Ezra without flesh or habits and certainly without politics, wholly self-contained and thus out of the reach of biographers or tour guides. While Frank discerned patterns and tensions I conjured up a doddering bard with failing eyes who ate porridge and needed to be led up and down the trails to the Sublime. I pictured myself leading him, in unmanageable nineteenth-century skirts and sensible shoes. I imagined feeding him an oatcake and tenderly wiping the crumbs off his chin. I imagined writing to his dictation yet another Ecclesiastical Sonnet. I knew where I was with him. He needed me.

But given the emptiness of the house, its secreted filth, and my pornographic project, he receded until I remembered him only sporadically and with irritation, as you might remember a decaying relative who is ready for a bedpan or a wipe-up. He exists at present as two bulging file folders, one upstairs in my filing cabinet, one in my desk at school. My pornographic narrative, on the other hand, exists in scraps, because nothing seems to go anywhere: every approach I've taken seems to lead me away from pornography. My conversations grow elaborate and bookish instead of degenerating into grunts and moans. My descriptions start with the less erogenous zones and stay there. The desk upstairs was full of pieces of paper I was afraid to throw away, envisioning the Pakistani graduate student going through my garbage, until school began, at which point I carted the whole drawerful of pages into my office, where I feel more anonymous. Somehow it's more secure throwing rejected purple passages into the institutional gray wastebasket: somehow I feel that if they're found they won't reflect on me personally.

I've taken off my bathrobe since there's no point in getting institutional scouring powder all over it. I don't really think of myself as naked until the phone starts ringing upstairs, and then I realize I'll have to crawl under the picture window in the living room to get to the stairwell. I could decide at this point that it isn't worth it, but I don't think I've ever succeeded in ignoring a ringing phone. Of course by the time I get there whoever it is has hung up.

It's my office hour again, beginning of the week, another fresh start if you're into rebirth. I've got my door open just a crack, which I hope will be discouraging. The early Bonehead class was a fiasco, with Louise Feitelson pinning me on restrictive and non-restrictive modifiers. It's the beginning of the end in that class. They're finding out there are things I don't know. I'm stealthily picking my nose. No one is watching, but nose-picking is   by nature a stealthy activity. I'm wishing I could go home, having already had enough reality for one day. In full retreat now I'm thinking about cunnilingus, one of Frank's words. He taught me a lot of words like that so I could read avant-garde literature and not get uptight, which is another of Frank's words, or one of the words a bunch of us hanging around Frank started using a couple of year ago, along with flipped out, freaked out and far out. The expressions were suddenly in the air and so we started using them—self-consciously at first, with little academic grimaces to indicate that what we *meant* was flipped, as they say, out or up, as it were, tight – but then with increasing authority and pride of ownership. Such words signal which side of the generation gap you're on, even if you do wear nylons to class. Flipped out is positive, as is far out. Freaked out and uptight generally are negative: what you say is "well don't freak *out* over it" or "don't get so fucking up*tight*." Generally when they say uptight they're accusing you of some-thing as in don't be so goddamned fucking uptight you goddamned fucking bitch. Frank was very concerned that I not be uptight about things like cunnilingus, which is natural and, in its own hairy way, like, beautiful.

I'm also vaguely aware of the possibility of an admirer

somewhere just out of sight, lurking, presumably admiring, although I'm not ready to admit this possibility to full consciousness at ten in the morning. Cunnilingus is the more defensible topic right now, since I'm moving toward the first climax of my porn novel. So to speak. Actually I'm not sure what climax is supposed to mean in the context of a pussy book for pussies. The Lenoreans have been coming practically since page one, after all, and the addition of a handful, so to speak, of sweaty prinks doesn't seem likely to make all that much difference, if you consider it as a technical problem. Or to be fair, it didn't make all that much difference in the case of Frank Nyland, sweaty bouncer and plunger and occasional practitioner of cunnilingus. The cunnilingus was okay.

Bearing all this in mind, my backlog of experience, I feel they ought to maybe, like, *ease* into copulation. A lot of licking of various things, going on for pages and pages. Perhaps moving on to some rubbing, with lots of emphasis on the hairlessness of the newcomers. Pricks are going to need working up to, but hairy rubbing has immediate possibilities. There's no denying, though, that this is all buildup, what Janet called fore play. Fore as in before. And before what, you might ask, but you *know* the event this is all in service of, oh so to speak, is that fireburst, that culmination of plot and, perhaps by analogy, all earthly desire, that climax. What they call it, their climax. When I was first in graduate school, in a criticism course, my newfound sexuality throbbing messily like a severed artery, the professor asked me out of the blue what I thought Longinus meant by the sublime. Out of the blue I responded, in my throbbing innocence, that the sublime seemed a lot like orgasm. "*Nooooooo*," he moaned at me, outraged: "orgasm is like when you build and build and build and then whaaaaa it all comes out. The sublime is completely different." The worst part about the incident is that nobody could figure out how I'd made such a mistake. I mean, they all thought orgasm meant male orgasm. So, climax. The point, frankly—oh so to speak, speaking of Frank—where you think oh shit and start cheering him on to new rodeo records, bouncy bouncy. To be fair, this has only been my experience in the case of Frank Nyland, bedroom cowboy, and to be honest there has only been

Frank Nyland if you don't count Janet and I don't count Janet. She never counted me, for that matter. She made a big point of the fact that she went to her hymeneal bed with hymen intact. I never told Frank about Janet. I didn't want to put him uptight.

Cunnilingus isn't a word you can imagine using in conversation, I decide, and mentally exorcize it from my dialogue. I've been considering variations on the proposition "I want to perform cunnilingus on you"; they come out sounding exasperated, "Look, you want me to perform *cunnilingus* on you or something?" Frank again, red-faced when he couldn't come, as if I had to have my quota of sperm to go into the requisite screaming ecstasies. It wasn't that I missed the sperm; it was where he had already put it that bothered me. At that point cunnilingus didn't help, nothing helped, but he'd keep at it, rearranging my legs, smacking down on my whappity whappity until in embarrassment, and not just for him, I'd begin rolling my eyes like Steppin Fetchit and playing raped, she *loves* it, grinding my pelvic bones into his stomach, hoping something, face it, to smash his balls, just like he'd always suspected. So: cunnilingus, potentially just another thing they use on you. In New York they said I want to suck your pussy and made wet sounds while you were walking down the street, although not with Frank around (did he know they did that? How could he possibly know?). It didn't sound pleasant when they put it that way, pursing their lips and making smacking, juicy noises, a plumber's friend in a toilet bowl, insinuating that I ought to be offended. I always pretended not to hear them because I was never sure how to take the information that they wanted to suck my pussy. With someone like Ralph Hamilton I know exactly what's expected. The point is that you're not a prude or not that *much* of a prude, and from there they can tell lots of dirty jokes that derive spice from your just faintly prudish presence. You give them permission to embarrass you: that's the first step toward acceptance. With the men on the streets it seems beside the point whether you're a prude or not. The point seems rather more hostile. At times I've wanted to shout back, what if someone said that to your sister? At other times I've thought, not suck, *lick*. Neither of these responses seemed appropriate for someone attending Columbia.

Of course, no one says anything about sucking pussies here; it's hardly the thing in Middle America. But with the suggestion of an admirer flickering around the edges of my awareness now I wonder how I'd feel if someone broached the subject tactfully. Not *I want to suck your pussy*; something more like, well, *I want to perform cunnilingus on you*. But without the exasperation. Or, very politely, *I want to lick your pussy*, no wet sounds. As if it would be an honor. As if he would never dream of telling the guys. As if it were my pussy, none other, that he aspired to lick. Somebody caring. Interested. We could fuck, for that matter.

"Miss Nyland?" I twitch upright, knees together, regressing to girdle-wearers' posture.

It's not, as I've been half expecting, Louise Feitelson. On the other hand, it isn't Tom Lippman either. "Yes," I say repressively, Miss Nyland, shepherd of the young. I swing around in the swivel chair, leaning back slightly, centrifugal force.

"Ah, are you busy?" It's a student from the blond back row of my World Masterpieces class. It astonished Frank when we first got here how many of them are blond. To me the fact barely registers. I think of blond as the absence of color. Not quite the case here though. His eyes are a startling blue.

"Come in," I say.

"Uh, I don't want to *bother* you—"

"Come in," I say. "It's my office hour. That's what I'm here for, to be bothered." I smile to let him know it's a joke. It's a pretty bad joke but to him I'm an authority figure and that always counts toward humor.

"Oh." He shrugs, looks around for the chair, spots it in the corner, and drags it to him rather than the other way around. I would never have done that. How many times have I been to talk with professors and ended up sitting scrunched in a chair in the corner by the door? Yet he manages to be diffident about it, eyes lowered now, sweep of smoky lashes against the pale gold of the cheeks, high cheeks, high-boned Nordic face, oh my God, I think, beginning to take him in.

"Ted," he says. "I'm in your, ah, World Masterpieces

class?"

"Ted," I say.

"I came to talk about my paper," he says.

"It's not due until December," I say automatically.

"You think I should wait to get started?"

"What?" I realize I've been staring at him.

"It's too early for me to start thinking about my paper? It's, like, *cumulative*? Like, I don't really know enough to tackle a subject yet?"

I blink. "I don't think I'm following you."

He shrugs, snots, a small sketch of a laugh, a trial huh-*hunh* with the lashes sweeping the cheeks, the cheeks turning faintly pink. I manage a sniffy empathetic chuckle and relinquish my plans to lord it over him. He's offering vulnerability. He's making fun of himself. And really, he is a breathtaking young man. Even in the classroom, where faces run together as I try not to speak too rapidly or hyperventilate, I should have picked him out. Not my type, of course. The good-looking ones never are.

"I'm not making myself clear," he says. "I have that problem not making myself clear." Shrug, snort. I nod encouragement. "I'm kind of excited about writing my term paper, that's all. I'm probably jumping the gun. I'm like that."

"Not at all," I say. "I'm not used to students who get excited about their term papers in October, that's all."

"No?" He looks worried.

"But it's wonderful that you're getting a head start." He still looks dubious. They hate being different. They're always trying to find out the way it's done normally.

"Maybe I should, uh, do some more general research before I try to specialize," he says now.

"Why?"

"To get ready." He's scowling into his lap. "I should get some background, probably. I've never even read *The Divine Comedy*."

"We're not doing *The Divine Comedy*," I say.

"I expect everyone's read it," he says.

"No," I say, catching on. "No. It's not that they're better.

You've got it backwards. It's not that they're so good they're deliberately not starting their term papers early, for some *reason*. It's never even occurred to them to try that hard, that's all. They'd never believe you were serious." I can't believe he's serious either. People like this don't show up in my classes. "*Good* students start their term papers early." He's looking more hopeful. "I mean, I always started my term papers early," I say before I can stop myself.

"Really," he says.

"Not to make myself out to be wonderful or anything," I gabble, "but yeah, right. All the time. I was famous for it. The other girls on my floor used to come look at me working on my term paper *months* before it was due. They finally decided it was a kind of cheating and then they left me alone."

"That's idiotic," he says.

There is a long, ungainly silence while we smile shyly at each other. "Of course, not everyone wants to be smart," I say. You have to act as if laziness were an acceptable alternative: otherwise they get worried you're discriminating against somebody.

"If you don't work as well as you can it's just a waste of time going to college," he says. "That's what I believe."

"Of course I wasn't doing much else," I say, wondering how much I'm going to blurt out. "Not like, you know, student government of sports or, oh *glee* club or like that." I've left out dating, to conspicuous an admission.

But he's gazing at me with his lips slightly parted, showing a bit of tongue, small teeth. Before I can interpret this he breathes, "Oh, me *either*."

It's an affirmation I never could have anticipated. People who look like that get made captain of the football team and student body president before they even learn there are people like me. Not having had the chance to be cast out, they never get around to rejecting the norm. But here he is, beautiful, acceptable, on my side. A gift.

"You like to read," I say.

"I love to read."

"And write."

"I love to write. I want to write a paper for you on Dostoevsky."

He said "for you." I tuck the fact away where I can get at it later and say, "You're taking Russian?"

"I'm full of shit," she says, eyes lowered, hint of a smile bending a perfect Greek-boy mouth. What they call an Adonis type, no doubt. He's probably used to having women go dry-mouthed at the sight of him. Having girls go dry-mouthed. Women might be different. Certain women. A certain kind of woman.

"I'd like to take Russian," he says, "but I'm not taking it now so I'm probably ridiculous thinking I can do anything with Dostoevsky. I'm just a freshman. I know *nothing*."

"You'll learn," I say. It sounds flat.

"You know what I want?" He has raised his head to look at me. His chin is square, faintly cleft. He looks like a poetic Joe Palooka. "I'll tell you," he says, emphasis faint but unmistakable on the "you." "I want to be a professor. Go ahead and laugh."

"Why should I laugh? I'm a professor. No," I correct my-self, "I'm just a lecturer."

"What's the difference?"

"Oh," I sigh, feeling worldly, "someday I'll tell you all about it, the hierarchy. It's something you'll need to know." I've managed that well, projecting a future. He nods soberly. "But right now I have a class," I say.

This brings him to his feet. He advances to the desk and stands over me. "I've been monopolizing your *time!*" he cries.

It's too much: I've never been this close to someone this beautiful. I want to reach out and grab anything that protrudes, to keep him from going away, ever. This is unlike me. I never grab.

"That's what my time is for," I say, Miss Brooks persona reasserting itself. I wonder whether I'll faint.

"I'm going to, like, do some preliminary research," he says anxiously. "Then maybe when I have something, you know, con*crete* we can confer about it. Have a conference. If that's not asking too much." There are two little grooves between his eye-brows, furrows of contrition.

"Not at all," I say.

"See you in class?"

"Right," I say. It sounds unnecessarily brusque. It can be remedied later. I do have a class, modifiers again. Everything I do in Bonehead I do twice, like the return of the repressed.

This class, more awake than the eight-thirty one, receives my news about restrictive and non-restrictive modifiers with polite incredulity. I keep telling myself it's nothing personal; it goes with being an authority figure. Writing my futile examples across the board while the class simmers with whispers and mutterings, I find myself wondering why I go on with an activity that involves neither teaching nor learning. It's hard to believe that I'm even failing, as restrictive and non-restrictive modifiers are hardly a burning issue outside this classroom, although I'm aware that this lack of commitment is far more subversive in me than it would be in, say, Tom Lippman or Ralph Hamilton. Part of my role seems to be that I'm supposed to care enormously about grammar and syntax, to have some loonily personal stake in the behavior of commas, so the class can mumble and snicker at me and the professorial types can pull rank. There's an odd sort of symbiosis at work in Bonehead. It requires a lady teacher to operate, and indeed "lady teacher" is the operative phrase. Or "schoolmistress," universal symbol of repression, natural prey of the young. It's part of what happened to me when I became an authority figure.

I'm relieved when the bell rings, less relieved to find myself walking back across the sunlit stretch of campus to Schwindemann in the company of two students, both male, both blond although less assertively so than Ted, both sulky, and evidently friends. As far as I can tell they belong to that portion of the back row that comes to class maybe once a week. They seem to be working as a team.

As a rule I dislike crossing campus with students, no matter what their intentions. For one thing, I usually run out of small talk within the first twenty feet. I've always been baffled by small talk anyway, both my mother's self-consciously prattling openers ("Y'know, the funniest thing just happened to me") and the more sophisticated repartee of the girls around me in school who, as my mother put it, got along ("Gee, that's a cute skirt you're wearing, kid"). I feel it's necessary to keep the conversation to small talk, however, because the students invariably want to complain about something and it seems unfair and a little dangerous to have them airing their grievances on a public walkway. I rarely get help from the students themselves, even those who are socially artful under other circumstances ("Thanks, kid, and gee that's a cute skirt *you're* wearing *too*"), so I work at eliciting chat, feeling awkward and timid and ready to concede almost everything at the outset. With these two I essay "You guys have a nice summer vacation?" which they appear to find too contemptible to notice. I follow up with "What did you guys *do* this summer?" which provokes one of them, Ken I think his name is, to say "I didn't go to *school*" so savagely that I want to scream that none of it is my fault, the modifiers, the Bonehead class, the exam that threw him at me, the 2-S deferment that keeps him in college, at least until he completes the long slide through remediation, counseling, and probation that will deliver him at last into the arms of the Army. The worst part of it is that none of it really is my fault although some of it may well be his fault. He's a healthy boy and probably representative of the patriotic sentiment in this part of the country that maintains American boys should fight gooks wherever gooks are found. I get papers on the subject.

The mail room is full of people milling around trying to see who got turned down for what. My box contains only a manila envelope, which I glance at pokerfaced and then slide under my arm. The students seem more subdued when I rejoin them, probably because of the disproportionate number of adults around this time of the day. We get into the elevator along with several lesser lights of the Boys' Club, two male graduate students in ties and sport jackets, and a wasted looking person whom I recognize after a few moments as the janitor for my floor, and I stare at my shoes while the graduate students and the Boys' Club boys swap anecdotes in bluff, tense voices. When the doors open I step out briskly without looking back, swing around the corner, and run up against Lois Lafferty, who is teetering on her high hells in the middle of the hall hugging her arms and looking up at Bill Powers, junior modernist and organizer of the departmental basketball team. Lois makes one of her squashed noises and lurches sideways. I drop the manila envelope. Bill Powers looks at this watch, say, "Oh wow it's time for my class," and dashes around the corner past the two boys who have caught up and are now watching me squat to pick up the manila envelope. "*I'm* sorry," I say, much too heartily.

Lois isn't about to respond to this. She has her hands on her hips or what you'd assume would be her hips. She is short and dark, like Frank, but amazingly indeterminate in outline if you actually start wondering where she begins and ends. She wears things that drape and flow and trail and generally hang off her, usually several at a time, and the other things she wears are gathered and tucked and flounced and pleated and yoked and cut on the bias and dripping with Third World embroidery and bunchy lace and occasional beadwork. She wears everything my mother and my Home Economics teacher warned me about, and for this reason I'd feel warm toward her except that she has never once said anything nice to me. Frank was openly scornful of her, the more surprising in that Frank can usually see some good in any woman who throws herself at him. The fact that she is a medievalist may have turned him off. The medievalists here have to be disciples of Ralph Hamilton; they're his core group and occasionally he has them herd together and make chilly remarks about the decline of scholarship. Also, Lois is quite overweight. I would have figured out this was what all the hanging, floating, dangling stuff was about even if I hadn't spent the last ten years of my life disguising my thighs. Crouching at Lois's hem now I note that the skirt covers Lois's knees, which is just as well, and that it is a woven, banded sort of thing, predominantly hot pink and greeny-yellow worked in vertical strips, presumably for that heightening, slimming effect.

"Why don't you look where you're going," says Lois above me.

I stand up. Even at five-four in my penny loafers I'm a lot taller than she is. "I'm sorry," I say again.

"You could have knocked me over," says Lois. "I just

barely caught myself."

I'm aware of a subdued shuffling behind me, students in high-topped sneakers growing restive.

"I may have twisted my ankle," says Lois. She has a long upper lip, like a sheep or a camel.

"I was thinking," I say. "I was lost in thought. I didn't mean to run into you."

"Just because you're thinking doesn't mean you don't *notice* people," says Lois. She bends down and feels her ankle.

"I hope you're all right," I say. "I'm very sorry."

"I *presume* you're sorry," says Lois. "I mean, that's under*stood*. But not everything." She flexes her upper lip. Lois has many expressions that might be implied in the phrase "mobile mouth." Many of them are quite repellent. She looks at the moment like someone who wants something but can't figure out what it is. She's taking a long time about it.

"Most people here don't get lost in thought," she says finally. "We think. We don't get *lost* in it though." She smiles, closed-mouth, long-lipped, supercilious. "The absent-minded professor is a myth," she says.

"I know," I say.

"I was sorry to hear about Frank," she says as if reverting to an earlier topic of conversation. "That he walked out on you, I mean. It was in the cards, of course, but if left you in a terribly embarrassing situation. You must feel terrible coming in every day just as if you were a member of the department."

No sound from the boys behind me. "No," I say, not very loudly.

"Most of us though you wouldn't even come back in the fall," says Lois with an encouraging smile.

"I have to talk to some students," I say.

"Students!" Lois flings back her head and squints to the right of my shoulder. "Yes I see. You're teaching Bonehead, aren't you?"

"Basic," I say.

"Most of us call it Bonehead," says Lois. "I won't keep you." She spins away, sending a string of beads and the long tail of a fringed piece of fabric into space. "My ankle is holding up," she says without turning her head. "Lucky for you."

I start toward my office again, reactivating the precession: I can hear behind me the circumspect padding of sneaker soles. Unlocking my office door, I force myself to consider what might happen next. If they gang up on me I'm going to cry, and then it will be a very long semester. I could have a breakdown maybe. Resign for health reasons. *And then?* Sneers a Frank-inflected voice at the back of my head. *And then?*

The key catches and I push the door open. On the floor at my feet is a cream-colored envelope. Typed neatly across it is

Elinor.

I stop short, and Ken, or maybe his name is Dave, slams into me from behind. I skitter forward over the envelope. There's some shuffling as they back off. "Sorry," says one of them, but I'm intent on getting behind my desk before anything more can happen. When I look up again they're standing just inside the doorway. It's a small office and they look as if they could take it apart. One of them is extending the cream-colored envelope to-ward me, holding it gingerly between thumb and forefinger. My shoe has a made a grainy smear across the name on it, *Elinor.*

"I guess this is yours," he says. I take it by the corner and drop it on my desk. "Um," he says.

"Well," I say.

"Um," he says again, and looks at his hands. The other student, who has kept one step behind him, looks at his feet.

"Won't you sit down," I say. There is only one chair, of course, but if I can get even half of them down to my level it will be an improvement.

He mumbles something. I nod encouragement, beginning to feel a little better. "I said," he says, "that lady sure was giving you a hard time."

I keep my face carefully neutral. "You think so?"

"Jeeze," says the other one suddenly. "I could of *mashed* her, you know that?"

I know that, but I do my best to look disapproving. *"We were going to give you a hard time,"* continues the first one, their spokesman, "but Jeeze—" He looks as though someone has stuffed a sock in his mouth.

"A hard time," I say.

"No offense," he says, looking miserable. "I mean, we do that sometimes, you know?"

"I know," I say.

"But Jeeze," he says.

"Maybe you could come to class a little more" I say. "And bring your books."

"Hey," he says, grabbing at the escape I've offered him. "Then maybe we might understand more, right?"

"It's worth a try," I say, feeling a lot like Miss Brooks again.

"Well, we'll just be *going*—" he says. His friend is already out the door.

"Glad to help," I say. "Any time." The real Miss Brooks would have said any time, *boys*, because she is by nature an authority figure whereas I can only hope to do a convincing imitation of an authority figure, of Miss Brooks as it happens. I don't feel authoritative. I don't even feel right most of the time. When they challenge me on the rules for apostrophes or my policy on late papers I have to mimic a bureaucrat defending the laws because they're there. Mine is not to reason why. Reasons are the prerogative of the regular faculty.

I pick up the cream-colored envelope. *Elinor.* Not the same typewriter, though; this is Elite, small and chaste. A high quality envelope too. Nothing shows through. I get up and shut the door. It isn't my office hour any more.

The manila envelope has a gummed label with my name and address centered neatly. Everything is spelled correctly: I typed the label myself last spring ("I have, of course, enclosed a stamped return envelope"). Inside is a pile of pages neatly secured with a paper clip. The top sheet is on letterhead stationery, *Romantic Poesis* in a small, square, ostentatiously tasteful typeface. My name and address are typed, again correctly, on the left side of the page under the letterhead. The typist used an IBM Selectric with the currently favored *italic* typing ball, and the squat, loopy letters huddle in little clumps, spelling out the date (*September 27, 1965*) and the greeting (*Dear Miss Nyland*).

The portion that follows is in a lighter typeface, more elongated and less loopy than the previous copy: *I regret to inform you that after careful consideration our editorial board has decided against publication of your essay (and then, in the italic letter of the address, date and greeting), "'There Was A Child': A Buber Paradigm for the Wordworthian Topos of Harmony With Nature in Biological and Spiritual Childhood."* There is a wide space below this, and then the longer, unloopy letters resume: *We receive so many articles of merit that we are forced to turn down a great many that are doubtless, in their own way, very fine. Best of luck in the future. Very sincerely yours, Randolph Littlewood, Managing Editor, RP.*

I run my hand over this last part of the letter. Even the signature has been commercially printed. RP? I think. RP? For some reason it's the initials that outrage me most. It's a little *premature* for initials, I tell myself. They only started publishing last spring. It's not as if they're a household word or anything, even if they did reject my article. It's a question of status, actually. I was sure they wouldn't reject an article that had both *paradigm* and *topos* in the title.

But they did, thereby putting to shame my attempts to pander with an obscurantist vocabulary and a geriatric prose style. Score one for Randolph Littlewood, Managing Editor and part of the growing movement to say the hell with Wordsworth, Buber and Miss Nyland, I think, but my eyes are burning so I practice saying "Fuck," for a while, very quietly and with varying emphases. It's a satisfying word to say even if you're in no position to shout it. For one thing you can prolong the *fffff* part indefinitely by making a face like a demented rodent. When I'm finally bored with this I consider the cream-colored envelope my last surprise of the morning, feeling like Alice with a piece of the mushroom: will it send me up or down? I could choose not to open it. I could put it in my drawer for later, or my purse for home, or the wastebasket for never. I know I'll open it. A phrase of Frank's is resonating through my sinus cavities. It's from Frank's newly nasal phase. He has Brooklyned most of his vowels, which is a trick of voicing invisible umlauts and losing the r's. People from Indiana, and from Kansas too, for that matter, make a big deal out of saying those r's. They phrase is "So what's the worst case scenario." He doesn't say "woist," which would be overdoing things. More like "wust." It's not a question because he goes right on to answer it. Right now, in the recesses behind my nose and above my larynx, he's saying, so what's the worst case scenario, you go screaming home to bed, right? Right, I think. But screaming home to bed is a live option anyway at this point. It's odd to be taking counsel from Frank's affections. I couldn't do it when he was around. I rip open the envelope.

It's a greeting card, expensive, featuring a high-gloss photograph of a sunset strong on fuschias and tangerines. In the lower right-hand corner is printed *For a Beautiful Person*.

I open it and am instantly impressed by my admirer's impeccable typing. This isn't, after all, Corrasable Bond. Around the printed message, *From One Who Is Thinking Of You*, he has typed,

Dear Elinor (I call you Elinor in my dreams),
> *You are so near and yet, so far from me. Someday the winds of chance will blow us together. When I first beheld you, I was fascinated by many things about you with few behold. I know you are not COLD. I know of your inner desires and longings. I walked past you this morning and could hear your thighs brushing. They stirred me. You understand how. I have a special KIND of dream about you. Do not feel offended for I know you were married and know of life.*

> > *Sincerely yours,*
> > *Your Admirer*

I find I'm staring over the open card at my door. It can't be someone in English, I'm telling myself. It's too clunky, not Bonehead-level-clunky but not professorial by a long shot. And of course there's the content. Things have progressed considerably since Saturday, when he declared himself. Here it is barely

Monday and he's already familiar with my thighs and alluding to a special KIND of dream that I know about, as it happens, only because Frank told me. I didn't believe him, either, until he got mad: he wasn't convincing about the details. "So the sheets would be all sticky and yechy," I said, urging him on. "So you took a shower. But what about the sheets?"

"I don't remember."

"What do you mean you don't remember? You washed them yourself? Or did you have the nerve to leave them for your mother?"

"I suppose I left them. I never washed any sheets."

"I wouldn't have dared let my mother see them. I'd have sneaked them down to the laundry room and run them through as soon as I got up. You mean the next night you just climbed in to the old, cold—"

"It dried right away," he said. "Anyway it was mine, it wasn't like foreign *matter* or something—"

"Gross!" I cried, although I really envied him. The closest thing I had like that was my period, when my mother left a box of Kotex and a little booklet put out by the Kotex people on my bed. I didn't know what to do with the used Kotex so I collected them in my bottom drawer for a long time. And the blood wasn't even revelatory; it didn't indicate I'd had a certain KIND of dream. My dreams tend to be compromising without being enjoyable, and usually feature me naked by mistake or accident under the scrutiny of everyone I'm currently afraid of.

Oh, but Elinor in my dreams, a certain KIND of dream: not good. *I know you are not COLD!* Does he really? It is *he* now, irrefutably, given those dreams of his, which is something to go on if indeed I want to go on. What does such admiration portend? Who slipped this thing under my door between 10:10 and 11:10 this morning? I'm simply sitting here now, looking at the card, further responses deferred while I consider my schedule, 1:20 World Masterpieces, World Masturbators, yech, then maybe into the library, then, well, home. Nothing else expected of me until 8:30 tomorrow morning, restrictive and non-restrictive etcetera with the examples already committed to mimeographed sheets. No one asks any more of me. If anything they'd prefer a bit less, especially if you believe Lois Lafferty, "Most of us though you wouldn't come back in the fall."

So nothing is exactly keeping me from checking out early, making a phone call to Dale, Norford's secretary, claiming female troubles. Female troubles. Humiliation, rage, sexual ambivalence. *I could hear your thighs brushing together.* Hell, it's not ambivalence, I just want to know who he is before I decide how to take this information. Brushing together. I've got to lose weight.

Anyway, World Masterpieces is the high point of my day, especially now that I know about Ted, his aspirations, his eyes. Ted. The association is unnerving. You get cards like this at the campus bookstore, across the street and down a block. Typewriters are everywhere, coin-operated in the library. It wouldn't take long, provided that you typed well. *I have a special KIND of dream about you.* It seems implausible, but so much about him is implausible already. It could be anybody, I remind myself. *I could hear your thighs brushing together. They stirred me. You understand how.* Suddenly I hope it isn't Ted, that those slapping sentences aren't coming from someone I'm prepared to like. There's too much harm possible; it's like a hand snaking out from nowhere, sliding up underneath my skirt. He hasn't asked my permission. My permission is beside the point, not at issue here. *I know you were married and know of life.* I know of life. I'm available.

The question now is whether I'm going to sit here until it's time to brush my thighs across the street to my World Masterpieces class of whether I'm going to put my worst case scenario in-to effect. I'm feeling flayed and unwilling to be looked at by any-one who might conceivably be my admirer, but to go screaming home to bed I need a decent story for Norford, one that doesn't suggest an unprofessional degree of susceptibility to emotional terrorism. I don't want to jeopardize my status, whatever it is. I wouldn't want it to get around that I got this letter, although I'm not sure why. I think they'd feel that somehow I brought it on myself. But I discovered last spring, when I took frequent days off to compensate for long nights spent in interminable discussions with Frank about who was morally superior, that Norford won't make solicitous inquiries if I claim to have female problems. Courtly and repelled, he regards "female problems" as a virtually mystical category of explanation and will let you stay home if you don't go into detail. Dale has no such compunctions, but it's possible to circumvent her questions by acting aloof and uncomprehending. Not only possible but wise. Last winter everyone was talking about the operation on Arthur Kott's asshole. It's perfectly acceptable to have problems in intimate locations and not to specify which locations. As if there could be any doubt. Female problems. On the other hand, what if my admirer found out?

I have to admit, I don't like the idea very much. It's one thing to create the impression that you're the sort to suffer from the demands made on your sex. There's a certain amount of cachet to having people think you're a martyr to your uterus. But it's quite another ting to call the attention of some horny weirdo who's already fixated on your thighs to the specific part of your body that has the alleged problems. Euphemisms do not conceal location: on the contrary. And thighs are intimate enough.

I have my knees pressed together again. If I keep this up I might as well go out and buy a girdle, one of those rubber things with holes for the sweat to ooze out of, the kind my mother wears or used to wear: presumably Bob, having assumed the position of husband, has a position on girdles. If I'm going to faint at the suggestion of sex it makes sense to have my thighs artificially squished together, loose and doughy under the taut rubber, surrogate muscle. Years of watching my mother stuff herself into encasing underwear and absorbing the attitude that this ritual assumes – "I think it's just silly when people make a fuss over sex because sex is just a little *part* of life, don'cha think?"—have made me skittish about bodies in general. Frank always said I had to work on that. I shouldn't be feeling such alarm at the evidence that someone admires me, should I? Admires. It doesn't feel like admiration.

"Well hello again, Eleanor."

What registers even before identity is how smug he is, how assured that I'll be overjoyed to see him. And perhaps this is why I'm overjoyed, or at any rate my heart gives a little bounce. He's leaning against the door frame. His head is tilted back and he's looking down at me from underneath eyelids that are almost closed. He's smirking. No, scratch that: *a little smile is playing about his lips.* I always wondered what that looked like. He gives me a few more seconds of the little smile and then sits down in my student chair and clasps his hands behind his head so that his elbows stick out like bat ears. I want to fill the silence but can think of nothing to say. He seems perfectly relaxed. His poise is seductive.

"Been a long *time*," he says finally. It hasn't been all that long, and I'm thrilled that he puts it that way. "I've been pretty busy myself," he says. "Just wanted you to know I haven't forgotten our plans to do *Hamlet* for your, ah, introductory class."

My two Bonehead classes aren't scheduled to read *Hamlet* until December. The literature is supposed to come last, a little content at the finish as a reward for having incorporated the rigors of commas, placement of, and all the rest, although the idea of using *Hamlet* as a reward is like promising a kid runny Brie as an incentive to finish dinner. "I'm looking forward to it," I say. "I don't know what they'll think though." We interrupt this session on restrictive and non-restrictive modifiers to bring you Hamlet and Ophelia in her bathrobe. They probably wouldn't think it was any weirder than the stuff they normally do.

"Knock their socks off." This is a Ralph Hamilton expression. "What do you say we have lunch on Friday and then spend the afternoon working up those bits. Gives you some time to memorize."

"Memorize?" I haven't been thinking that far ahead. "Oh, but Friday's out," I remember, almost grateful to Norford. "I'm having a conference in the afternoon about my status."

"Conference?" I watch him furrowing his brow, putting two and two together. "About your status – you mean with Norford? Oh, well then, I can see you're tired up on Friday. That old guy can spend *hours* going over a file." I must look as appalled as I feel because he goes on, "Well gee, I bet you're pretty nervous about that." I acknowledge my nervousness by nodding and widening my eyes while drawing my lips in around my teeth like a small child working on mmmm-sounds. I've done some practicing in front of the mirror myself lately, and this is one of my most appealing expressions.

He's now sitting hunched forward with one elbow on each knee. "I didn't realize that was coming up so soon," he says. "Look I can put in a good word for you but you're the one that's going to have to convince him. I mean, I *know* you're sensitive and caring and dedicated—" he's looking down at his clasped hands now, getting into it— "but what you've got to show Norford is what a nurturing person you really are." He meets my eyes. "I mean, I don't know how to say this but sometimes that doesn't come across."

I make myself stay quiet, occupying my hands with stashing the card from my admirer in the top drawer of my desk, the drawer containing the more likely sections of my pussy book for pussies. "I know," I say.

"I *knew* you knew!" I wonder if he's going to throw his arms around me, but he only clasps his own thighs just above the knees. "Look, you're going to need a drink when you get out of there," he says. "How about I buy you one and we go over the whole thing together. What he said. What you said. Strategies. Like that."

I can't think of anything to say to this.

"I went through this myself," he adds. "And you know, it even made me a little, oh, anxious?" He purses his lips. "Well, not anxious really. Somewhat anxious. More like excited, you know? But of course that was an entirely different thing, just a formality in my case." Evidently deciding that the analogy is specious he goes on quickly, "I'll stay in my office and you can come by and get me when you're through. Ah, when Norford is through with *you*."

There have been too many surprises today. I'm not sure what to make of this one. Hanging around my office is one thing, but this is almost a date. Although perhaps I'm reading things into it. It's unwise to jump to conclusions about someone like Tom who, after all, has already demonstrated that he will go to incredible lengths to convince me of his superiority. Although – and here I begin to feel hemmed in by so much complexity – the desire to prove his superiority to me is itself and indication that I matter to him, isn't it?

"Okay," I say, not looking at him.

"*Okay* then," he returns, too hearty.

"If you can't make it that's okay," I say in case he wants to back out.

"Okay," he says, letting me down. We both look at our hands.

He says at last, "By Friday you can have memorized Gertrude's lines in the closet scene. I went over it last night. It's a very *telling* scene."

I suddenly realize I'm exhausted. "Okay," I say.

"See you Friday afternoon then. If I decide to come in."

"Okay," I say. I'm thinking of my admirer. *I have a special KIND of dream about you.* Tom Lippman doesn't, I'm willing to bet. Unless he's got a whole other side to him. It's hard to imagine a whole other side to him. He'd have to be a very subtle bastard, and I can't believe that either Tom or the anonymous letter-writer is at all subtle.

*O*nce again he awoke, this time to discover before him two ladies of such astounding beauty that for a moment he
believed himself still dreaming. Without haste or explanation they led him through an aperture and down a corridor curiously
irregular in shape and serpentine in progress, less like a hall in a man-
made structure than a tunnel dug by some deviously burrowing crea-
ture, and less like either of these than like the internal conduit of
some vast organism. It was as if they were passing through channels
of the earth's own body, wherein dwelt his captors.

I check my watch. *Wherein dwelt his captors?* I try mouth-
ing the words, hearing Frank's intonations, his incredulous yelp.
Behind me the rain slides in sheets down my one window. Regular faculty get at least two windows, full professors have three, so
someone must have planned this office anticipating
people like me. It's a sort of wedge of building but somebody
went to a lot of trouble to avoid putting windows in on both sides
of the wedge, and this one looks out on the faculty parking lot,
full of puddles now and relatively empty of cars. Most of my department is somewhere else to day. They rarely come in on
Fridays, especially during what is locally termed the monsoon
season. Tom Lippman may be a notable exception. His office is at
the other end of the hall, but I haven't gone out of my way to see
if he's in it.

I work the words over in my mouth: *Wherein dwelt his
captors.* It's so goddamned precious, Frank's word, even his
emphasis. I've internalized him so perfectly that I really don't
need him anymore, or perhaps he's mine forever now, my super-
ego with a phony accent. You can't say *Wherein dwelt his captors.*
Never mind why not, you just can't. We don't, it isn't done. But
suddenly I'm convinced that preciosity notwithstanding, Frank

Nyland notwithstanding, this is exactly what I want to say, what I mean, how I mean it. It's the language of my formative years as deployed notably in all those Fairy Books with their variegated covers—Green, Blue, Red, Gold—and their neo-Beardsley drawings of princesses who are mostly hair. Books of that sort favor archaisms, also inversions, also a speciously high-sounding diction that has little relation to any form of English spoken at any time anywhere by anybody—which I *know*, I know . . . . But it's also in a sense my language, the idiom of Romance as I've always experienced it, remote, ethereal, hopelessly alien. And here I am at last, having slid into the mode proper to erotica for the discriminating female reader, back with the forms of my earliest seduction, when I learned the prince would come if you waited, despite the machinations of stepmothers and stepsisters. And my earliest betrayal. I'm still waiting.

As he followed them through the twining corridors he brooded over means of escape, but at every turn more women joined the procession, silent, soft-shod women who appeared to him beautiful but disconcertingly serious in the pallid light shed by the irregularly glowing walls. Opportunities were passing, he chided himself, trying to rouse his torpid body to action, but his limbs were heavy and numb, and the idea of flight suggested only the futility of trying to thread his way through an underground labyrinth.

I've given up smoking again. By way of oral gratification I'm whistling tunelessly *I can't GET no-o* (rest) *Satis-is-FAC-shu-un* as I write. His limbs were heavy and numb, poor baby, because doubtless they'd given him one of those literary drugs, laudanum, morphia, opiates, draughts of Lethe, some such thing I should probably check out in the library. But the rain is slopping against the window like a wet dishrag and I'm not feeling all that scholarly. Or perhaps it's nothing so specific as a drug, maybe a spell or a potion and the reason his limbs were heavy and numb, poor baby, was that he was enchanted. Poor baby. Here I have to stop whistling and wonder how ruthless, predatory Bik Chaggard, the throbbing shape of his desire making a teepee out of his rough-spun nether garment, got my sympathy.

He's in their power, granted. But this state of being overpowered is virtually a defining condition of erotica for the discriminating male reader, as in "I have you in my *power* my pretty, heh heh heh" and variations. Everybody knows the object of desire must be wholly subject to the whims of the desirer or –ers: that's what pornography is. I put in a lot of time in the back room of that library. I'm disappointed now to find that it's not particularly arousing having him drugged and captive and being led to a place where I'll do I know not what to him. I find I'm beginning to want to invent escape routes for him, turncoat sex goddesses, *caring* relationships that evolve out of his distress. He will become one of them. He will become their leader. He will have them all shipped until they beg for more. I can't keep rooting for the underdog: no wonder my side never wins.

It's not only the conventions; he deserves to be in their power, given what he is and what he represents. What he is is unimaginative, which is where all that confidence comes from. He's confident that he's right, and if you disagree he simply *repeats* that he's right, louder. Occasionally he'll threaten to hit you, but that's a late development; usually he relies on disapproval. Or he'll ignore what you say as if you hadn't said anything, or as if your speech is so redundant that courtesy requires him to pass it over without comment. He also likes to tell you what you already know in situations where it should be clear that you already know it. The reason it never occurs to him you already know it is that it never occurs to you're really *there*, that you exist, that you're a little center of converging perceptions yourself, a locus of cognition, a human being with feelings, a conscious subject. Say it in as many ways as you can, odds are none of them will penetrate.

I stare at the sheet of paper half-filled with lines of spidery script, cross-hatching, arrows leading out into the margins where threads of even tinier handwriting curl and rise to the top of the page like smoke. Overwhelm a man and he's unfairly victimized; all justice is on his side. Overwhelm a woman and hey, it's *The Story of O!* I'm damned if he's going to get my sympathy.

"Got to get my men," he muttered huskily between dry lips, and then glanced nervously at the two women flanking him. But they made no sign of having heard him, and in relief he turned again to his

own thoughts. He loved these men, loved the fierce comraderie of their three years' voyage in search of fame, of riches, of adventure. In the face of insurmountable obstacles they had dared, venturing finally above the polar ice-caps into uncharted waters, into—finally—the forbidden reaches of exotic Nyland, whence no man had ever returned.

They had taken whatever stood in their way: taken jewels, matchless tapestries, richly embroidered silks, costly perfumes, rare parchments. But above all they had taken women.

The lush, dusky women of the southern sea towns with their luxuriant growths of wild, dark hair between glossy, sweating thighs. The frail, ethereal women of the inland waterways, with the perfume from their powdered bosoms mingling with the rank odor of musk that emanated from the lubricious passage his men forced. The white-skinned, red-haired women of the outer islands, who shrieked in terror when the throbbing cocks penetrated their flame-colored thickets until their shrieks turned into moans of desire.

I've crossed my legs again.

All this they took. And after they had taken, they destroyed.

It comes easily: all that back room reading was good for something. My legs are crossed, right over left, and I'm describing little circles with the toe of my right foot. I'm feeling quite pleasant, even a little tingly, when I realize that someone out in the hall has just put a key into the door of my office.

Before I can think any further I get a jolt of adrenalin that makes me feel as if I've just dropped down two floors. It occurs to me to scream, but I don't seem to have any noises in me. Then the door swings gently inwards and the janitor peers around it. We blink at each other for a frozen moment, and then he vanishes and the door closes again.

I slip the manuscript pages into the top drawer of my desk and go open the door again. I want a good working relationship with the janitor, who has access to all sorts of cleaning compounds not sold over the counter. When he appears a few minutes later I smile reassuringly and swivel away from my desk so he can get at my wastebasket. "You kind of startled me there," I tell him.

He flips the wastebasket from one hand to the other and vanishes with it for a moment. When he reappears he says, "Didn't expect anybody to be around," and slides the wastebasket along the floor until it comes to rest inches from my kneecap. I do my best to look impressed.

"That's because faculty in this department don't teach on Fridays," I say, but he is already out the door. I decide it's better not to think of this as a rejection. "Lubricious passages," I growl, stretching my lips around the words, but I know I can't keep that part. Even if it's only a pussy book for pussies I don't want female masochism getting into it, not even my own.

Suddenly the passage curved sharply and dipped, and without warning he found himself in a vast chamber. Far away he could discern a throne mounted high above the glistening floor, and on that throne—

He was shaken by the savage shout that arose all around him. He had heard nothing like it in all his travels. And now he was seized by eager hands as if he were not vital flesh, mind, will, as they were; and hoisted above the crowd. They were bearing him now, helpless, toward the throne high above them, and on that eminence—

He had known from the first, he realized. Perhaps he had known all his life that this was where the currents of his Fate were carrying him. For it was she: the woman of the heath, she of the alabaster breasts.

They carried him to the foot of the throne and set him on his feet. He fell to his knees and gazed up at her. The great green eyes held his own. The lips parted. There was a profound silence.

"You are a prince?"

He trembled. "In my own land, yes," he whispered hoarsely. "My people are—"

"This is not your own land," she interrupted. "We are not your people. Indeed, we find your people interesting in only one respect." She gestured toward the enormous protuberance that lifted the front of his warrior's garb. "Disrobe!" she commanded.

"Majesty," he whispered. "Your women. Your court. I cannot."

"We will teach you to have less modesty," she informed him, her lovely mouth curving in a faint smile. "You will discover that your

customs ill prepare you to serve a Lenorean queen." She glanced at the assembly and added, "And her ladies. But the queen first."

"Majesty," he pleaded. "I am a soldier. I can guard your kingdom. I can repel invaders. I can be of immense service to you—" He broke off, riveted by her gaze, although the sea-green eyes were not fixed on his face. In shame, he looked down at the enormous shape of his desire, a shape he was powerless to hide. The vast chamber had become very quiet.

"You will be of great service to me," she breathed, her eyes flashing emerald darts. Her whisper seemed to resonate through all the honeycombed passages of the wondrous domain she ruled. "You will disrobe. And then—"

"Kill me, Majesty!" he cried. "I cannot endure such humiliation!"

"And then I will take you," she murmured.

Actually, he's going to have to find those men. There have to be more men hidden away somewhere while their leader undergoes ritual debasement. Not to put too fine a point on it, you can't do much with one man among several hundred lissome maidens. You certainly can't have a gang bang, that staple of erotica for the discriminating male reader, it's a mechanical impossibility. In fact, bang of all kinds are out unless the protagonist is, ah, *up* to it: that's certainly one thing I learned from Frank. Once you've degraded them they're limp, which curtails the possibilities for role-reversed rape unless you give the women dildos, and where's the fun in that? I've thought of having them sit consecutively on his face but it's hard to believe he'd be any good. Licking is an art form: I learned that from Janet, who used to say things like, "Shit, your tongue melt or something?"

Obviously there have to be more men in the wings, a lot of them since the Lenoreans like to come a lot, which requires relays of men, waves of men surging and breaking, falling exhausted to be succeeded by still more men, very picturesque. But then I'll be giving them numerical superiority and that's asking for trouble; anyway, I don't intend to write this thing on an epic scale. Two hundred pages, large type, crummy paper. Cover photo of those alabaster breasts, looming large. Well, all right, but still the plot is moving along here isn't it; something is building, a little suspense, a little *thrust*? *"And then I will take you," she murmured* is one great chapter closing, although talk about tenterhooks, nothing is ending at this juncture, far from it: from here we go to the men, who have to be shuffled in very quickly like an opera chorus. Otherwise the book will get diddled to death with all those drawn-out gibbering orgasms. You have to have a point, something you reach for after a reasonably prolonged, ah, rising action.

I check my watch. Not quite yet. Norford said one-*ish*, which presumably means on o'clock on the nose. I wish now I had a cigarette. I've been here since nine, having awakened at four-thirty in the morning with little shocks of anxiety pricking up and down my spinal column. I lay brooding paralytically for at least an hour, alternatively rehearsing deft responses to unlikely questions Norford might ask and speculating on when the Pakistani graduate student's party broke up. The party worries me. It's out of character: he generally prefers one-on-one. Furthermore, Thursday night doesn't seem quite the time for so much shrieking and breaking of glass and playing "Stop! In the Name of Love" over and over—apparently it was the only record anyone had— so that I finally sank into sleep over Diana Ross's sultry nasal pleading:

> *Think it o-wo-ver*
> *Haven't I been GOOD to you?*
> *Think it o-wo-ver*
> *Haven't I been swe-eet to you?*

I probably should say something to him. I know I'll do nothing of the sort.

If I want cigarettes I'll have to go to the Pub, which means I'll get wet because my poplin raincoat absorbs water like a towel. If I'm wet this will be still another thing Norford has over me and will probably prove detrimental to my status. Then again, nicotine withdrawal is nothing to fool around with, I read that in the *Ladies' Home Journal* last year, the article bracketing a two-page full-color cigarette ad. Anyway, the rain seems to be letting up. I tune in again to the drumming of water on glass and concrete and notice, for the first time, the shouting.

Not really shouting. You could just as well call it chanting. The voices are in ragged unison and whatever the words are, they're rhythmic and repetitious, just like the cheers I learned in high school, where we were required to go to all the pep rallies and yell

> *Swing to the left!*
> *Swing to the right!*
> *Stand up! Sit down!*
> *Fight! Fight! Fight!*

energetically swinging left and right, standing up and sitting down, our eyes fixed on Juli, Earline, Di, Dee Dee and Kim, who performed Rockette versions of these moves in very short stitched-down pleated skirts and opaque red underpants. They do these things here, too, but I don't have to go. Occasionally one of my students mentions "the game" with reverence. "The" game, as I know from my mandatory pep days, is always the most recent one, usually last Saturday's, as in my mother's sure-fire conversation opener (she drilled me in it before I went clomping off to school in my saddle oxfords) "Dja see the *game* last Saturday?"

But today isn't Saturday and classes are in session right now. I try to think of other campus activities that might involve shouting: initiation into something, hazings, a fight between rival fraternities. Suddenly it seems pointless to be sitting here listening. I pull my coat off the hook by the door and shrug into it.

The coat is so wet it's a whole different weight. It clings to my shoulders and arms, sending clammy shivers down my back. The corridor is empty and silent, except for one typewriter that clacks haltingly in the little warren of offices beyond the elevators. My elevator is empty. I go out the main entrance to Schwindemann and look around.

The rain isn't letting up, and cars tear by throwing up great wings of water that fan out toward the sidewalks. The shouting is only across the street on the other side of the parking lot, in front of the Pub. I pull my collar up, hunch over and run across the street. Water fills my shoes even though I run prissily on tiptoe. I keep to the sidewalk bordering the parking lot, which now looks like a wading pool, and work my way down to the shouters. There are six of them marching in a circle. They're so wet that their hair is flattened against their heads. On the steps of the Pub, underneath the overhang, twenty or so people stand watching.

I skirt the action and get under the overhang myself, aware that some of the spectators are now watching me. My hair is dripping. "What are they saying?" I ask the stocky man at my left elbow.

The man shrugs. "They're saying 'Hey, hey, LBJ, how many kids have you killed today,'" he says as if reading from a phrasebook.

"LBJ?" I echo. "In the Pub?"

He squints at me. "Nah. They're just saying that."

I nod, although it doesn't make much sense to me.

"Trying to get attention," he explains. He has curly gray hair and a gray topcoat that matches almost exactly. Science type, I decide. Social scientists would want to make more out of it.

A tall, eager-looking boy with a flattop pushes in between us. "Damn right they're trying to get attention," he says, craning down at the gray-haired man. "They just want to be noticed, that's all, to be different, that's all. So what do they do, they spit on their country that gives them freedom of speech. I call them scum!" He looks alertly from the gray-haired man to me and then back at the gray-haired man.

"I was in Normandy," mutters the gray-haired man. I shrink into my raincoat.

"Scum," says the boy, looking hopeful. "One of them's even *old*."

I peer at the circling figures. It's hard to tell them apart when they're this wet—water is a great leveler—but there are certain distinctions. One of them, it hits me, is a Negro. I think Negro is what you say here if you're not holding it against them. Sometimes you say Afro-American or black; it depends on the context. There aren't many of them in school here. This region produces blonds and hasn't historically been, ah, welcoming to other racial types. I watch this man trotting around the circle, un-hurried, graceful, looking faintly amused. I'm impressed. His presence somehow gives the whole demonstration authenticity. According to Frank this is the kind of reaction that proves I'm from Kansas.

"Oh the old guy's just Herb Kiley," a woman's voice declares behind me. "He's always doing this sort of thing. He's one of those Ban-the-Bombers too. I feel for his wife, I really do."

"I could say a few things to him," growls the boy, who is now standing at my left, the gray-haired man having disappeared. I reflect that generally it's better not to know what other people are thinking.

"Oh Herb Kiley likes that," says the woman. "He's talk your ear off. That's what he likes to do best, ask you if it's *right* and if it's *good* and if it's *just*—"

"Commies don't care about right and good," says the boy, but he looks uneasy. I've picked out Herb Kiley. He's their cheerleader, the one who has just cupped his hands and shouted, "Okay now, we're going to do War on Poverty Not on People, you got it?" He's a compact, athletic looking man with a ruddy face. He doesn't look particularly old, but he's certainly not a student.

"I say shoot first and ask questions later," says the boy in the flattop. "That's the way we do it in Vietnam." Herb Kiley is smiling as he shouts. The smile crinkles his eyes into little slits and draws his face into horizontal creases so that he looks like a manic elf. As he swings around toward where I'm standing I realize that he's looking at me. I smile back. I'm still smiling as the next marcher swings around, catches the smile, and waves. It isn't until he's on his way around again that I recognize him, Ted of my World Masterpieces class.

A group of young men is gathering under umbrellas at the near edge of the parking lot. "Go back to Russia," one of them calls.

"Go back to *Berkeley!*" shouts another, inspired.

Looking at my watch, I discover I'm already five minutes late for my appointment with Norford. I hunch over and scuttle back out into the rain, feeling a little as though I'm abandoning them. I wave as I pass, arm limp, fingers curled, two of them less curled than the others in what might conceivably be interpreted as a halfhearted V-for-victory sign.

In Norford's office Dale is pushing her cuticles back with an orange stick, an instrument I've seen on sale at Woolworth's but have never had occasion to use. The orange stick has a splayed and flattened tip, which Dale presses carefully against the skin at the base of each tear-drop-shaped Pink Pearl nail in turn. "You've got to get at these things while they're *soft*," she explains without looking up. "I just spent twenty minutes soaking them."

"Really," I say, wondering whether by "them" Dale means her hands, her fingers, the tips of her fingers, or, miraculously, only the cuticles. I keep my own hands in the pockets of my raincoat. Usually I'm enthralled by other people's beauty rituals but right now I'm certain that a discussion of hands would only call attention to mine, and I don't want advice; I don't have it in me to be grateful at this point. I stare at the framed Degas print on the wall above Dale's head while Dale spreads her hands like a Balinese temple dancer and surveys them critically. I'm aware of the dank chill penetrating my coat and settling into my most adult-looking skirt and blouse.

Dale looks up. "What happened to *you*?" she asks.

"I got rained on. It's raining."

"Jeeze you're all *wet*," says Dale. "Look, you're even dripping on the floor."

"I know," I say. "I just came in. It's raining like anything."

"Your hair looks like it drowned," says Dale, wrinkling her nose. Dale's own hair is an improbably homogeneous dark brown and looks like a cushion. Along with many women in this part of the country she still favors what is known as a modified bubble, the modifications in her case being two symmetrical spit curls, one at each temple, curving in like miniature ram's horns. The spit curls serve to emphasize a faint but unmistakable resemblance to former Mouseketeer Annette Funicello.

"I know," I say. "Look, is Professor Norford in?"

"One-thirty," says Dale.

"I have an appointment to see him—"

"One-thirty," she says. "It says here one-thirty. Eleanor N." She indicates the spot on her desk calendar with one pale talon. "Don't come any closer," she adds. "I don't want you getting my desk wet."

"Sorry," I say.

Dale lowers her voice. "If I were you I'd dry myself off," she advises coldly. "I wouldn't go in to see Professor Norford looking like that."

"Sorry," I say again. "I mean thank you, I won't. Good idea." My face is stiff with smiling. In the ladies' room I swipe at my hair with brown paper towels. My collar is rumpled and puckered and the sleeves of my blouse are mottled with damp. My shoes have stretched out of shape and I can only keep them on by curling my toes, hard, whenever I take a step. I'm shivering a little.

Norford is behind his desk when I go in, apparently absorbed in the contemplation of two typewritten pages spread out on the shiny veneered surface. On the desk also are a standup calendar with little openings that divulge the day of the week and the date, a memo pad in a matching holder, and a small gold-framed photograph of an English Springer Spaniel. "Ah, Eleanor," he says.

"Hello, Professor Norford," I say, articulating his name very clearly.

"Do sit down." He nods at the single chair directly in front of his desk. It's a nice chair as office chairs go, better than mine: rather low, foam backed and seated, covered in textured black vinyl. Norford's own chair is done in the same vinyl but is higher off the ground as well as in back, has arms, and swivels. I decide this makes sense inasmuch as Norford is taller, older, and has more to swivel at. I know, of course, that this isn't why.

"Your semester is going well I trust," he says resonantly. I smile and nod. "Good, good. The Shakespeare working out. Well good, good. Mm." He looks down at the papers on his desk and then up again. "*Hamlet*, wasn't it? Yes. Mm. Professor Lippman says he's been giving you a hand."

My face feels warm. "He's been very helpful," I say.

"Good man, Lippman. Good mind. Also socially adept, if I can call it that."

"Yes," I agree. I don't feel socially adept.

"Not like some," says Norford, and I shrink into the vinyl chair. "Stereotype of the absent-minded professor," he explains. "Wholly invalid, of course. We who have the responsibility for young minds must never have our heads in the clouds."

"No," I say.

"Responsibility, that's the key word," he says. "Responsibility for young minds. Wouldn't you say."

"Yes," I murmur.

"A little learning, Eleanor, is a dangerous thing, do you know that?"

"Yes," I say, hoping he doesn't mean this personally and wishing I had the temerity to identify the quotation. I've noticed that around here if you don't identify quotations they're apt to assume you don't know them.

"Alexander Pope, the *Essay on Criticism*," says Norford. "Many people think it's a little *knowledge* is a dangerous thing. But it's a smattering of learning that can lead astray, can lead to the disruptions of the body politic, politic coming of course from *polis*—"

"I know," I say.

"Greek," he says. "Well. So what can we do, we who are in the learning profession, when some of our, ah, students seem likely to be led astray by a *little* learning?" He raises his eyebrows and stares at me.

I have no idea what he is talking about, but I have the sense that whatever it is might be my fault. Feeling inane, I smile and shrug.

He frowns. "As you know, Eleanor, illiteracy is a breeding ground for rabble-rousers. Insurrection raises her head wherever there is room for her to take root and grown, where the land lies fallow and untended. The mulch, if I may put it that way, of such tendencies is improper education. As I see it, universities today must heed the summons to counteract burgeoning unrest, to be the DDT on the growth of insurrection. You see? Illiteracy is the breeding-ground and insurrection is the growth."

"Yes," I say. "It's a metaphor."

His face creases into a wan smile. "An *extended*

metaphor," he says. "I suppose you're wondering what all this has to do with you."

"Yes," I say.

He brings his hands together fingertip to fingertip and stares at them intently. I start examining y own fingernails and decide this isn't a very good idea. "Well," he says. "I've been looking at your file here. Practically the first thing I noticed is that your position here is rather unclear, wouldn't you say?" I nod and for good measure purse my lips judiciously. "Yes, well I'm very glad you um perceive this as it makes my task much easier."

My heart drops straight as a plumb bob into my stomach. I lean back against the foam of the chair keeping my face expressionless.

"Now we do have in this department, as in English departments across the country, a few people who don't have, um."

What it takes, I guess. All their marbles. A penis.

"A doctorate," says Norford. "Although they're generally *good* people, *good* teachers—"

"I'm working on my dissertation," I say.

"—often more willing to spend time with students than their more, ah, *scholarly* colleagues," he finishes without acknowledging the interruption. I wish now I hadn't mentioned the dissertation. Frankly it sounds incredible, even to me, that I expect to finish. Lots of people don't finish. They meet men in graduate school and get married and drop out when the men get jobs.

"But Eleanor," he continues, "there is room in this university for such people. Times change. More of our faculty have the Ph.D. than in previous times, true, but we must never forget that we are first and foremost a teaching institution and that our primary responsibility is to the student."

Bonehead, I think, the pieces beginning to fit together.

"For such demands we must re-think large sections of our curriculum," he says. "We must, in a sense, redefine the concept of a liberal education, liberal stemming from the Latin—"

"*Liber*," I say with him.

"Mm, yes. Take, for example, our Basic program. In which, of course, you currently play an important role."

"I'm also teaching a class on World—" I begin, but he rumbles over me.

"And teaching it very well, if I may say so. There have been reports." I lower my eyes demurely. Flattery always throws me. "It takes a very special gift to teach Basic classes, do you know that, Eleanor?"

Even as my face heats up under the praise I get the feeling this is leading somewhere I don't particularly want to go. "I try to do my best," I murmur.

"No, really," he insists. "I, for instance, could not teach such a class, so I never *would* teach such a class. I'm too impatient, Eleanor, and long ago I recognized this as one of my fundamental limitations.

I understand that I'm supposed to applaud his self-knowledge. Instead I discover I'm furious. I'm reminded vividly of the evening when Frank informed me that it was pointless for him to help with the dishes because I was so much better at that sort of thing than he was. Keeping my eyes averted I say, "I'm not all that patient either."

"You underestimate yourself," he booms. "Don't forget, I've heard reports."

"I'm *not* patient," I say, very softly because I want to scream it.

"Come now, Eleanor." There is an edge to his voice; I'm not playing this right. "Modesty is hardly appropriate here. I wouldn't be complimenting you if I didn't value your particular, ah, strengths in the classroom."

"Thank you," I say. I know I don't sound grateful.

"Perhaps I should ask if you have *plans* beyond this academic year." His voice has risen. It's now high-pitched and chilly. He enunciates with exaggerated care. Clearly I'm not the sort of person to have plans. I'm the sort of person who ought to be thankful for what she can get.

I shrug, wishing he wouldn't pin me down. It's like the question of what you're doing Saturday night. You want to think there are options, anything could happen. You don't want to commit yourself to the statement that you're going to the library, as always. "I'm just not sure at this point," I say, hoping I sound like someone juggling alternatives. "I mean, it's too early to say, isn't it?"

"Nonsense!" he thunders, and I jerk upright in the black vinyl chair. He is glaring at me, looking, I find myself thinking, exactly like Charlton Heston in *The Ten Commandments* during the incident of the Golden Calf. "May I remind you, Mrs. Nyland, that it's not too early for appointment committees to be meeting," he says, and I note the way he clips his syllables, coming down on the consonants as if he were biting me. It catches me by surprise, the self-righteousness of his bullying. *His* strength is that he actually believes what he's saying. I'm so outraged that for a moment I can't even see. I can feel my face burning, my jaw muscles twitching. And then suddenly it hurts so badly that I want to wail and tear my hair and Oh my God, I'm thinking, it's happened again, it's all being transmuted into pain. I'm blinking rapidly to keep back the tears. I don't trust myself to speak. I just wish he'd stop looking at me.

What I say finally is "I hadn't really thought about appointment committees."

"Evidently not." He's not a gracious winner.

"I'm sorry," I say.

"Mm. Well, shall I *proceed*?"

I nod. One tear plops onto my skirt, already blotchy with rain. I hate going out of control. It's as if my insides were leaking out in full view of everybody. I might as well let loose and sob in front of him; a lot of them like that. I keep on blinking.

I don't look up until I hear him subsiding, settling back in his big chair and then swiveling from side to side as if rocking him-self. When I do look up he's peering at the photograph of the English Springer Spaniel. I wipe my eyes with the back of my hand and straighten in the chair, trying to make as little noise as possible.

He clears his throat. "I have a reason for inquiring about your plans," he says. "If you have other plans, of course you should tell me."

"I don't," I say meekly.

"Mm. What I was *going* to say," he says. He meets my eyes for a moment and then returns to the English Springer Spaniel. "was we, um, contemplate making some basic changes, you might even say radical changes, radical in the root sense of, um—"

"Root," I say, and then wonder if I shouldn't just tape my mouth shut.

"Root, yes," he says. "Radical stemming from *radix*, root, meaning um, root in the *root* sense. As it were. We contemplate changing the Basic program radically, given new demands, the new student. You see, not only are there more young people of college age than ever before, but more of them are in fact *going* to college. The whole academic profile is changing, as our admissions people are fond of telling us."

I'll bet they are, I reflect. More students after upward mobility and evading the draft. More tuition money. More grants. More allocations from the legislature. All the departments are expanding. Even English can get into the act if it can come up with something this new bunch can use.

"The main thing is to wrest Basics from the grip of the schoolmarms," Norford says.

This throws me completely. I just stare at him. His jaw is squared and his eyes glitter. "The what?" I ask.

He takes a deep breath and lets it out slowly. "All right," he says, and I feel like the most backward student in the class. "Now I want you to think of the word schoolmarm. What does it suggest to you?"

I pull my lips over my teeth and suck them in. I'm aware that when I do this I look particularly waif-like. "Old lady. Gray hair. Maybe *blue* hair. In a bun. Makes you memorize," I say. "Mean. Hits you with a stick. Makes you use a lot of commas."

"Very *good*, Eleanor." I begin to feel hopeful again. "Now needless to say, schoolmarmish is only a figure of speech, a sort of, ah, shorthand way of referring to a situation. But the word connotes—" He pauses. "You're familiar with the distinction—"

"—between a connotation and a denotation," we chorus.

"Yes," I say.

"Um, yes. Well, schoolmarmish connotes an ah, antiquated way of teaching and the antiquated priorities we need to revise. Replace. Transcend even. We must eradicate the influence of the little old lady schoolteacher, metaphorically speaking of course. Do you follow me?"

"Yes," I say, please that for once I do follow him. The Basic program is run by a little old lady schoolteacher, Jo Michaelson, who has blue hair in a bun but no stick. Word has it she pisses Norford off. "It's like Momism," I contribute.

Norford considers. "Momism," he says. "Schoolmarms. In a way they're both aspects of the same insidious, ah, phenomenon, wouldn't you say?"

I choose to appear alert but noncommittal. I'm not certain yet whether he groups me with the schoolmarms.

"A lot is being done in that area of teaching basic skills," he continues. "It's become a very *vital* area. Some very big names involved. As I see it, it's time we took the business of basics away from the schoolmarms and put it in the hands of professionals."

"How?" I ask.

"A good question, Eleanor. I've convened a committee to consider the situation and to suggest the actions that are deemed necessary. It's chaired by Ralph Hamilton, have you met him?"

"Oh yes," I say.

"Good man, Ralph, good mind. Medievalist, you know."

"Yes," I say.

"Philologically minded. Can't say I see the *point* in everything he does but top of his field, good man."

"Yes," I say, noting the possibility of a rift, maybe between Norford and Ralph, maybe between Norford and all medievalists.

"It has occurred to us, Ralph and, oh, others on the committee, that we lack what you might call the feminine element. The element of concern. Nurturing. Also, you teach in the Basic program as it stands so you'd be able to, ah, report on how it's run, problems that arise, that sort of thing."

"I'd love to," I say. I don't see that any choice is involved.

"There's no guarantee, you know. About next year. Just an idea we've been throwing around."

"Of course," I say.

"I shall let Ralph know, then, that you're on board, so to speak."

"Yes," I say. "Good."

"Well then, that's very good, isn't it, Eleanor?" He rises, so I detach myself from the chair, which is sticking to the skin above my stocking tops. The back of my skirt is all wadded up and damp. I'm pulling at it as he offers his hand. "It's been pleasant, Eleanor," he says. "I feel as if I know you better."

"Yes," I say, feeling outclassed. It hasn't been an hour; it's only been twenty minutes.

I climb the stairs with my skirt sticking to my legs and riding up on my thighs, and make a long leisurely stop at the third floor ladies' room where I pull my underwear back into position. When I get into my office it's still too early to drop in on Tom, so I remember the demonstration, if that's what it was, in front of the Pub and get out my faculty directory. Kiley, Herbert turns out to be an associate professor of philosophy, office in Stone Hall, home on Delmore Drive, one of the roads leading to campus. If he is, in fact, old, he ought to be a full professor. Troublemaker, no doubt. It's a type I'm drawn to. I try to grade a paper but I can't keep my mind on anything, so at last I give up and start down the hall to-ward Tom's office, figuring that if he's in I can say something witty about why Norford took up so little time. I don't want to think directly about my meeting with Norford. Maybe later, when I feel less skinned.

Tom's door is shut but light shows underneath. I knock, feeling strangely furtive. Rain is beating on the roof and windows. Except for the ghostly clacking of a typewriter down the hall there is no other sound. The corridor is dim and vacant except for the janitor's cart standing in the middle of it.

Then Tom throws open the door and smiles in a way that turns my legs to pudding. "It didn't take long," I begin, but he seizes my wrist and pulls me in, closing the door behind me. I make no decisions; I'm purely a physical object governed by laws of force, and when he stops propelling me forward I'm swung around to face him, just as he turns from the closing door to face me. His expression is difficult to read: peremptory, perhaps even cruel. I take a step backward. My leg encounters the seat of this armchair and I sink into it, gazing up at his face. He steps forward and looks at me.

"Now, mother, what's the matter?" he says.

My mouth goes slack; otherwise I remain perfectly still. I continue to stare up at him. He hovers over me expectantly.

Mother? I'm thinking. Mother?

It must make sense. It's just that I can't get a fix on the connection, the pattern, the way it all fits. Schoolmarms. Momism. Mother. It's a way they're thinking, defining me, using me, but I can't understand what it means or why he is doing it now. I feel horribly vulnerable.

He's watching me. "Now, mother, what's the matter?" he repeats, more slowly this time and with a trace of irritation.

My mind is clogged, but a dull throb of anger moves in my throat. He has stepped back and is standing with his hands on his hips, still looking at me.

"You may not be aware of this," I say, "but I'm a hell of a lot younger than you are."

He clinks. "For Christ's sake, Eleanor, *you* say Hamlet, thou hast thy father much offended, and then *I* say Mother, thou hast *my* father—"

"Hamlet," I say, comprehension dawning. "Oh. Hamlet. Oh hell."

His arms drop to his sides. "Eleanor, you haven't forgotten again?"

I'm still punchy but momentously relieved. "Oh Tom, I'm terribly sorry, really."

He drops into his desk chair and swivels around until he has his back to me. "That was the whole point," he says truculently.

I thought the whole point was to make me feel better after the meeting with Norford. "I'm sorry," I say again. "Maybe I could just read the lines—"

"That won't do any good," he snaps.

It's not intuitively clear to me why it won't. "Oh," I say. I think about it. "Well, I guess there isn't much we can do, is there?" He doesn't answer. I start to heave myself out of the armchair and notice that my skirt is wadding up around my hips and both sets of garters are showing. I yank at the skirt and settle back into the armchair. "I guess I was so wrought up about my meeting with Norford that *Hamlet* just slipped my mind," I re-mark.

He says something that sounds like "Mmf," but I know he's interested. I put my hands together fingertip to fingertip, the way Norford did, and stare at them. It's quite soothing, actually.

"I'm very close to Norford, you know," he says.

"I know. You told me."

He swings around to face me. "No kidding? Funny, I don't talk about it a lot." I nod gravely. "Huh. What did I say?"

"I don't remember."

"Oh come on, just a general idea."

It isn't the basis I would have chosen for increased intimacy with Tom, but I do manage to lure him to a cocktail lounge known as the Hyacinth Room, which is the only place I can think of that isn't a student hangout. Tom is emphatic about not going to a student hangout, which I regard as a positive sign although once we're established within stroking distance of the flocked wallpaper I wonder if the students don't have a point. Drinks are exorbitantly priced. We go Dutch treat, Tom's idea again. I drink scotch on the rocks, which I loathe but which seems suitable for an assignation between consenting adults. Tom talks about his special relationship with Norford, his most recent successes in the classroom, his special relationship with Pete Wanamaker, who is the Associate Chairman, his dissertation and what everybody said about it, his special relationship with all the guys in the department who get together every other Sunday night to play poker, and Michael Drayton's *Poly-Olbion*. He does not talk about his special relationship with his wife Patsy, which I regard as another positive sign. I concentrate on staring into his eyes as he makes these revelations and drinking the scotch very rapidly so as not to taste it. I know that it's important to stare into his eyes. According to the innumerable books on developing a neat personality that my mother used to bring home, you've got to keep encouraging the guy or he might stop talking and then where would you be? "The gal who knows the score gets guys to talk about themselves," my mother would counsel at odd moments, usually while I was taking a bath and thus a captive audience, cringing beneath a thick layer of detergent foam (my mother thought bubble bath led to pimples, even on your bottom) and refusing to give her a chance to comment on my body ("Dear, have you ever noticed that your hair down there is, ah, skimpy?"). Gazing at Tom now I wonder why it's supposed to be so hard to get guys to talk about themselves. I assumed it was. I hadn't had much opportunity to test the thesis.

When he leaves, I walk home in the rain with an ashen taste in my mouth from the scotch and spend the early part of the evening drinking Tokay with the Pakistani graduate student, whose name does turn out to be Abut and who has been thrown out of the university for moral turpitude. I'm fascinated by the idea of moral turpitude but he proves unexpectedly reticent and keeps murmuring things about shame and his family in a pathetic, drunken, Mel Dowd kind of voice. I don't even have to fight him off. When we get to the bottom of the bottle he retreats into his basement murmuring and hiccupping. I wonder what I'm going to do without a tenant. I manage to get to sleep without going over the conversation with Norford even once.

I wake up with a headache and a diminished tolerance for light. At the foot of my bed the radio is buzzing, the Pepsi Generation song again: *Come alive!* My neck feels as though it's been wired upright. I sit up, trying not to move my head and getting little angry jabs right at the base of my skull, red sparks under my eyelids. I don't want to think about the Tokay but it's back there waiting for me whenever I get around to it, puddling up at the bottom of my stomach collecting a lot of really unpleasant additions, chips of Spanish peanut, little drowned pieces of bar pretzel, acid green now, fighting back. Come alive. I make it to the sink, which makes me feel ignominious. I mean, I might as well have done it all over the Colonial bedspread where it would have at least been a nice color contrast. Not much there, actually. Most of it coursing through my cardiovascular system by now, polluting blood, dissolving tissues. I've never been what you'd call into drinking.

I know why I woke up, of course. Even hanging there over the washbasin trying not to look up because if I even turned my eyes a little I'd be looking into the mirror and seeing myself hanging there, mouth in spasm, big scooped-out crescents under my eyes and little bits of stuff dropping slowly down to stick to the porcelain, I was thinking: Mailman. What I hear from upstairs is the flap of the box snapping shut, maybe two inches by four inches of lightweight metal coming down. Most people wouldn't be able to hear it with theirs ears smashed up against the door. It's one of the noises I'm conditioned to respond to, whiff of the outside world, surge of saliva. As if I were expecting a love letter. Or any letter, for that matter. Hanging over the basin gagging on the last grainy bits now I'm thinking brush teeth, brush tongue, brush teeth again, put on bathrobe. Anything to get down to the porch. Make coffee, I'm thinking, sit in the breakfast nook. Read mail. Drink one cup of coffee first. If there is any mail.

But there is mail. There is even a package propped neatly against the shingled wall under the mailbox when I finally go out, hugging my arms and holding the bathrobe together. It's cold and I have a residual shudder going, but I stand there examining every-thing in the bright sunlight and listening to the sedate thrumming of neighborhood traffic going by. As my mail goes, this is a bonanza. The package. A bill from Union 76 addressed to Dr. Francis C. Nyland, Ph.D., currently in possession of the car. My *Newsweek*, cover story "The President's Operation." A letter Elinor Nyland, no return address.

Loose spidery handwriting on the package, purple ink, *Eleanor Perry*. Janet, I decide, just faintly disappointed. I go ahead and open it while the water comes to a boil. It turns out to be a kind of book I've never seen before, with an absolutely plain buff dust jacket except for the title, printed in the center in little black letters, *Beaver Country*. I know enough to figure this is no Walt Disney True Life Adventure but I don't have the code; I don't get what's implied in "Beaver." Buck teeth, I think. The Ipana toothpaste ads, coats, *Leave it to Beaver*, Hamlet's father's ghost: he wore his beaver up. I give up and flip the book open to find on page 24 that Hank is ramming it into her succulent slit. She writhes convulsively, in ecstasy beyond her wildest imagin-ings. On page 27 a dusky Indian maiden joins Hank and uses her deft tongue to bring him to throbbing manhood. On page 28 *she* goes into writhing convulsions with her mouth still full of throb-bing manhood, presumably *because* her mouth is still full of throbbing, etc., post hoc. I don't find this physiologically persua-sive. On page 31 someone named Trapper Dick arrives on the scene. The whimsy strikes me as misplaced. None of this explains why beaver, but it's certainly enough to think about for the mo-ment so I align *Beaver Country* with the upper right-hand corner of the table in the breakfast nook and make myself a cup of coffee. Then I sit down to work through the rest of the mail.

The Union 76 bill gets readdressed and forwarded. Dr.

Francis, Ph.D. In certain respects Frank was just your garden variety prig. I wonder about the President's operation for a while, but my heart isn't really in it. I'm not opening the letter to Elinor Nyland until I've had two cups of coffee.

The phone rings while I'm making my second cup. I take the stairs two at a time, bathrobe flying open, face bloodless, wondering if I'm going to faint. By the time I get to the bed I'm dizzy.

"Hey, Eleanor."

"Yes," I say.

"Hey, I hear you're going to be on our committee."

"Yes," I say.

"I think that's just neat."

"Thank you," I say. "Who is this?"

"Arnie Stutke," he says, and I fish around in my memory for an image. I come up with thinning hair, a soft horseshoe-shaped face, spongy lower lip. Wife makes the cheese balls.

"Oh hello," I say.

"Hey. You know why I called you?"

"No," I say.

"Well, just to tell you it's neat you're going to be on the committee. I was one of the ones that really wanted you."

"Thank you," I say again.

"All those guys, you know. There we were at the conference table and I looked down the table and I said hey. We're all guys. You know?"

"Ah," I say.

"Great guys though," says Arnie Stutke. "You'll love it."

"Who all is on the committee?" I ask.

"Ralph Hamilton's the chair. You know Ralph."

Once again it's not a question. "Yes," I say.

"Bill Brewster, he's a character. Petie Havermayer, you know him? Linguist. Solid. And me and Tom Lippman, you know Tom."

"I know Tom," I say, the first warmth of the day making it into my face.

"I'm secretary," says Arnie Stutke. "That's really what I called you about. Oh also I called you to say it's neat you're on board, you know? But that's the way we started out, Ralph being chairman and me being secretary. That's when I suddenly thought, hey."

"Oh," I say.

"I mean, it kind of hit me all of a sudden that here we were all getting together you know to discuss how to get those, ah, difficult students to use grammar and things like that and here we were without the feminine mind."

"The feminine mind," I say.

"I figure we're nothing without the feminine mind," he says.

"Thank you," I say.

"Really, Eleanor. So I said we should get you on. I thought of you right away."

"You did?" I wouldn't have thought of him right away. Or in the first twenty minutes, even.

"Well, we'd kind of been talking about you, not what you'd call officially or anything."

This is amazing news. "Really?"

"Oh yeah. I mean, you teach Bonehead. Ralph says you're good."

This seems to be the prevailing sentiment. It makes me nervous. I don't feel as though I'm good. "Thank you," I say, and wonder if I'm saying it too much. Arnie doesn't seem to mind.

"So last night Ralph and I were sitting around, oh you know, shooting the bull, and I said Ralph, you know what we should do with Eleanor, make her feel right at home since she's coming in late, you see? We've already had two meetings, you know that."

"No," I say. There's no particular reason I should know that, but he seems to feel I'm at a disadvantage.

"So I thought you should be secretary. Ralph thought it was a great idea."

"Thank you," I say.

"It's a great idea, don't you think? That way you'll feel, you know, needed."

"I've never been a secretary before," I say. It's true, I

never have. "Do I take minutes and read them at the next meeting?" I ask. When we had assemblies in high school they'd get Bonni Bentham up on stage and she'd read the minutes of the Student Council meeting in her breathy little voice and everybody would shout "Louder!" or all the boys at least, and she'd breathe a little harder into the microphone and you still couldn't hear but it didn't matter. Bonni Bentham had a voice like Marilyn Monroe's, and no one worried about what she was saying.

"Right, Eleanor, you'll be great. Sometimes we ask you to fix up stuff to send to other members of the committee, too."

"I think I can do that," I say. I'm telling myself that this is secretary as in Dag Hammerskjold, not secretary as in Ann Southern in *Private Secretary*, my mother's favorite TV show. It's not as if they expect shorthand or anything. More of an honor. Madame Secretary.

"Sure you can, Eleanor, that's why we wanted you. Like I said, welcome on board. I'll leave some stuff in your mail box on Monday. You have a mail box, don't you?"

"Yes," I say.

"Just some stuff that needs, ah, fixing up before we give it to the other guys. You'll understand when you see it."

"Okay," I say.

"Swell to have you on board, Eleanor."

"Thank you," I say. "Arnie." It sounds too informal.

"Just call me Arnie," he says.

"I did," I say, but he's explaining he has to go now and I feel vaguely that I've been keeping him. After I hang up I go down and find that the water has boiled away and the bottom of the saucepan is glowing pale orange, the color of the upper stratum of cloud in the postcard of the sunset that my admirer sent me last week. I put it in the sink and open the envelope for Elinor Nyland.

It's a letter this time. I spot an erasure in the opening paragraph, first sign of vulnerability.

My Dearest Elinor,

Words cannot express the feelings I hold for you in the most sensitive part of my being. I yearn to be with you in your intimate

moments which you know are frequent. You know what it is to be
loved by a man. You need this love. I can see into your inmost long-
ings.

Some night I will come by your window and it may be I will
contact you then, maybe not. I have called you on the telephone. You
can not hide from me for we are so close. Sometimes I think of you
and am transported to a heaven of BLISS to which we two will go
someday together when the time is right. You understand this, for
you are experienced with men. You understand my desire and what I
do when I am thinking about you. Perhaps you too will have BLISS
when reading this as I am THIS VERY MINUTE.

Yours truly,
Your Admirer

The frightening thing is that I do respond a little; I'm a
little more aware in a physical way, although not aroused exactly.
I mean, the odds are that this is some disgusting human being, or
that's the type that gets drawn to me insofar as any type gets
drawn to me. Pudgy, sweaty hands. Slobber. Although I have to
allow for the off-chance that it isn't that type, that it's some other
type entirely since nothing is wholly predictable, after all. I'm still
thinking of Tom, of course. Or not exactly thinking: it's his hands
on my wrists, pulling me through the door, spinning me around,
I still feel them. He touched me. Well, grabbed, but that's still
supposed to mean something; contact takes it to a whole other
level, doesn't it? Or ought to. I think it ought to.

What bothers me most about the letter is that it keeps
telling me how I feel, that I feel, well, horny. Which I am, of
course, but not for just anybody, that's the part that gets lost
every time, not for every heavy breather, peeping Tom, oh hell,
peeping Ted, peeping Arnie. It's as though being sexual makes
you fair game, as though there's no middle ground between chas-
tity and succulent slit. If he were just creeping around on his own
making molesting noises it wouldn't be quite so threatening
somehow, be-cause at least it would be clear that I was unsuspect-
ing and innocent, a victim instead of an accomplice. But he seems

to think he's actually responding to *me*. Hell, he's even trying to anticipate my reactions, *Perhaps you too will have BLISS while reading this as I am THIS VERY MINUTE* – oh creepy, creepy.

Having gone over all this, however, I find I'm not quite into it because there's still some ground for complacency in having been singled out for special harassment. Why me, after all? I'm not an obvious candidate for admiration, especially in a town full of slim-thighed coeds ripe for the centerfold. I'm the type you don't notice, given that sort of environment. It would be like choosing Jane Eyre to be Playmate of the Month. So there's some judgment working here, some power of insight that can discern the passion lying dormant beneath the phlegmatic exterior. Maybe it's because my hangover is dissipating in the cold sunshine or because the Pakistani graduate student is moving out today, giving me my solitude at last and an empty apartment to fill, lacuna of a fresh beginning. But I feel as if I had secret depths. Duplicitously now I go upstairs and put on jeans and a sweatshirt, student uniform, and trudge off to the IGA, partly because I didn't go yesterday and there's nothing in the refrigerator but baking soda and a softening cucumber, partly because I don't want to be around when the Pakistani graduate student evacuates, but mostly because it's somewhere to go and I feel like going somewhere, skulking around where there are people, pretending I'm nobody in particular. It's the unobtrusive ones you have to watch.

I'm standing in line waiting to put my purchases on the rubber conveyer belt when I realize that the woman behind me is Patsy Lippman. Something jolting happens to my insides and I nearly fumble the lemons I bought with the vague notion of warding off scurvy, while I'm explaining to myself that what I'm reacting to is a sort of fetish, a link to Tom, although this is his wife and not some glove or ballpoint pen. She doesn't recognize me, of course, being absorbed in *Family Circle* to the point where I can only see the top of her head, blonde with a neat pink part, no roots on Patsy. On the cover of this *Family Circle*, holiday issue, is an incredible cake made up of layers and layers each about an eighth of an inch high. You could spend days making a cake like that, which is probably the point. After you've scrubbed around the little screws and things on the back of the refrigerator with a tooth-brush and repainted all the mouldings around the light fixtures you might find yourself casting about for something to do. My mother always wished she had the time for thirty-five layer cakes and gelatin desserts shaped like things, lambs or bunnies or chickies with coconut sunk into them like seaweed. She wanted me to have all my friends over for parties with a theme, like Sweet Sixteen and Never Been Kissed or Spring Into Summer—they told you how to do these in *Seventeen* and my mother was a great reader of *Seventeen*—but I wasn't the party type. For one thing is was much too obvious that I'd never been kissed. My mother worked all day for a construction firm where she took modest pride in being indispensable, but she yearned for the kind of home life celebrated in *Family Circle*, where you crocheted your place mats your-self and saved old nylons, which make wonderful throw rugs that look as if they're made out of old nylons, or can be used to strain things: you can always think of something to strain. My mother supervised my cleaning, disconsolately, on Saturdays, and spent Saturday nights reading *Family Circle*, *Good Housekeeping*, and occasionally *Better Homes and Gardens* and staring off into space as if she could see there the hand-tatted evening bags and whimsical pajamas for your teen's slumber party that she was missing out on. I knew I had failed her, not only because I never had slumber parties but because I was indigent and the reason she stayed year in and year out at Fred Barclay and Son Builders, Inc. A satisfactory daughter would have had an independent income. Or a father who wasn't a rat.

There's no sign of the Pakistani graduate student when I get back. No sign that he's moved out, either, but I don't feel like checking on him just yet, so I put the groceries away and sit down in the breakfast nook, which has warmed up in the thin afternoon sunlight. I read two chapters of *Beaver Country* very carefully before I decide there's something very wrong here. It's not that it's obscene, more that it's someone else's obscenity, as if I'd wandered into a culture where the big toe was the principal fetish. The women of *Beaver Country* are very into fellatio. Fellatio is another one of the words Frank taught me, although it wasn't one of his more successful words since he couldn't figure out occasions on which to use it. What he wanted was a verb, but nobody seemed to be sure what the verb was. Do you say fellate me, baby, or what? Anyway, the women characters, if you can call them that, get off on fellatio in this book, do the eyes-rolling-back-into-the-head number that is supposed to signify intense pleasure and frequently remark on the quality of what they're getting in their mouths—"Mm-*mm*" and other Madison Avenue expletives. I don't believe it. If sperm really tasted that good they'd be selling it in the IGA. And then there's all that gagging on mammoth members, pleasant for those attached to the members presumably but not for the gaggers unless they're into vomit, which I also don't believe, having been intimate with vomit quite recently. But I'm uncomfortable with my reactions. They might well be the wrong reactions given my upbringing and the number of times Frank has called me a prude. We fought horribly about it, in fact, me wailing why was it prudery to dislike things that don't feel good and him shouting that if I weren't such a prude they *would* feel good. I still don't see how. As I pointed out to him, I'm quite clear where it is that I get excited and it isn't anywhere near my mouth. Frank said I was supposed to have erogenous zones all over my body, but I shrieked over him that he always came out of the same damned penis and not his nose or his middle finger, and whatever erogenous zones are supposed to be they're certainly not alternative genitals, at which point Frank announced with great dignity that perhaps men and women were different and stalked off to the shower leaving me to wallow in retrospective guilt at not being as mysterious and paradoxical in my desires as women are supposed to be.

So of course now I'm questioning my own simplicity again, wondering if I did, in fact, get it, as if sexuality were a dirty joke that I might have missed the point of even if I did laugh. Janet initiated me into orgasm immediately and none too soon. I had been creeping around right before curfew peering vampirishly at the necking couple scattered among the lawn trees around our dorm, and sooner or later somebody was going to catch me at it. It didn't occur to me until much later that this was what Connie Chatterley finally discovered with Mellors. It wasn't as if my very being was shaken, more like being overwhelmed with satisfaction at the scratching of an insistent itch. It was gratifying, if deflating, to find that Janet could go unerringly to the source of the central problem of my last five years and produce immediate results, requiring only that I do it back, an equitable if not particularly passionate basis for sexual relations.

With Frank, however, I learned that reciprocity wasn't the whole story—wasn't, generally, even part of this story. With Frank I was supposed to be thrown into rapturous convulsions by such anatomically removed events as *his* orgasm: I learned early he was proceeding on the assumption that whatever felt good to him necessarily felt good to me too. "You didn't come," he charged on one such occasion, and I had to swallow grimly several times before I could say, "I hardly ever do, there." Comments of this sort damaged him seriously, he told me, and thus damaged me in his eyes. Always the good student, I learned to sound a lot like the women in *Beaver Country*, although I did try to be more directive in my amorous pantings. "Yes, *there*," I would gasp hopefully, although he resented being prompted. I tried, with more subtlety, to remain neutral when he wandered into erogenous wastelands and to reinforce potentially exciting moves, but quite often I felt as though I were playing that game where you've hidden something and have to direct the other player toward it by telling him whether he's warmer or colder. After a while I stopped coming entirely, so I relaxed the rules and began making gratified noises at indications that *he* was coming, on the theory that one of us might as well have fun.

Frank believed I'd improved, although he still had criticisms. I wasn't eager to be tied up, for instance, and I wasn't into pain. I wasn't, he informed me more than once, truly feminine, and the information alarmed me as I'd been verging on the same conclusion. If you're feminine, I gathered, you enjoy things that are fundamentally unenjoyable, take pleasure in actions that are intrinsically painful, and derive most satisfaction from the gratification of someone else's desires, anyone else's. Not only was I unable to imagine what might constitute feminine fulfillment but I was beginning to respond to Frank's efforts to make a woman out of me with murderous rage, perhaps the most unfeminine of the emotions and—I wasn't an English major for nothing—the least universal. I didn't encourage the rage. It was just there, another thing between us.

Sunday morning I open the cellar door and peer down into the basement. It stinks of spilled beer. No one is there. I spend most of the day washing the apartment with Lysol and taking out old garbage that was stashed in paper bags in the bathroom, where I also find four unused condoms. I take them upstairs and put them in my bathroom feeling a little excited; you never know. I've never had condoms of my own before. In the evening I hear on the radio that there have been antiwar protests on over forty university campuses over the weekend. My immediate reaction is to be impressed with Ted, that he was in on it, that he knew. All that marching around in the rain in front of the Pub begins to take on a sort of significance even if it is only the Pub, not the Pentagon.

When I come in Monday after my first class he's leaning against the wall beside my office door, books tucked under one arm, head down, apparently absorbed in kicking the heel of one tennis shoe with the toe of the other. Light from the narrow window across the corridor catches a cheekbone, jawbone, some shoulder, the curve of his back. He's frowning slightly in concentration. People going by shoot little looks at him, but he doesn't appear to notice. He's probably used to collecting small crowds whenever he isn't moving. He doesn't see me until I'm right in front of him, and then he smiles so radiantly that I have trouble getting my key into the lock.

"I brought you my proposal," he says, after I've made a production out of hanging up my coat and getting behind my desk. "I mean, it's nothing formal, it's just something I've written down. I expect it's really naïve."

I take a look. It's really naïve. He wants to write about the human condition. "Malaise," I say, thinking of the Existential Theology seminar, and spell is for him. He writes it in his note-book and gives me another radiant smile. "Angst doesn't have a k in it," I tell him. It occurs to me that what I'm doing is teaching, telling somebody something he wants to know.

"I shouldn't even be bothering you with this now," he says. "It's not even a topic yet, just a lot of ideas I've sort of been brooding about."

"You'll have to narrow it down, but you can do that later," I say.

He grimaces, eyelids down cheeks flushing a delicate peach. "That's what Tyrone said, he was just disgusted with me. But I said I wanted to talk to you first, before I got too into it, you know?"

"The black guy," I say. Something about the way he said the name, Ty*rone.*

"Yeah, he lives down the hall from me. They've got him with another black guy, can you believe that? A senior who's a football player. And Tyrone's, like, an actor."

"That's crazy," I say. We smile at each other. Another bond.

"What I want to talk to you about," he says, and stops. "I mean, Tyrone was right, I'm being just incredibly vague but I wanted to sort of get your sense of whether I'm going off on a tangent or what." He's looking at the tips of his tennis shoes, leaving over in the chair, elbows on knees. The light grazes his cheekbones, leaving little hollows underneath. "I mean, the whole idea of being hyperconscious, of thinking too much, you can't just say it's bad and leave it at that can you? I mean, you can't yell stop thinking too much, it doesn't *work* for one thing. And anyway, I can't get my mind around the idea that Dostoevsky was just showing us what happens when you think too much, like watch out, this is what you'll turn into if you don't get dumb. I mean, I can't believe that's the point."

I shrug. It's not that I don't understand him. I'm trying to figure out how I'm supposed to react to this demolition of the approved reading, what my role is when students start making good points all by themselves.

"I feel like *I'm* the Underground Man," he says suddenly. "Of course, I imagine everybody says that."

"No," I say, trying to imagine a class full of students who said that. "No, they don't."

"I suppose I'm being incredibly pretentious," he says, so violently that I wince. "I mean, here I am thinking I'm somebody in a *book*. It's a phase, isn't it?"

"I don't think so," I say. "But I don't think I'd know. Actually I've never known anyone like you."

He looks up, startled. "What do you mean?" he says after a moment.

I shrug again. "Like you. I don't know people like you. If you're a type I don't know the type."

"Oh," he says, and seems to relax a little. "Do you know a lot of types?" he asks after a moment.

"I'm not that old," I say. I wasn't going to say it, but it seems like something I want him to know. He looks at me hard and then nods. After a moment he slumps down in the chair and swings one foot across his knee.

"I waved at you Friday," he says. "Did you see me wave?"

"I waved back," I say. "Sort of."

He doesn't say anything. I know what I'm supposed to do now. I'm supposed to tell him where I stand on this war so we can go on wherever this is we're going. And of course I don't know where I stand, even though the question has been occurring to me a lot lately. Everybody I've spent any time around has been against war in a general way, but never in particular. When my mother talked about it she would sigh and say human nature would never change: it was like Bambi's mother being killed by hunters, a technicolor inevitability. Frank thought Vietnam was probably a mistake but you couldn't just leave after you'd gone in there, and anyway the idea of putting an end to war was naïve and ignored biological drives. I used to agree with my mother and then I agreed with Frank. In fact they weren't very different, which as least makes me consistent, in a waffling sort of way.

"It was very brave of you," I say carefully.

He's watching me closely. "A lot of people didn't think so. A lot of people were saying we were cowards."

"It must be scary having people yell at you like that."

He rolls his eyes. "I thought they were going to come get us and beat us up, five on one, six on one. I've never been in a fight in my life. Anyway, that's what we're against, fighting. Professor Kiley showed us beforehand how to go limp, but it's not like feeling prepared, you know?

I can imagine. I can imagine what the fraternity types would do to him, too, and to Tyrone if they thought they could get away with it, and the scene is so vivid that I want to throw myself across the desk and on him, want to wrap him up in my own body and hide him somewhere they can't get at him.

"A lot of the protests got violent," he says. "We watched the coverage on television, in the dorm. And even just watching TV there were guys making remarks, really vicious remarks. I would never have guessed they were so—" he shrugs. "Mean. Stupid." He looks at me. It's a challenge.

"You threatened them," I say. "It's harder to talk back than it is to go along." He nods again, confirming me.

"Then they say *we're* cowards," says Ted. "It gets confusing." We smile again at each other. We're on the same side now, and while I'm not completely clear what's entailed I know I'll always be able to spot which side it is. It's the side with the fewest people on it.

"Were all the protests coordinated?" I ask. I don't know the mechanics of these things. I've never thought about how they happen.

"There was a lot of publicity through the peace groups and SDS. A bunch of us meet fairly regularly with Professor Kiley, and we decided how we were going to demonstrate, what kinds of slogans we'd use, where we'd march. Not everybody showed up. They said it was the rain."

I'm allowed to be amused by this, part of my new sense of belonging. "It was awfully wet," I say.

"You're telling me. Our signs all, like, dissolved right at the beginning. We figure one person in three had some idea what our issue was. Next time we make sure it's a decent day, right?"

Next time. That sense of a future involving both of us. "Professor Kiley's in philosophy, isn't he," I say.

"You'll like him," says Ted. I feel honored.

Arnie Stutke's package shows up in my mail box after my

second Bonehead class. It's a fat manila envelope containing maybe sixty pages, most of them yellow legal paper covered with penciled notes, most of these in what surely must be Arnie's cramped, backward-slanting scrawl. I try squinting, but the result isn't illuminating. Isolated phrases like "goals and objectives" and "interim measures" emerge from an indecipherable sludge of soft-penciled bumps and dashes. I leaf through the entries, feeling more and more dismayed, until I come to several pages in different and generally more legible handwriting and finally to one that is actually typewritten. The name in the upper left-hand corner is "Lippman." I twitch reflexively, feeling my predictable blood leaping up into my face.

> *Procedure: break down into manageable steps – Arnie*
> *Questions: What specialists do? How different from current Bonehead staff?*
>   *--What needed? Profile Bonehead student – Ralph.*
>   *--How other institutions of higher ed. handle?*
>   *--Tom (me): library research and correspondence*
> *TIMETABLE?*

I'm not sure why I stop there but I do, and then I realize that it's those capitals: they're familiar. Then I wonder if I'm crazy. Typewriters are fairly standard; there aren't a lot of variations even in typeface; they exist to be standard, after all. This is absolutely normal type, plain old pica, and you probably find it on eighty per cent of the machines on campus. Still I'm staring at those capitals, something about them, maybe only the fact that they're capitals at all. It's all very suggestive. I slide Tom's contribution out from the pile and put it in my top drawer.

Arnie and I end up having what he calls a preparatory session in his office Wednesday afternoon. This means that he sits on the edge of his desk and reads aloud from his notes, emending them as he goes, and I type what he's saying directly onto ditto masters, using his big Remington upright. I'm not that great a typist, but then Arnie's notes aren't all that coherent either. In fact, if they were my notes I'd do a lot to stop people from typing them onto ditto masters and distributing them. "I'm not trying to make this, you know, a finished product," he tells me early on. "I just kind of spill out things spontaneously, the way they come to the surface, and that way we can fool around with them when they're still, you know, wet." Shortly after he says this he says "No, scratch that, scratch that whole paragraph," and I tell him I can't do this without throwing out the ditto master I'm working on. "Just *ignore* it then," he says irritably, and I type on, feeling like Ann Southern in *Private Secretary* after all. We end up with thirteen and a half pages of Arnie's notes, single-spaced, and slightly more than four pages of everybody else's notes. Arnie says great, great, now all I have to do is fix it up so that everyone has a copy, which means running off the dittos and collating the pages. I get home at ten-thirty.

At the meeting the next day Arnie proposes that I be given a vote of thanks for having fixed up the notes so neat at such short notice. Tom Lippman cries "Second the motion!"—his specialty at these meetings, I discover, is seconding motions—and everybody murmurs things like "Terrific" and "Good job" without looking at me while I feel my face warming with pleasure. We're sitting around one end of the big lozenge-shaped table in the conference room of the main office, Ralph at the head with the coffee urn gurgling behind him. In front of each of us is a fresh yellow legal pad and two very sharp No. 2 ½ pencils. I've already tried one of the pencils: I've written *Nyland* in small gray letters at the upper right-hand corner of my legal pad. After the vote of thanks subsides, Tom's foot comes to rest against mine under the table and remains against mine for the duration of the meeting. It takes me a while to be sure it's Tom's foot, but he's directly across from me, and given the seating arrangement anyone else would be snaking his leg out from an angle that would make constant pressure over an extended period of time virtually impossible.

Above the table Ralph is explaining that Norford has given this committee a mandate to ah explore and as it were reevaluate the Basic program as it currently operates and also to investigate the range of available alternatives. He then nods at Arnie, who hunches over the table with the intensity of a coach laying out his game plan. "Like Ralph here was saying last week, gang," Arnie says earnestly, "we've got a mandate and that's a pretty serious thing. So what we've got to figure out now is what's the best way of exploring these alternatives, really digging into them, getting the meat out, you know? Because as many fine minds as are here today, that's how many perspectives there are on the whole can of worms, the whole ball of wax, the whole Basic thing. We've got to ask ourselves now what's the best way to take advantage of all these neat perspectives we've got?"

I blink and look around to see how other people are reacting to this, but all I see are bulldoggish expressions that appear to denote toughmindedness. Arnie is a full professor, I remind myself. I looked him up in the faculty directory. I write at the top of my legal pad, *perspectives* and, after a moment, *take advantage of*.

"Now this is only my opinion," Arnie says, "but speaking off the top of my head, kind of spontaneously now, I see us laying out the groundwork, you know? So here's what I see us doing first, see, first we've got to accumulate different ideas on how to improve the Basic program. Accumulate." He holds up his hands about two feet apart, as if he were displaying the word. Everyone is writing, so I write on my legal pad, *Arnie's Groundwork: (1) accumulate ideas.*

"Next," says Arnie. "This is only a bar outline," he adds. "I'm working on a more, ah, fleshed-out version, you know? Anyway, next we collate ideas so that everybody can take a look at everybody else's and compare notes and like that. See, first accumulate, second collate." I write *(2) collate ideas* on my legal pad, although I have a feeling this will all show up on the fleshed-out version.

"That's where Eleanor comes in," says Ralph, and everyone looks at me. "We couldn't do any of the collating part without Eleanor since if I may say so it's, ah, *beyond* everyone else at this table." I smile shyly at him. The toe of Tom's shoe brushes my instep and settles down against my arch again.

"I'll say," cries Arnie. "You know how long it would have taken me to fix up these notes myself, Eleanor? I knew you were going to be great, I said so, didn't I guys?"

I'm just beginning to catch on. "You mean," I say, "that

when you accumulate more ideas I'll type them up on dittoes again and then run them odd, like last time? You mean I'll go on doing that?"

"That's right, Eleanor" says Arnie. "Only last time I kind of gave you a hand."

"It took a long time," I say.

This is clearly not what anyone wants to hear. There is some embarrassed rustling and scraping of chairs. In the corner the coffee urn goes into a little cadenza of chortles and then stops.

"Um," says Ralph, looking pained.

"It took *you* a long time!" cries Arnie heartily. "you know how long it would have taken me, Eleanor? You know how fast *I* type?"

"I use two fingers," says Bill Brewster on my left.

"Everything in longhand," says Petie Havermeyer, next to Tom. Tom is examining his thumbnail. I know he can type. I've heard him.

"The general idea was that you had agreed to take on these responsibilities, Eleanor," says Ralph finally. "I thought Arnie and you worked that out."

I feel horribly isolated. "I didn't mean—" I begin, although I'm not sure there is anything I didn't mean, but Arnie cuts in.

"Ralph, you know Eleanor's just been fitting in so great I didn't really get around to filling her in on the whole thing ahead of time so it's really my fault, you know? I mean, I don't think Eleanor has anything *against* doing the accumulating and collating, do you Eleanor?"

I find myself shaking my head before I'm even sure what I'm negating, but the tension is ebbing. The others ease back in their chairs and cross their legs again. After a minute Ralph says, "Well, Arnie?"

"Do I have to move we have some coffee?" says Arnie.

"Second the motion," says Tom wittily, but I'm already rising from the table, mindless, hooked by their expectations. I'm the secretary. It makes sense. Who else could be?

We adjourn after resolving that everyone will prepare a

statement detailing his ideas about a renovated Basic program, to be accumulated in my mail box so I can collate everything by next week. "In time for us to discuss them," says Ralph.

Arnie looks worried. "Not discuss," he says. "The way I have it here our next step is to analyze all the different ideas. I mean analyze in the root sense, break down into their component parts, see where they're similar down into their component parts, see where they're similar and different. You see, these steps kind of naturally fall into pairs. First we accumulate and collate. Then along with analyzing the various ideas that are accumulated and collated we prioritize them. See? Analyze, prioritize. Then we end up proposing and disposing."

"What?" I say. It's the first thing I've said since I served the coffee.

"It's an allusion, Eleanor," says Ralph kindly. "As in man proposes, God disposes, you see?"

"No offense to the Lord," says Arnie.

After I go back to my office I spend a long time starting at the various letters from my admirer and Tom's typewritten page of notes that I've kept in my desk drawer, but Tom doesn't come by. There's a little chip out of the dangling part of the p in Tom's notes and also in one of the letters from my admirer, but only one of the letters.

Whoever he is, he calls on Friday night while I'm doing sit-ups on the shag carpet to the Four Tops singing "I Can't Help Myself." I know it's my admirer even though he doesn't make any noise. I don't make any noise either, after the initial "Hello," which strikes me immediately as a mistake: I should just have lifted up the receiver and held it to my ear. It takes a long time be-fore I stop hearing echoes of my own voice. I stand there listening, with the mouthpiece under my chin so he won't hear my breathing, but there is nothing on the other end, nothing at all. Finally I reach out and press on of the little buttons that cuts off the connection, very slowly so he won't know exactly when I stopped being there. I stand with my finger on the button for a good two or three minutes, but he doesn't call back.

On Sunday morning the telephone rings again but it's only Jo Michaelson asking if I'm free for lunch on Tuesday. I tell her I'll have to look at my calendar, which is uncharacteristically devious of me since I have only one calendar and it's in my office. Then I scuttle into the bathroom, which strikes me on some primitive level as a safe harbor, and stare at the ceramic wall tiles and wonder what would constitute strategy at this point. The wall tiles are arranged in what the landlord kept emphasizing was a random pattern, as if we had to be discouraged from looking for dirty words spelled out in squares of white, pink, beige, and seafoam green. I think they probably are random; at least I haven't discerned any regularities although God knows I keep looking. After about three minutes I scuttle back to the phone and tell Jo that Tuesday would be great, just great. I think about calling Arnie or maybe even Ralph for advice, but that seems cowardly and probably premature. Anyway, at this point I'm still a free agent. I also think about calling Tom, who is after all the logical confidant since he presumably knows all about the schoolmarm problem and has escalated our relationship to the level of footsie, but I decide to hold off. Now that I have something to ask Tom's advice about, I can call him any time; there's no hurry.

Ted walks back with me after class on Monday afternoon. There is a steady drizzle, very good for the skin. Neither of us has a hat or an umbrella. We discover that we are both afraid of having an eye put out by an umbrella. "I have this, like, vision of it suddenly just being there, impaled, going off on somebody's *spoke*," he says. "Like, they wouldn't even notice till they got home and there would be this *thing* with all these nerve fibers hanging off it?" My entire face screws itself up around my eyes. "Actually it's better not to think about it," he says, looking down at me anxiously. I decide it's too early in our acquaintance to compare mothers. "Oops," he says, having run into an umbrella. The girl behind it does a double-take and turns all the way around to watch him go by. Me with him. What he sees in me. I must have a neat personality. "I really enjoyed reading *Faust*," he says shyly.

"Yes," I say, watching his profile.

"About striving," he says. He has his hands shoved into his pockets and is looking at the ground about two feet ahead of him. I keep a weather eye out for umbrellas. "I kind of relate to that," he says.

"Right," I say. He's slowing down and people are surging around us now. It hits me suddenly that he's only on his way somewhere, that he isn't coming back to my office at all. I try to think of something more to say but I'm winging it; this is the first time I've taught *Faust*.

"Hey," he says broodingly. "Want to get a coke or something?"

"Sure," I say, take it or leave it.

We go to the Pub, where everyone goes except, ordinarily, the faculty, who go to the faculty club. I get a chocolate coke in honor of the adolescence I never had. Ted has a chocolate shake and two orders of French fries. I pay for my own coke but Ted grabs some extra napkins, which shows he's thinking of me, "Hey," he calls, waving the shake, and I stand on tiptoe behind him trying to follow his line of sight and remembering that standing on tiptoe elongates the calves, very flattering to, ah, heavier legs. "Professor Kiley," he says over his shoulder. "Far out." Also Tyrone, I dis-cover, and end up sitting beside him.

Herb Kiley shakes my hand across the table. "Miss Nyland?"

"Eleanor," I say.

"Eleanor. Herb. This is Tyrone." I shake Tyrone's hand, although it's a little awkward since we're elbow to elbow. "Eleanor," says Tyrone, shocking me just slightly. Student to teacher, first names. It's never done. I can see Ted is thinking about it, Eleanor. It does put a new slant on things.

"Tyrone and I were discussing the Fifth Avenue march this last weekend," says Herb Kiley. Subversive, I think, feeling as if he has just drawn a circle around out booth. Behind me two boys are talking, as ever, about the game, their dialogue punctuated by soft coos and giggles. Pretty girls: I can tell just by listening. "An extraordinary turnout," Herb Kiley says. "My New York friends estimate twenty thousand."

"I read ten," I say, grateful to *Newsweek*, my finger on the pulse of the nation.

"You were supposed to think ten," says Tyrone on my right. His elbow brushes mine. I find it hard to look directly at him. We're so close together I'm not sure it would be polite. "Ten was the least they could get away with reporting," he continues. "You know it's going to be at least twice that number."

I look at Herb Kiley. He's nodding confirmation. I feel chastened. "Twenty's probably accurate," he says. "It's amazing how much discrepancy there is between parade marshals' figures and police figures. The media follow the police, of course, unless they're our media."

"Oh," I say, grudgingly accepting the new information. Police figures. Parade marshals. Our media."

"They keep saying it's a bunch of extremists, too," says Ted. Both Herb and Tyrone smile at him. Evidently he's everybody's prize student.

"Even with a figure like ten thousand they'd have a hard time maintaining that," says Herb. "There just aren't that many extremists, not even in New York City."

I'm not sure how to keep my end up, so I start stirring my coke to get the chocolate off the bottom. If you don't keep stirring, it globs up down there around your straw and doesn't flavor anything. My mother said flavored cokes were neither one thing nor the other, which made them wrong somehow.

"Extremists," says Tyrone. I find that I have to look at him now. He's watching me from under long eyelids, not smiling. Broad lips, beautifully shaped cheekbones that push up the corners of his eyes. A straight, flat nose. Thick eyebrows, short hair like fur, very smooth dark bronze skin. He is, I acknowledge, another incredibly beautiful young man, Ted's double his dark twin. I've never know any Negroes personally, not really. Once, before I had really *bonded* with Frank, there was a rally at Columbia for SNCC, where we stood in a circle and sang We Shall Overcome and I held the hand of one, a real SNCC member, but that was luck: I just happened to be standing in the right place.

"I don't really know," I say, smiling too much. "I mean, I'm new to all this."

He nods, once, confirming a point. "You're afraid they'll make the movement look bad," he says, not a question. "Herb here thinks we got to watch out for those extremists. What do you think?"

I look at the chocolate ice in the bottom of my paper cup. Herb Kiley ought to be intervening at this point but he isn't saying anything so I suppose this must be some kind of test. I should have known no one was going to accept me simply on Ted's recommendation. "I don't know what an extremist is," I say.

"It's contextual," says Herb Kiley.

"I *know* that," I say, surprising myself and, evidently, them, for they all pull back a little. "That's the point, that it's contextual. It tends to mean what we disapprove of, whoever *we* happen to be at the moment." It was his tone, I realize, that professorial tone. He's treating me like a student.

"But some of them are talking violence," Ted murmurs. "You can't be anti-war and try to achieve that end by violent means. It's a contradiction in terms." I don't need to look at Kiley to know this is his line. He's staring into his coffee cup. Tyrone, beside me, is drumming his fingers lightly on the table top. The atmosphere around the table is so taut that it's almost erotic.

"The whole concept makes me nervous," I say. "I'd rather deal with the situation at hand, what we want to achieve. It seems to me that if you make intensity automatically bad you're leaving yourself open to the charge. I mean, lots of people think opposition is extremist by definition."

"Good," says Tyrone, very softly, almost in my ear. I hunch over my coke and suck at the straw until I'm making unladylike slurping noises. My mother would be appalled. I suspect that Herb Kiley is a little appalled.

"So you'd rule out the word entirely," he says now.

Socratic double-binds. Now I get pinned as an advocate of censorship. "Oh hell," I say. "You can use it. I just want to know what you mean when you do. It seems to me that extremist is one of those words that gets everybody screaming and it turns out they're all screaming about different things."

"Right on," murmurs Tyrone, and for some reason the tension seeps away. Unexpectedly Herb Kiley smiles at me, and little wrinkles radiate from the corners of his mouth and eyes. All right, I concede, this is a charming man. I can feel the charm lifting me out of my anger even as I'm thinking that he's got some sort of leprechaun identification going, some goddamned fey persona that really sucks them in and probably gets him great teaching ratings. But it's sucking me in too, the very light blue eyes tilting up now at the outside edges. I don't really mind all that much. And with him two beautiful young men. An assembly of gods with the right politics. And here *I* am, I think, and wish that somebody were watching. Louis Feitelson even.

Tyrone is looking at me. I let him look. It feels good. "Got a nickel?" he asks after a while, and I dig one out for him. "Back in a minute," he says, and I slide out to let him by. Ted looks a little dazed. I sense that Kiley is looking at me too, but I avoid his eyes, unready to define my position any more just yet. I feel as if I've come a long way in a very short time. I'm not sure how far I've gone, what I've committed myself to, or what commitment entails.

The music starts up as Tyrone ambles back toward our table, shuffling a little, loose-kneed, loose-hipped. He dances, I think, a little thrill travelling up my backbone although I don't dance, have never danced, haven't got beyond doing exercises to the radio. But Tyrone definitely dances, I tell myself, sensing possibility. "Move over," he says to me, and I slide into the corner. He slips in beside me making no particular effort not to brush hips, legs. I glance up at Ted. He looks radiant.

"Get off my cloud," I say to Tyrone.

"Hey," he says.

When the chorus comes up we sing it, mugging, Tyrone on the beat, me on the afterbeat, coming together on the refrain: *Hey (Hey) You (You) Get offa MY CLOUD–* We're swaying from side to side together after the first chorus. Ted twitches his shoulders a little. Kiley is watching us as if he's recording some sort of rite, which in a sense he is. When the record stops he's the one to fish out a quarter and tell Tyrone "Play it a few times. I think I like it." I wiggle my shoulders at him and imagine teaching him about rock and roll, a new acquisition of mine. I imagine teaching him how to dance, even though I don't dance or haven't so far. Tyrone could teach me. Tyrone and Ted. I think about the four of us getting together to practice our dancing. It would have to be at my house, that's the obvious place. Kiley could bring his wife, I suppose, although it would be okay if he came by himself. He looks like the type who goes a lot of places without his wife.

"You're coming to the meeting on Friday?" he says now. I feel like the prom queen. "I haven't been asked," I say.

"Come. We need you. Ted will tell you all about it."

I incline my head graciously, the bow I tried out on Ralph Hamilton a couple of weeks ago. It's some sort of coping mechanism, I guess.

"See you there, then?" It's almost an order. But what the hell, this isn't exactly a social engagement. They do need me. They need everybody. Not only that, though, or I don't think it's only that. They need everybody, especially me. It's a just a little shift in emphasis.

Late in the evening I put on a slip and try moving my body around while Wilson Pickett growls at Mustang Sally, but I can tell I don't have it anywhere near right. If I had a television I could maybe watch American Bandstand: that was how the pretty girls figured out how to dance back in junior high. They danced with each other in their garages. I know because a lot of times they used Sheri Willey's garage across the street. I suspect, however, that Tyrone doesn't dance like anything Dick Clark could put a name to. I have a feeling Tyrone dances re-ally dirty. *All you want to DOOOOooo is ride around Sally*, Wilson Pickett shrieks, and I try swinging my pelvis in an ungainly circle: ride, Sally, ride. Sometimes they call him the *Wickett* Wilson Pickett, flavor of the ghetto permeating even Middle American DJisms, even here. Of course, what I want most of all is to dance dirty. To be taught to dance dirty. It's not the sort of thing you get very far with all by yourself.

Jo Michaelson takes me to the faculty club for lunch and I have a Manhattan, which turns out to be one of those brown drinks, not bad after the initial shock. Halfway through it I find I'm telling her about the committee while she nods like a sybil. "Hamilton's the one you have to watch out for," she observes after I'm done with my blurting. "The other are basically hangers-on." She extracts the olive from her new martini and lays it, still impaled on its ornamental toothpick, on the linen tablecloth. "Hamilton's got the clout. Furthermore he's got it in for me."

"Really," I say helpfully. I could have said I knew, but it doesn't seem polite to tell somebody you're aware she's not, um, *liked.*

"So has Norford, for that matter," she says. "Not that he's normally on the same side as Hamilton, who's aspiring to the throne. The Middle-Aged Pretender, you know, but Norford picks his own successor thank you although he's not ready yet, not by a long shot. Actually he still hasn't found a *pure* asslicker. But this one they're together on. There's a story behind all this but I'm not going to tell you."

"Okay," I say. The Manhattan has put me in an accepting frame of mind.

"Like Elizabeth," she says, and picks a shred of tobacco from her tongue with the maroon nails of her thumb and third finger. "Elizabeth the First." I have been helping myself to her Lucky Strikes ever since my defenses went down, and now I'm practicing blowing smoke out my nose. It gets into everything; you can taste it in places you didn't know tasted.

"They're supposed to be hiring somebody for next year," I tell her.

Her smile is closed-mouthed, a thin streak of mottled red.

"They don't have the line," she says. "They have to get the line from the Dean. They think they're going to get it but they're not."

"Ah," I say, not about to ask what a line is. I get the general idea.

After that I cope muzzily with World Masterpieces and the inscrutable Part Two of *Faust*. The Eternal Feminine lures us onward: now what do you make of that, Suzi? Jim? Ted? Even Ted shakes his head morosely and looks down at his desk. It's not just the alcohol, either: I'm having trouble with this one. I thought I could pin down the Eternal Feminine without any trouble, if only by association with things like the True Cross and the Vagina Dentata—what you might call your favorite images of Western culture. But it turns out that I haven't a clue, probably because I keep trying to imagine *being* one, although clearly this is all wrong. If you were the Eternal Feminine you couldn't know it. It's part of the definition of the role that you can't have any awareness you're it. Or any awareness of anything, actually; like all the rest of those sexual ideals the Eternal Feminine has no insides, not even in her case gynecological ones. I keep coming up against this. Here I am a literature major when all of literature is crying out to me that what I ought to be is a symbol. I expect it's the translation, I say guiltily, and everybody perks up. You can blame a lot on the translation. We end class on that note, conspirators for once in the plot to leave it at that.

I'm so deflated by the experience that I seek out the janitor for a restorative discussion of floor wax. I find him swabbing down the hall by the elevators. "Listen," I say, hoping to impart some urgency to the interruption. "I've got white linoleum, streaky but basically white. It doesn't get clean anymore."

He stops swabbing and leans on his op, tucking his long chin into the collar of his shirt. "Kind of blotchy, you mean."

"Not even what you could identify as blotches," I say. "More subtle. As if there's something wrong with my eyes."

I can see he's giving it some thought. At last he nods as if satisfied with his diagnosis. "Wax buildup," he says.

"But you gave me the wax. It's industrial wax."

He nods again. "I keep forgetting the layman doesn't understand wax," he says.

I've never thought of wax in quite those terms before, as if there were a priesthood devoted to its mysteries. I feel rebuked.

"You can't just keep waxing and waxing," he explains. "You're putting stuff on but you're never taking it off. I can get you some remover, but it's strong. You have to be careful with it, like you ought to wear gloves. It's not available to the general public." He shoots me a dubious glance. "Not for, ah, domestic use ordinarily."

"I'll be careful," I say, and wonder if I appear mature enough for the responsibility. I'm getting resigned to the fact that my life is made up of this kind of metaphor. What I need right now, clearly, is a strong remover.

"Just the person I want to see," calls Tom Lippman from the end of the hall, and I'm unsure for a moment whether he means me or the janitor until the janitor goes back to his linoleum. Tom catches up to me and we stroll back down the hall to my office as if it were the most natural thing in the world for us to be walking together. "So why were you talking to that guy?" he inquires.

I shrug. "Don't you ever talk to him?"

"What about?"

It occurs to me that with the janitor I have the kind of collegial relationship I dreamed of having once I was established in the profession, a passionate shared interest in a recondite subject. "Cleaning," I say.

"Cleaning." Apparently the word conveys nothing to him. "What do you mean, cleaning?"

"Cleaning *things*," I say. "Floors, woodwork, carpets, dishes. Laundry. Counter tops. Ovens."

"*House*work?"

"Schoolwork too," I say. "I mean, you can clean other things than houses, you know. He cleans this building. He cleans your office, Tom or hadn't you noticed?"

Tom snorts. "Since when am I supposed to notice who cleans my office?"

He probably doesn't notice who cleans his house, either.

It's probably some deficiency in me that I notice. If you're serious about the profession you probably just throw things on the floor and figure God will take care of them. Frank was like that.

We're back to my office now, and he drops into my student chair and slings his ankle across his knee, exposing a couple of inches of white calf above the ribbed sock. "The hair is auburn and sparser than I would have guessed. Not as curly as I'd imagined either. "You're a kook, Eleanor," he says conversationally.

Teasing, I interpret. I'm getting better at this. When they call you names it's so you'll act bothered. It's supposed to be a positive sign when they bother you. I give him my tight classroom smile. "Kook as in kooky?" I ask.

"Kook as in wacko," he returns.

"Why am I wacko?" I ask, feeling like Miss Brooks again.

He smiles joyously. "Oh Eleanor, at the meeting. You were just *out* of it, you know?"

"No" I say, alarmed.

"Oh, it's okay," he assures me. "I mean, everybody really thought you were great. A load of laughs."

"They did?"

"Oh yeah, nobody knew you were so much fun, you know?"

"Oh," I say. It doesn't seem like the best thing to be on a committee but I've obviously made an impression.

He squints at me. "You're going to be a definite asset to our team," he says. "That's exactly what Ralph said."

"Oh, that was *nice* of him," I say, my mother's training asserting itself. I'm thinking that if they're a team I'm their cheerleader. It's the only possible role they could have for me. My mother would be so gratified if I could finally be a cheerleader.

"He's a great guy," says Tom huskily, and we both avert our eyes in recognition of what a great guy Ralph Hamilton is. It's one of the conventions of our committee that when you mention the name of somebody on it you're supposed to be overcome with emotion. The emotions differ hierarchically, of course. When my name is mentioned, for instance, presumably everybody laughs.

I want to know how, exactly, they think I'm fun, but I can't figure out how to work up to it so Tom does his version of Oh what a rogue and peasant slave am I for me instead. "I just did it for my class yesterday," he confides. "They couldn't get over it. One girl even called me last night, she was still brooding over it." The nerve, I think, full of envy. "You should figure out when we're going to do this for your students," he says. "I'm not going to be as fresh once I get beyond *Hamlet* in my own class. Tomorrow would be a good time."

Tomorrow we begin our concerted attack on the comma splice. "I don't know that they're primed for you yet," I say.

After he leaves I bundle myself up in my extra sweater and raincoat and muffler and walk out the other end of the building toward Schwindemann Annex, where the Basic program is officially housed. The Annex is a squat half-cylinder of corrugated metal, ostentatiously temporary, dating from the war. When the light is on, as it is now, you can see right into Jo Michaelson's office. I tap on the pane.

Jo waves me toward the front door and comes to open it. "You're just in time for a little sherry," she says. "I always take a little sherry this time of the afternoon. Gentlemanly practice."

I accept a brimming paper cup. Offhand I'm not sure why sherry has more class than Tokay. They smell about the same.

"Back in the gentlemanly days of this department," Jo says, waving me to her couch, "there were faculty sherries every Friday afternoon. Culture. Meeting of the minds. Ladies not invited. The great tradition."

I have too much sherry in my mouth to swallow gracefully so I have to cough several times before I can ask, "Why weren't ladies invited?"

Jo raises her paper cup to me. "I wondered that too at one time. I asked Norford. It was Norford then too, you know. It's always been Norford in this department, since something like 1946. Anyway, he said Josephine *dear*, sometimes the boys just need to sit around together and scratch their balls. Just came out and said it, you see. Levelling with me. A great compliment."

I sip at the sherry. I can see how you might get used to it.

"Some other things about that committee," I say, and she nods like royalty granting an audience. "I'm supposed to serve coffee and type up all their notes onto ditto masters," I say. A lot of people wouldn't see that as grounds for complaint. "I mean, I'm supposed to be a member—"

"Hah," says Jo, and goes into a fit of coughing. "Short mirthless laugh," she explains as she emerges and picks up the stub of a Lucky Strike still smoldering in the ashtray.

"You think I'm pretty naïve," I say.

"You're learning," she soothes. "Every day in every way." I feel pretty naïve. We make another luncheon date and I stumble out into almost complete darkness. Walking home I sober up enough to reflect that all this stumping around in penny loafers and a trench coat is getting unworkable and that I'm going to have to get either a car or a good winter coat and boots. The coat and boots are a lot cheaper but irrevocably associated with my mother and my plodding high school persona, zipped into scratchy wool and sturdy fleece-lined rubbers. My past is getting in my way, I decide. If I don't transcend it soon I'm going to freeze to death.

I compromise by going to Penney's the next day and buying an imitation Navy pea jacket made of scratchy wool and a pair of bell-bottom jeans. The drawback is that I can't wear either of these garments to school, where even the graduate students go around dressed like insurance salesmen, but I figure they're accessories to my fantasy life, part of another identity congealing out of my amorphous off-hours in the upstairs study and on my knees on the linoleum. Lenorean autoeroticism and I'm gonna wash that man right outta my floor. On Thursday I discover an unmarked quart bottle full of a liquid the surreal blue of swimming pool water sitting on top of my desk. I make a note to buy rubber gloves on my way home.

Tom comes by again that afternoon while I'm typing Bill Brewster's Ideas on the Teaching of Composition In The Basic Program on Arnie's Remington upright, which is in my office for the duration of the accumulating and collating portion of the committee's work. I would have preferred an electric, but Ralph looked pained when I brought up the subject and Arnie, who was sitting on the edge of Ralph's desk swinging his legs, said he didn't mind loaning out his possessions for the good of the whole, which displaced the problem and made me look petty. As I poke at the keys now, I reflect on Arnie's earlier admission that he can't type and resolve not to correct any of the numerous errors I seem unable to avoid on this machine, since I have no evidence yet that anyone actually reads the material I transcribe and duplicate. Bill Brewster's Ideas are in the form of a list, and Bill is developing a distinctive laconic tone. *Let them know they're out on their ears if they can't cut it,* he has written in a bold, sloping hand almost two lines high, and under this, *Revisions mandatory, only flawless work accepted!* Tom fidgets in my student chair and stares at the quart bottle, which looks quite pretty in the afternoon sunlight. When I finally look up he sighs and says, "Eleanor, I hate to say this but it strikes me you're being pretty evasive about this *Hamlet* business."

I move the bottle so I can see him. "How do you mean, evasive?"

He gazes at me levelly, and I am struck again by how dark and wet his eyes manage to be. "If you don't want to do the closet scene then why don't you just come out and say it?" he says finally.

I shrug, feeling ashamed and a little aroused again. It's the unseasonal sunlight probably, along with being stared at like that. No one stares at me under normal circumstances. "You know how busy I am," I begin, but he has risen from the chair with sudden energy.

"Let me show you how I see that scene," he says. "Now I'm just going to give you your lines and you say them and I'll show you what happens. Just say what I tell you."

I can't think of any reason to refuse. "Right," he says, stepping back into my doorway. "Right. Now I come in and you're just sitting there, right? Expecting me. And I say, Now mother, what's the matter? and *you* say Hamlet, thou has thy father much offended. You got that?"

"Hamlet, thou hast thy father much offended," I say obediently. It's almost a tongue-twister.

"That's it. Only on cue, you know? After me. Okay, now I'm coming in. Now, Mother, what's the matter?"

"Hamlet, though hast thy father much offended," I say tonelessly.

"Mother, you have *my* father much offended," he says, leaning over the desk toward me. "You see? It's a play on 'father.' *She* means Claudius but *he* means—"

"I've read it," I say.

"Yeah. Well then you say Come, come, you answer with an idle tongue."

"Come, come, you answer with an idle tongue," I say.

"Like that," he says. "Only preferably with more, you know, zest, but that'll come. Okay, let's start from my entrance again and I'll show you how it plays." He backs up to the doorway again, nearly falling over the student chair and kicking it negligently out of the way to disguise his recovery. "I see coming in *briskly*," he says from the doorway. Behind him in the hall, Lois Lafferty is standing transfixed. "Now, Mother, what's the matter?" he cries, striding up to my desk. Lois covers her mouth with her hand.

"Hamlet, thou hast they father much offended," I say, and lean back in my chair as he lurches forward across the desktop. "Offended," I say again weakly, for he has clasped one hand around my jaw and brought his face so close that our noses are almost touching.

"Mother," he murmurs, "you have my father much offended."

"Ah," I say.

"Come, come—"

"Come, come," I gasp, "You answer with an idle tongue."

He licks his lips and tilts my face up toward his. "Go, go, you question with a *wicked* tongue," he hisses.

"I see you're busy," says Lois Lafferty from the doorway. I'm not sure which of us she is addressing. Tom simply waves her away without letting go of my jaw, and I roll my eyes to watch her moving slowly out of view. Then I focus on his eyes, only inches away. His breath warms my lips.

"You see?" he whispers ecstatically. "It's Oedipal!"

"Right," I whisper back and close my eyes, but he lets go of my jaw and straightens up.

"We wouldn't have a desk, you know," he says. "Just a chair. And I see myself really, ah, caressing you so that it's be explicit. I mean it's got to be explicit or they just won't believe it. I mean, even some of my students don't really believe it and we've gone over and over this passage—"

"Right," I say again. My jaw is burning. "You see him having an, ah, thing for his mother," I say.

"Well yeah, it's right there," he says, and retrieves the student chair for himself. "I mean, here he's killed his father and what does his mother turn around and do but—"

"Hamlet killed his father?"

"In a manner of speaking," says Tom airily. "It's symbolic, you know, that's the main thing. Also, why else would he be so upset? Anyway, I see this scene as just incredibly erotic, you know Gertrude ready for bed—"

"In her robe?" I ask, inspired.

"Good idea. Yeah, kind of coming open—"

"Do I, ah, caress back?" I ask casually?

He leans back in the chair, considering. "We could try it both ways," He says at last. "I mean, she's got to be hot for him, that's for sure, but I don't know if she's, ah, saddled by conventions or just waiting for him to move or an out and out hypocrite or what. I mean, there's a certain amount of leeway for interpretation there, so maybe we should try it a couple of ways and see what happens."

I think about some of the things that could happen and cross my legs under the desk. "Fine," I say. "Sounds fine. When do we try it?"

He wrinkles his forehead and considers again. "What about this weekend?"

Weekend. Private life. "Sounds okay," I say, and look at the bottle of blue liquid. Now we're both looking at it. Eye-beams intersecting, triangulation of gazes. How illicit is he intending to be? "When this weekend?" I ask.

"Ah, Sunday's better."

"Sunday's okay for me," I say.

"Three, maybe?" he says. "My office?"

"Sure," I say to the bottle, and add as an afterthought, "I'll learn my lines."

After he's gone I uncross my legs and wonder whether I shouldn't do something about finding a robe. I'll have to order it from somewhere, maybe from one of those places that advertise in the backs of magazines. When I try to resume my transcription of Bill Brewster's Ideas my hands are trembling so badly that I end up on the wrong keys for *No late work accepted—fixed deadlines!* and have to pull out the whole ditto master and start over. It occurs to me while I'm doing this that Bill has chosen to view him-self as a prison warden, or perhaps a reform school master, for the purpose of rethinking the Basic program, and that Jo Michaelson would view this persona as terribly threatened, whereas Tom Lippman if I asked him would only purse his lips and point out to me that fixed deadlines are a necessity. Like the rest of the committee he seems to assume that the Basic program should be a mechanism for showing them—and undefined but presumably hulking, proletariat, and of course male Them—who's boss. Yet Tom Lippman can make my hands tremble and, I'm assuming, other parts of me as well, and in fact it's Tom Lippman who is making all the moves, or not making them as the case may be, while I wait, quivering but otherwise inert, to see how far he plans to go with Hamlet's mother. "Asshole," I murmur, nasal-voweled. It wasn't a word you heard in Lawrence. I got it at Columbia, not initially from Frank. It's meant to apply to me, too, although secondarily, by association.

I spend Thursday night looking over the most recent papers from the two Basic classes, which take on the subject of My Name and What It Signifies (To Me, To Others, In My Family, In My Culture). I had hoped that the innocent narcissism of the topic would provoke some reflection, even some creativity, but aside from a few predictable effusions (Kimi Kelly wrote that her name *makes one think of a person which is basicly full of fun and good-times but with a little "something" which is very unique to the person themselves*) the responses are even more terse than usual. The one exception is Louise Feitelson's essay, which manages to be four pages long and ends with an impassioned coda: *Some persons feel they can change there names to such as: Gloria, Angela, Michelle, Nicole. Not so. You are who you are. It is important, above all, to be your self.* I note the list of current pretty-girl names, powerful temptations for a Louise, and the homiletic conclusion, which represents the party line for college girls right now. Be yourself. Don't try to change: that's phony. But why, I ask myself, and then write *Why?* At the bottom of the paper. It's not a question she's likely to have considered. After a moment I write below it a grade: C-minus. Now she'll consider it, I think, feeling rather pleased with my intervention into Louise's intellectual development.

My real concern, however, is my pornographic manuscript, which has been languishing since my meeting with Norford. I've resolved to deal with the situation of Bik Chaggard tonight, since he has been due to have someone slide up and down the greased pole of his manhood for almost a month now, stuck in that uterine amphitheater with his protuberant member hoisted and the Queen on her eminence poised to take a flying leap. But there are problems. It ought to be clear what happens next, but there are problems.

"Disrobe!" she repeated, a faint moue of frustration downturning her perfect lips. No sound in the vast hall, although her courtiers encircled the throne in their serried ranks. He stood before her, tunic outstretched in admission of his desire, but unmoving. Her own robe, she realized with exasperation, was falling open, revealing more cleavage than she had intended at this point; with an impatient gesture she pulled it together and retied the belt. Satin was so slippery: there were drawbacks to all these raiments of authority, authority of course being the issue at hand. He was gazing steadily at her, and she composed her face hastily into its usual mask of serenity. "Perhaps the outlander is modest," she proclaimed to the assembly, evoking smiles and faint chuckles all the way to the back row, for everyone recalled his braggadocio the night of the troupe grope orgy orgiastic religious rites rituals ceremonies in honor of the Goddess.

But his face remained set and his gaze never wavered. When the laughter had died down, his voice rang out. "Your majesty," he called up to her, one eyebrow lifted ironically. "I'll take off my clothes if you will."

A palpable shudder ran through the hall. All the conventions indicated he should stand bare and defenseless before them while she remained swathed in her satins voyeur to his exposure, Dejeuner Sur L'Herbe, so to speak, although presumably at some point she would spread her skirts are squat over him in the manner of someone taking a pee in the shrubbery—"

Taken aback by his arrogance, she found herself plunged into speculation. How was she going to do this? It was all very well to adopt the premises of pornographic rape sequences, but when you reversed the usual victim and victimizer roles you couldn't always control the connotations. Even regally garbed, she involved herself in a symbolic descent by getting off the throne and onto his prong: even with her own cheering section the lines of dominance blurred; any sex at all was somehow, inevitably, lowering . . . .

This business of dominance isn't working itself out or even turning out to be much fun, *Beaver Country* and all my other exemplars to the contrary. She can't just be in it for the sex, that's what's coming out of this. Maybe she should have a *relationship* with him; they rule the kingdom together or maybe she rules and he pots, getting right into the non-intellective. Actually she's going to have to watch out or she'll be making the pots while he revises the protocol for the ceremony in honor of the Goddess to include dancing girls in garter belts and a backup chorus of hearty adventurers with whips. He's not the type for a relationship. I know his type.

I'd hoped this snag in the pornographic process would work itself out, though, given my current condition, which is practically writhing in my desk chair in anticipation of Sunday afternoon in Tom's office. Not that I really expect Tom to molest me in iambic pentameter. It's enough at the moment that we'll be there alone, with innuendo hanging heavy in the air and a lot of lines about tongues to flick snakily at each other. The point is that this is a step forward and that I'm willing to settle for a step. Not even settle: I'm not sure I'd want to rush into anything with Tom even if I did have any choice in the matter. It's been occurring to me this evening that I'm rather counting on having a long, slow escalation of erotic tensions to give some direction to my school year, lots of meaningful looks and pregnant pauses accompanying the transition from footsie to handsie, for instance. Horny as I am, I'm not eager to do anything with Tom Lippman that might give him more of an edge on me, or maybe it's just that Frank was right in his initial accusation and I do take a hell of a long time to come. Still, I had thought that an atmosphere of sexual expectation might ooze over into my writing and resolve the libidinal paralysis that has kept me away from the Lenoreans for so long. If it's not going to work out that way, subliminally, instinctively, then I'm going to have to start thinking.

I go to sleep instead, and spend most of Friday in bed or in front of the bathroom mirror contorting my face to look simultaneously intellectual and as if I had cheekbones, in preparation for the meeting at Herb Kiley's house. Late in the afternoon I put on my new bell-bottoms and walk around trying to keep them from being caught under the heels of my penny loafers. Then I try on my entire wardrobe of blouses to see which one looks best with the bell-bottoms. None of them looks very good. My new identity is going to require more planning than I'd realized.

It's almost eight-thirty by the time I get to the Kiley house, which is large and white and lit up like an ocean liner behind bare, dripping elms. I can hear the voices even on the sidewalk. I climb the porch steps feeling a little like Cinderella on the verge of the ball, although I know I'm one of the loser stepsisters or at best someone else's fairy godmother. As soon as I knock, the door opens and a small, vivaciously pretty woman pulls me in by the elbow. "I'm Mary Ellen Kiley," she whispers breathlessly. "I don't believe I've met you?"

"Eleanor," I whisper back. "Nyland. Ah, English Department."

"Ooooh, *faculty*," she whispers, and squeezes my elbow. I wonder if I'm supposed to squeeze her elbow back. I wasn't brought up to fondle people: my mother touched only in order to steer. "We always said we'd know things were picking up when the faculty started to come over," Mary Ellen confides.

"I'm only a lecturer," I say, and then wonder if they've

heard me in the next room. It's awfully quiet. Just one voice rising and falling. A lot of muted rustling and thumping, though.

"Well I'm off to get coffee," she hisses conspiratorially, and squeezes my elbow again before she lets it go. For one awful moment I believe she has recognized me as a kindred spirit and is about to ask me to join in the coffee-getting, but she disappears through a swinging door, not quite closed, and through it I can hear the monotonous cadences of the voice. After a moment of faint-heartedness I slip inside.

There are perhaps thirty people in the room, most of them sprawled on the beige wall-to-wall carpet. I edge in and drop to the carpet myself, dislodging a very lean young man who grunts and hitches himself sideways. At that moment the voice stops and everyone looks at me. After a long pause another voice demands, "Can I have the conch?"

There is some twisting and fumbling from the sofa by the fireplace before someone produces a large pink shell, which is passed from hand to hand until it reaches a plump young man who has arranged himself cross-legged on a hassock. He fingers it languidly as if drawing inspiration from it and then says, "Too long."

There is a chorus of muttered "Yeah"s and a single more assertive "Right on." I decide that they're not discussing me and begin to relax. "There's a *reason* it's too long," says the plump young man. I've identified the original speaker or rather reader: he's clutching several smudgy pages of typewritten copy, Eaton's Corrasable Bond I'd be willing to bet. He too is elevated above the floor-sitters, on an old-fashioned piano stool twisted up to its highest position so that he appears at first glance to be impaled on an iron pole.

"The reason is there's an ambiguity in the conception of this letter," says the plump man. He has the kind of beard I'll always associate with Columbia, the kind where each individual hair is doing something different. "As I see it," he continues, "Charlie's basically conflated several possible responses. I boil it down to three courses of action we could take. One." He raises his index finger, everybody write it down. "We indicate our general approval of Miller's action without committing ourselves to any position on its illegality. Two." Another finger. I resent him already but I have to admire the fact that he isn't even using notes. "We declare ourselves in full support of an action we acknowledge is illegal. Which would make us accessories, if anyone feels like pushing it." Several people are nodding. A creak from the piano stool. "Three." He looks around for a moment until he is satisfied that everyone is paying attention. Then he drops the shell into his lap and raises his hands, palms up. "We declare our willingness to burn our own draft cards," he says.

The room explodes into applause and "Right *on*"s and I murmur, "Someone finally did it."

"Yeah, where you been?" growls the young man next to me. "Catholic Worker guy, did it today right outside Whitehall Street. That's what all this is *about*."

"No, it isn't," says a young woman who has leaned around behind him. She looks vaguely familiar, one of our graduate students I think. "This was just a regular meeting. Nobody even knew about the draft card burning until Professor Kiley announced it."

"How d'ya *know* nobody knew?" snaps the young man.

"You would have said something, Kenny," she tells him firmly.

The man on the piano stool has the shell. "The ambiguity was deliberate!" he is shouting over the general uproar. "We can't commit everybody to one position. That would be undemocratic!"

"Hear, hear!" calls a middle-aged man sitting on the carpet with his back against the couch. Alliances forming. I spot Professor Kiley now, deep in a wing chair by the fireplace.

"Undemocratic, bullshit!" the young man whose name seems to be Kenny shouts belligerently. "We either put our bodies on the line or we're just talking."

"You'll lose your exemptions." It's Kiley's voice, dominating the room although the tone is conversational.

A pause. Beside me Kenny mutters, "Exemptions, bullshit!" but seems only to be trying out the phrase. It occurs to me that one function of these meetings must be to allow people to say words there is no context for anywhere else in this town.

"Now Paul's right that we need to examine the kinds of responses we could make," Kiley continues. "But of course Charlie's right too, in that we can't reasonably demand that everyone have the same response." Charlie and Paul, I observe, are softening. Although they haven't actually made eye contact they're shooting little dubious glances at each other.

"Why can't we *reasonably* demand—" Kenny again, strident with anxiety now at being left out.

"Because some of us have more at stake than others," Kiley says patiently. "I'm not eligible for the draft any more, and neither is Will—" a nod at the middle-aged man on the floor—"or Paul, for that matter, who's 4-F." Little surprised murmurs. Not everybody knew that. Setback for the emerging student leadership here. Kiley, I'm beginning to see, is very good at this.

"Well that makes it a question of priorities then." Kenny is vibrating with irritation and making spasmodic gestures with a newly-lit cigarette. "I mean, whose protest is this finally? The *old* guys'? I mean I'm talking leadership here, like who's making decisions about our bodies, right? First it's the old guys in Washington and now it's the old guys on campus and as far as I can see it's just lot of old guys—"

"I'm not eligible for the draft," I say.

He stops short and swings around to face me, lip drawn back from his upper teeth in feral consternation. Around us people are saying "What?" and someone across the room shouts "Louder!" "Give her the conch!" someone shouts, and another voice contributes, "Hey you're not supposed to speak unless you've got the conch." It occurs to me to point out that there has been quite a bit of speaking without the conch already, but I know they wouldn't get it, any more than they get the fact that they've made me invisible in this division of humanity into old guys and young guys.

The shell is unexpectedly pleasant to hold, cool and rather heavy. "I was just pointing out—" I say.

"Who are you?" someone shouts.

"Eleanor Nyland," I say, more emphatically than I had planned, perhaps because I have only just decided not to add my identifying tag, English.

Across the room someone calls faintly, "Yay, Eleanor," and people crane around to look and then back at me. I don't have to look. My face is suddenly warm, partly because I have dared to come into this group and demand attention, partly because in this room I have an admirer. "I'm not eligible for the draft either," I say. "And I'm not an old guy. I mean, I'm not a guy at all."

"Right on," says somebody near me, and there is perfunctory laughter. They don't get it.

"*Your* body isn't on the line," Kenny points out, and gets a few sniggers. My body obviously doesn't command the reverence that his does. It seems, rather, to suggest dirty jokes.

"Don't you see, that's the *point*," I say. "So in a way, people like me, not just old guys but all the rest of us, the half of the population that won't get drafted no matter what, are in a better position to support, ah, this guy's—"

"Miller's" supplies somebody across the room.

"Miller's action," I say. I've just learned that action is what you call it. "Which was what Professor Kiley was saying," I finish, feeling uncomfortable now. I realize that I've been gesturing with the conch and set it down carefully on my left, well out of Kenny's reach. He strikes me as a grabber.

"Um, how support Miller's action?" It's the girl on the other side of Kenny. She's hunched over with her forehead wrinkled in concentration.

"Well," I say, improvising out of air now, "we could have two statements of support, two letters, one for the guys who could get drafted and one for the rest of us. I mean, their bodies are, ah, on the line, so it's their business what they say. But the way I see it the rest of us are in a position to make the government pretty uncomfortable about prosecuting Miller if we want to."

"I think I see what you're getting at, Eleanor." It's Kiley's voice floating across from the fireplace, setting me up. Of course he sees what I'm getting at. It's his point. But evidently I'm the one who is supposed to explicate it, to remove the stigma of old-guyism. I'm annoyed but then I tell myself this is the way politics works. We've just formed a coalition. And there's no doubt that they're listening carefully now. There's a new tautness in the silence surrounding me.

"The point of this letter is that it's an open letter, as public as we can make it," I say. "We send it to the student paper, to the town paper, to the legislature, oh to the New York *Times—*"

"All our Congressmen," someone calls.

"Shit," says somebody else, "we send it to Rusk, to the Joint Chiefs, to *Lady* Bird—"

"Right," I say, "right." It's coming now, it's like class discussion once you get it going. "Of course we take a risk but it's a public risk and they'll be making all their moved in public—"

"So what should we say in this letter?" Kiley again. It crosses my mind that I'd hate to have him against me. "Well," I say, "I can tell you what I'd write if it were just me doing the letter." That's the classic defense among my students, particularly the girls: *Well, this is only my opinion and of course I could be wrong but.* "Speaking only for myself, of course," I say carefully, "I'd want to declare myself an accomplice or even a conspirator. And say it's my intent to help and support anybody who plans to burn his card or resist the draft in any way."

Unexpectedly, there's a burst of applause. I look down at the conch, trying not to look as if I loved it. I do love it. Has anyone ever clapped for me before? "I mean," I continue, breathless, "there no *way* they can send me to Vietnam and I'd just like to see them try sending me to jail—"

But people are on their feet shouting "Right *on!*" and stamping and clapping, and someone is pounding me on the back. No, I'm thinking, but it's useless now, they believe I've volunteered for martyrdom, they believe I'm setting up to be a hero. And I only just got here. Of course I didn't mean I was going to write the letter of I was daring the administration to send me to jail. Not alone, not me personally, that was a figure of speech, a convention you use when you don't want to seem to be telling other people what to do. I meant us, of course, thousands of us preferably, an academic mass too weighty and respectable to be carted off to jail without shrill public outcry, a reevaluation of the draft system, withdrawal of the troops. It doesn't matter what I meant.

Someone presses a mug of coffee into my hand, Mary Ellen Kiley looking misty-eyed and fond. Behind her is the girl who was correcting Kenny, carrying a fluted silver tray with silver cream pitcher and sugar bowl. My mother would have approved. It's extraordinarily pleasant having someone else serve the coffee. They drift off into the crowd and the cigarette smoke, and Ted pushes through and makes himself a place beside me. "You were terrific," he whispers. "Did you hear me cheering you?"

"Um," I say, but at this point the plump man, Paul, plops down on my other side. "I'd like to work *with* you on that letter," he says significantly. "It's important to move fast, don't you think?"

"So as not to lose momentum," I respond sagely. Both he and Ted go into energetic nods. I feel around for the pack of Marlboros that I brought along with me in case I needed moral support. They both grab for matches. "I think I can find time in the afternoon," I say, extracting a cigarette with difficulty and accepting Ted's light. "Around two, maybe? Two-*ish*?"

Ted and Tyrone drive me home in Tyrone's Studebaker coupe. "Like, this is a *loser* car," Tyrone reports with satisfaction as I wedge in between them. A little giddy with the pressure of thighs, I invite them in for a beer, which they accept so gratefully that I'm forced to reflect on their ages again. "You here by yourself?" Tyrone inquires, eyelids at half-mast as he leans against the kitchen counter, and I shrug and tell them about the Pakistani graduate student. "Hey," he says. "Can we see the apartment? I lead the way down to the basement and they poke around opening cupboards and examining the tiny refrigerator with exaggerated care.

"Cool," says Ted finally. "Offhand, what do you want for it?"

The question takes me by surprise. "I thought you guys had to live in the dorms," I say, not trusting my luck yet.

"That's *girls*," says Tyrone scornfully. "They can't make us live anywhere, even though they'd like to. I mean, they won't come out and say so, but they don't want us rooming together and they're doing everything they can to stop it. So we really have to live off-campus unless we want to go along with institutionalized racism."

"Forty," I say. "That counts heat and electricity. And garbage. But I don't mind noise. Or, ah, political activity." We all smile in complicity.

Tyrone nods at Ted. "Twenty apiece. You want to go talk about it?"

Ted shakes his head. "The hitch is we can't move in till Christmas break," he tells me, with a smile that forces me to sit down in one of the two butterfly chairs in the apartment's tiny living room. "Is that okay with you?" I can only nod. I'll wait a lot longer if I have to.

Paul and I get together Saturday in his office, which is even smaller than my office because he is only a teaching assistant, albeit in Political Science, a department far better funded than my own. Above his desk is a poster with a drawing of Che Guevara's head, social realist with curls, floating above a lot of foreshortened peasants who are looking up awestruck from what they're doing, exactly as if they were witnessing a manifestation of the Virgin. Below the drawing is a quotation: *Permit me to say, at the risk of seeming ridiculous, that the true revolutionary is motivated by feelings of love.* When I remark on the poster Paul says yeah, most of the guys in Poly Sci are Maoist now, and I nod gravely as if I get the connection. Later he adverts reverently to my Columbia background and I realize that he's got me fitted into a context that I'm only dimly aware of: hotbed traditional left, the Marxist remnant. Not *that* Columbia, I want to say, but I don't.

The session is a smashing success inasmuch as I dictate while Paul types. The reason for the apparent role-reversal is that Paul doesn't want me screwing up his typewriter, but I still find it a heady experience being the initiator. I stride back and forth across Paul's cubicle gesturing with my pencil and feeling like Lois Lane while Paul hunches over the machine muttering "Yeah, right," and feeling, I suspect, like Ernest Hemingway, even though what he is typing is essentially what I am telling him. Man with typewriter is a whole different image than woman with typewriter.

Herb Kiley calls that evening. "About the letter you and Paul drafted," he says. "I want to go over some changes I've made in it."

"Right!" I snap crisp and paramilitary into the receiver, but I'm a little shaken. I hadn't realized that Paul was going to run our offering directly over to Kiley—he hadn't said anything about giving it to Kiley. But then I hadn't really been assuming a chain of command either. The true revolutionary is motivated by feelings of love, I remind myself, and concentrate on subsuming my individuality to the democratic process.

"I've toned it down a bit," says Kiley. "And tightened it. Let me read you what I came up with." He does. It's very different.

"You've put a lot of time into this," I say after he's finished. I don't know what else to say. I liked my version better.

"Not really," he says. "I'm just used to the specifications. You figure you give them two paragraphs they'll print it, otherwise, they cut. Also, you can't come out sounding hostile. They jump all over hostile."

"I'm new at this," I tell him.

"I've been doing it for nearly twenty-five years," he rejoins. I can tell he's pleased at the opportunity to let me know. "Look, I've got to have it in a form we can all sign on Monday. Do you supposed you could drop by to pick it up tomorrow?"

"I've got an appointment," I say, thinking of Tom and *Hamlet*. "Maybe earlier though." It sounds intimate, just me and Kiley in his living room on a Sunday morning. And Mary Ellen, of course, who will give me coffee. The leadership cadre. "I don't have a typewriter," I say as an afterthought. "Paul typed it."

"Oh," says Kiley. "Oh, well, I suppose I should call Paul then."

"He types *very* well," I say, feeling snubbed, but I agree to get copies to the group members who have offices in Schwindemann, meaning the group members who are in modern languages and history.

I'm awakened on Sunday morning by the telephone, which I knock off the dresser as I lunge for it. "Hello," I gasp after a short scuffle.

"Ah, Professor Nyland?"

"Speaking."

"Ah, this is, ah, Professor Lippman."

"Tom!" I squeak, and burrow under the covers with the receiver.

"Ah, about our meeting to draft that report."

"Report?" I echo, slow as ever to catch on.

"That report we were going to meet on today to draft. Um, about that."

"We were going to rehearse the Closet Scene," I say.

"That one. Could we, ah, take a rain check?"

"You're backing out," I say into the sheet.

"Pardon?"

"Forget the Closet Scene," I say. "I don't want to be your damned mother."

"Fine, then we'll discuss it tomorrow," he says.

"Fuck yourself," I say, but it's safe, he's already hung up. Women don't say fuck yourself. If a man says it, it's grounds for a fight maybe but it doesn't really convey a specific image. If a woman says it, it betrays an unseemly interest in, well, fucking. An interest that I have, of course.

Louise Feitelson is leaning against the wall beside my office door when I show up on Monday morning, ten minutes into my office hour and clutching two cardboard containers full of coffee. From down the hall I can see she's wiping the back of her hand across her eyes. When she sees me she wails, "It isn't *fair!*" and I have to hustle her into my office and shut the door. She lowers herself into my student chair and swipes at her nose, smearing mucus across one cheek. I have no Kleenex, so I can only watch in fascination. "You know how much *time* I put in on that paper?" she demands.

"No," I say. "That's not the point," I add realizing she's about to tell me. "I have to judge the product on its own merits. I can't just pay you in grades for the hours you put in."

She takes a long shuddering breath and I find I'm breathing in with her, fearing the worst. But she only pulls off her glasses and wipes them on her skirt. "Look," I say, "a C-minus isn't the end of the world."

She puts the glasses back on and stares at me blearily. "I'm a B student," she says with finality.

It's important, above all, to be your self. In Louise's case that means a B student. "You ever want to be an A student?" I ask.

Old Nick here.

She takes off her glasses again. Her eyes look pink and naked. "You are what you are," she says. "You shouldn't try to be what you aren't." An absurd claim for someone ostensibly here to learn I think, but I recognize it only too well. This is Middle America speaking, a voice that carries considerable authority around here and sounds a lot like my mother. Despite myself I'm intimidated, as if in that statement Louise had dug out my entire past and tied it to me so that it bumped along behind, my sensible saddle shoes trailing the car on which I'd optimistically painted *Just Married*. Or, to put first things first, *Just Brilliant*. I became someone different. I had to; there was nothing else I could do; I was my mother's creation, summarily abandoned. But when I went home after that first year at Lawrence, grubby-nailed and blazoned with commendations from the Dean and the Honors Society, I was still expecting something, some grudging word of acknowledgment, and I hung around the kitchen while my mother fluttered back and forth shooting me little betrayed glances when she thought I was getting too comfortable. "We never wanted you to be a grind, dear," she hissed finally, the "we" presumably implicating Bob, taciturn in his E-Z-Boy recliner lounger in the next room. "We don't want you turning into one of those girls who think they're so smart. *You* know." I just stared at her but of course I did know: I had been my mother's overlooked daughter, a Future Librarian, groomed for emulative mediocrity. I spent that summer in my room, reading, and all subsequent summers somewhere else.

"What about change?" I ask Louise. Best to lead up to this gradually. "Some change is for the better, don't you think?" She sniffs and shrugs. "You could chance this *paper*," I suggest. "I mean revise it, make it more, ah, persuasive."

"It's what I believe," she says.

"Very *good*," I say. They're supposed to have beliefs. "Um, but you need to persuade your reader to believe it as well, and that means giving reasons—"

"Will I get a better grade?" she demands.

"Uh, if it's significantly improved," I say, feeling cornered. She stands up and reaches for the paper. "One thing you could change," I say before I can stop myself, "is those socks." She freezes in mid-reach. "It wouldn't affect your personality or anything," I say.

She straightens up and surveys me. "You have to wear socks," she says. "Otherwise you get germs in your shoes."

"Not those socks," I say and she stalks out the door, probably to report me to somebody.

After that I trudge through the halls distributing copies of Kiley's letter to the seven group members who have offices in Schwindemann. Mostly I just shove the letters under doors, but I do come face to face with the middle-aged man, Will, who occupies a comparatively sumptuous space within shouting distance of the History Department secretary, and with someone who was down on my list as *Linda Bertelson (sp?)* and who turns out to be the graduate student who helped Mary Ellen serve coffee. "Hey, this looks good," she says shyly after I've thrust the letter at her.

"I didn't write it," I say. "Kiley wrote it."

"I thought you and Paul Fisher were writing it," she says, providing me with a last name for Paul. I shrug, too tired to go into explanations. "Kiley kind of takes over, doesn't he?" she says, and I look at her in surprise. She smiles, and I smile back, feeling a little better.

The letter, signed by 22 group members, comes out in Thursday's edition of the student paper, the *Daily*. It's so hedged about with editorial disavowals that it's hard to find, despite the two-inch headline across the top of the page, *CRITICISM OF THE DRAFT FROM SOME STUDENTS, FACULTY*. But the trail of signatures, each with student or departmental identification appended, looks gratifyingly long. My own jumps out at me, *Eleanor Nyland, Lecturer, English Department*. At least they've spelled it right, I tell myself, but I'm not especially comforted by that fact.

"Well, people are paying attention to it," says Kiley when I finally get through to him. His phone has been busy for almost four hours: mostly crank calls, he reports cheerfully. "We'll be seeing some new faces at tomorrow's meeting," he continues. "This has generated a lot of interest."

"You don't think they're overreacting?" I ask. The *Daily* ran a special notice to the effect that its policy was to print all letters no matter how ill-informed, deviant, or reprehensible. I hadn't expected agreement exactly, but I wouldn't have used precisely those words.

"They're underreacting. The *Daily's* taking a risk printing our letter at all. They're students, you know, and the administration could just cut them out of the budget," says Kiley. "By the way, do you think you could bring along some cookies tomorrow night? I don't want to be caught short-handed if there's a big turnout." Impressed by his calm, I promise to bring cookies. It seems to be the least I can do.

On Friday the *Daily* runs two full pages of letters denouncing our group, bleeding hearts, comsymps, outside agitators, longhairs, Mario Savio, gooks, and the *Daily* for printing our letter in the first place. The *Daily* chimes in with an editorial decrying extremist elements in our midst. It's a remarkable show of unanimity. Attendance at Friday's meeting is down despite a sprinkling of the new faces Kiley had predicted, and I keep the cookies for myself. I'm not as sanguine about the new faces as he is, either. I'm not sure all of them are on our side. I sit with Ted and Tyrone and feel vaguely infiltrated while Kiley reports on the anonymous telephone calls he's been getting and how visible we've suddenly become. No one else seems particularly enthusiastic. Visible sounds like a good idea until it occurs to you that you could be a target. Even Paul and Charlie are subdued tonight. Only Kiley seems to have been prepared for the backlash we got in the *Daily*. I at least expected some balance, some support, some conversion even. I avoid looking at Paul. Our letter was longer and stronger and would have been even worse received.

On Monday, Louise turns in her revision, same thesis, no reasons, spelling somewhat improved. I change her grade to a B-minus, feeling like a hypocrite. I'm staring at her title page (*My Name!*) as Linda, the graduate student from the meeting and another, chunkier girl walk into my office. As I sweep Louise's paper into my top drawer, the one where I keep my pornographic manuscript and my more humiliating correspondence, they sidle over to the framed print of *Guernica* that Frank gave me last

Christmas. Frank gave me a lot of things like that toward the end of our marriage, as if he had given up on intimacy and was concentrating on raising my cultural tone: a boxed set of Proust, a facsimile issue of *Blast*, a recording of a baroque opera in which all the female parts were sung by boys. He took them all with him too, except for the *Guernica*, probably because it was the wrong shape to pack. I've never particularly liked it on my wall but it's something to look at. My students assume it's a comic strip.

"This is Lee," says Linda. "My office mate."

"Eleanor Nyland," I say, extending my hand across the desk and feeling very mature.

Lee shakes it gravely. "Good print," she mutters, and we all stare at it to avoid looking at each other. "My grandfather was in the Abraham Lincoln Brigade," she adds. "Not at the bombing of Guernica, but close, you know?"

I don't know, in fact. Now I blink, and the picture slides momentarily into focus: an agonized horse with some sharp thing jammed down its throat, a woman wailing with a dead baby in her arms. I must have seen them at some point, but around Frank they didn't figure. For Frank it was enough that this painting got a while room to itself in the Museum of Modern Art; it was art, aesthetic. I wonder suddenly if he ever knew what it was a picture of. But then Frank was perfectly capable of maintaining that the subject didn't matter, that such considerations simply misled. If he didn't convince, he could at least make you feel trivial. The picture slides back out of focus and becomes a composition in blacks and grays, austere, a tasteful thing to have in an office. "Was he?" I say politely.

Lee shrugs and turns away from the picture. "We were just going to lunch," says Linda, "and we thought maybe you'd like to join us. Just to the Pub. No big deal."

I'm touched that they've thought to include me. I could do with some huddling for warmth at this juncture. The Pub turns out to be jammed with students and we end up sitting at a long table with a number of raucous undergraduates, any one of whom could have signed one of the letters to the *Daily* denouncing us. Linda and Lee seem impervious to this realization, however, and make cheerful conversation about organizing strategies as we eat our hamburgers and French fries. They treat me with exaggerated deference, as if I were an emissary from the dominant culture, and early on I consider pointing out to them that technically we're all graduate students in this together, but I end up doing a lot of nodding and pursing of lips instead. I'm pleased by the deference, actually. Not even my students defer to me in the ordinary course of events. I have the sense of things unsaid, of questions they're not quite sure they can ask me, but on balance that's positive too. I don't have any answers.

Tyrone and Ted are leaning against the wall beside my door when I get back to my office. Both look unusually wary, and in my present mood they strike me as a little ridiculous, types of the handsome young subversive in the tradition of James Dean, Marlon Brando, and any number of English rock stars. They don't even speak to me until they're in my office and Tyrone has carefully closed the door. Then Ted slumps into my student chair and Tyrone leans over the back of it and stares at me so intensely that I feel my smile congealing into a grimace of idiotic condescension. I look quickly at Ted. His eyes are cast down, and his lashes tremble slightly over cheeks the color of eggshells.

"Guy set himself on fire today on the steps of the Pentagon," Tyrone says. "Pacifist. Quaker. Because of the war."

I'm still looking at Ted. Picked out by the light from my single window his features seem impossibly fine-drawn, but his face is colorless; even his lips are pale. It's just occurring to me that he might be in shock when he raises his eyes and gives me a little embarrassed shrug. I drop my own eyes, feeling envious that he can react this purely to tragedy.

"Is he dead?" I ask, and Tyrone nods soberly, but I catch the elation in his face, the ghoulish complement of my own. I know what he's thinking. This makes it real; this means opposition to the war is important; it's something someone is willing to die for. And even though I'm trying to concentrate on the horror of it, on scorched flesh and hair and Ted's stricken face, I have the exhilarating sense of doors blowing open all around me and the outside world rushing in. This matters, I think. We're not just isolated freaks meeting in Kiley's living room out of sheer perversity. I'm startled at how much of a relief it is to have grounds for taking myself seriously.

Kiley appears in my office the next morning in crisply pressed gray flannels and a sports jacket in a faint plaid that picks up perfectly the blue of his eyes, looking a cut above anything else that turns up for my office hour. My first thought after I've considered the impact he's likely to have on any colleague who might stroll by my door is that I hope Mary Ellen chooses his clothes. I'd hate to think he was capable of accessorizing himself so consciously. "So this is where you live," he says, examining in his turn the print of *Guernica*, and I smile and decide it would be gauche to explain that I actually live in a rental house near the IGA. "I don't often get to Schwindemann," he explains, drifting from the wall to a spot behind my desk disconcertingly near my right shoulder and peering through the window. He's more of a physical presence now that he's out of my line of sight, as if his compact body were radiating heat, and I find myself thinking he'd be fun to fool around with before I encounter the implicit corollary: more fun than Frank was, I'll bet. I could never imagine why anyone would want to fool around with Frank, but of course that was sour grapes. Lots of women wanted to, did. I wonder how many women have fooled around with Herb Kiley and how Mary Ellen feels about them, but at the thought of Mary Ellen I have to abandon my nascent awareness of Kiley as a physical presence. If you go in for fooling around you have to avoid noticing wives.

Kiley moves away from the window and back into my line of sight. "Not much of a view," he pronounces.

"I don't rate," I say, watching him prowl over to my student chair and inspect it. He looks up at me, uncomprehending. "I'm just a lecturer," I add by way of explanation.

His eyes crinkle. "You mean you think the fact that you're a lecturer has something to do with the fact you've got a view of the parking lot" he says, sinking into the chair.

I blink. "Of course."

"Oh, Eleanor," he sighs, and swings a neat black-socked ankle across his knee. "You sound just like Paul and Charlie."

"Oh," I say, wondering if I'm supposed to ask what he means. "Paul's office is even smaller than mine," I point out.

"I suppose you're going to read something into that," says Kiley. "Not everything's political, you know."

It occurs to me that Kiley's office is doubtless much larger and better situated than mine and that this fact would not occur to him in precisely the same way. That is, if I brought up the subject he'd either deny he had a better office or deny there was any significance in its being better. He'd certainly resist linking such de-tails of his physical surroundings to his status as an associate professor. That's something about status I've been noticing lately. If you've got it you tend to deny that it even exists. It's another one of those things you apparently see only from underneath.

"But speaking of political," he says: but seriously folks. "I came by because I think we've got to get some things together right away. You heard about Saturday's draft card burnings, I suppose?"

"Paul called about them," I say, trying to sound nonchalant, as if Paul and I were in continual contact.

"There's going to be a follow-up action Thanksgiving weekend. Big show of support. In front of the White House, no less."

"Terrific," I say. It sounds inadequate.

"Isn't it," he says, also sounding inadequate. Neither of us, I realize, can possibly go. The White House is too far away. Thanksgiving weekend is too short. No one on this campus would really consider missing a class for the Vietnam War. Maybe at Berkeley, or Columbia for that matter, they could be that committed but not here. Here it's possibly to take the outside world too seriously. "So I was thinking," he continues gamely, "that some of us here should get up a sort of support demonstration. Picket with the guys in front of the White House, even though we won't actually be in front of the White House, you know."

"Good idea," I say, trying for enthusiasm. "What shall we picket?"

He offers me a little rueful smile. "Well actually I was hoping you'd have some ideas. We could do the Pub again, of course, but since it's Thanksgiving weekend there won't be a lot of people on campus. There won't be a lot of people in *town* actually."

"I see what you mean," I say. "Maybe we should do it sometime when it isn't a holiday."

"But then it wouldn't be a support demonstration," he says.

"I see what you mean," I say again.

"So I'm thinking of calling a meeting Thursday afternoon," he says, rallying a little. "Not of everybody. Just people like Paul and Charlie and Will. And you, of course."

"Ah," I say.

"What Charlie would call the leadership cadre," he says, raising his eyebrows to show me he's only joking.

"Ah," I say, having no alternative noncommittal response. I like the idea of being in the leadership cadre but I know better than to act flattered. "Wait a minute," I say now. "Thursday afternoon? Oh hell I've got something on already. Just a committee meeting but I'm secretary. Could we make it another day?" Despite the fact that I'm finding the composition committee more and more irritating, I'm pleased that Kiley has had this opportunity to discover I'm necessary to other ongoing concerns. There's such a thing as being too available.

He only looks mildly regretful. "I'll get someone to fill you in on what happens," he says rising to his feet. "On what we decide, I mean. You'll be able to come to the demonstration, won't you?"

"I guess so," I say. I realize I sound pretty tepid, but this will be my first demonstration and I see it as the end of my political virginity. Picketing some token establishment while everyone is out of town strikes me as equivalent to being deflowered by a Tampax, something that also happened to me. My life is punctuated by anticlimactic ruptures.

On the same night that Paul calls to tell me the group will be picketing the Post Office, Tom calls to say that Patsy will be flying back to Minnesota to visit her parents over Thanksgiving and perhaps we'll run into each other. I'm so taken aback by this escalation of our relationship that I mutter something about rehearsing *Hamlet*. "Oh right," he says. "How did that go, anyway?" With more presence of mind than usual I say that I'll tell him if we run into each other over Thanksgiving.

At the next committee meeting Bill Brewster uses the phrase "political irresponsibility" twice in one sentence and I slide down in my chair and concentrate on the security of Tom's foot pressed against my own until I realize that he doesn't mean me. No one knows I have a deviant political stance, it turns out, or any political stance at all for that matter. It's only when Ralph begins making expectorant references to Youth that I see he is in effect identifying the caste to which we all presumptively belong. Don't trust anyone *under* thirty is about the size of it. Clearly they've all become at least dimly aware that there is some sort of activism on campus, but they haven't bothered to investigate its source and so as usual are blaming it entirely on students, with preference given to the students who can't spell. I pour coffee and take notes, radiant with duplicity. It's the first time I've ever thought of myself as subversive. The idea that I'm an infiltrator helps some when Ralph and Arnie inform me buoyantly at the conclusion of the meeting that I'll be expected to type up and mimeograph more of the committee's Thoughts on the subject. I manage to stay com-pliant by telling myself how insidious I'm being, but it takes some effort. I no longer contribute to the Thoughts pool myself. My own Thoughts, I've discovered, embarrass them, even when I hold to the party line. I'm not supposed to be on the thinking end of this operation, just the typing end.

I trot down to Jo's office after the meeting, stoolie reflex or perhaps only a blossoming addiction to sherry, and discover that Jo has actually noticed my name signed to the letter in the *Daily*. "Ralph wouldn't like that," she says, pouring me a liberal slug of sherry. "Luckily he never reads the *Daily*. None of them read the *Daily*. Student paper. Low."

"They think the Basic students are outside agitators," I tell her, gulping gratefully. "Due to be nipped in the bud. Or caught in the act." Bill Brewster had waxed especially metaphorical on the subject. "They're having me type up and mimeograph off a lot more stuff for them this week, their ideas on affirming traditional values, that sort of thing."

"You get me a copy, okay?" She raises her paper cup to me. "Well, here's to the revolution."

I wince. "We don't say things like that. We represent a whole spectrum of opinion, actually."

She arches her eyebrows at me. "*We* used to say things like that. You want to hear all the verses to 'Union Maid'?"

Once she's mentioned it I'm not surprised. I ask her if she wants to come to a group meeting, but she only snorts and refills my paper cup. "They don't have a place for people like me," she says without rancor. "You've heard that slogan, don't trust anybody over thirty. Well then." I think about saying that Kiley and Will are over thirty, but remember the dispute about old guys and decide against it. It occurs to me that most of the group probably regard me as over thirty.

Kiley comes by my office the next day to report on the decisions of the leadership cadre. "We were thinking about asking you and maybe Linda and Lee to take charge of the, ah, production end," he says.

"You mean type things up on mimeograph forms and run them off," I say. It's a foregone conclusion. "You thought of us because we're all in English, right?" I mean because we're all girls, but I don't expect him to get that.

"Well actually I did," Kiley says. "English has an automatic mimeograph machine, doesn't it?"

My initial reaction is horror at the idea of doing something that could get me in genuine trouble with the department, but it doesn't take me long to come around. On the one hand it's secretarial work all right, but on the other hand it will be my first genuine subversive activity. The mimeograph room is for departmental use only, locked and labeled to that effect, and even teaching assistants are only allowed to enter it under Dale's supervision. But as a faculty member, and moreover a faculty member acting as secretary to the composition committee, I can use the facilities at night, thus avoiding Dale and anyone else who might be watchdogging the equipment. Craftily I allow another pile of Thoughts On the Teaching of Composition to accumulate in my mail box before I arrange a tryst with Lee and Linda. As part of my newfound subversiveness I type these virtually unedited onto mimeograph forms, although in the case of Arnie's contribution this leads me to some fairly liberal interpretations of handwriting, as in the remarkable sentence ending of *profound significance, then, that conceptulax be ventory a wom wom wither.*

The posters feature a rather good line drawing of a G.I. clutching at this throat in the act of falling (*Do You Know What You're Being Asked To Die For?*), which Linda acknowledges as her work. We make five hundred copies, and then run off and collate the twelve single-spaced pages of the committee's Thoughts. "You know," says Linda, riffling through one of our collated copies, "It's taken me a long time to realize what *ass*holes professors are." Then she blushes and turns away from me so abruptly that I don't know how to say I'm not really a professor, just another graduate student.

Ted isn't coming to the demonstration. His parents told him that if he doesn't make it home for Thanksgiving he won't have money for next semester. He confessed this to Tyrone and me in the car after last week's meeting as if it were somehow his fault. "It's not like I couldn't defy them," he explained, and I had a momentary vision of supporting a disinherited Ted in my basement apartment. I wasn't sure I was ready for the responsibility. "But really, shouldn't I be taking this opportunity to reeducate them?" he insisted.

"You can work on reeducating them when you go home," said Tyrone, more nastily than the occasion demanded, I thought. "You're going to have enough trouble explaining to them why you're planning to live off campus and who your new roommate's going to be."

Ted winced. I was sitting next to him and felt his whole body contract. It occurred to me then that he hadn't been planning to tell his parents about his new roommate. To do him justice, I imagine that if his parents heard about Tyrone they'd not only withdraw his funds; they'd pack him off to a nice local Bible college, racial purity guaranteed in the charter. I could tell

Tyrone had caught on too. He didn't say anything, but he straightened up in the driver's seat and looked coldly out at the curving tree-lined street that serves as the arterial for Kiley's neighborhood. Watching his profile out of the corner of my eye I thought he looked like the kind of mask that might be magic or the kind of stone head people erect to worship. I felt enormously distant from him at the same time that I felt how lonely he must be here, and I wished I could think of something to say, but nothing seemed remotely appropriate.

I spend Thanksgiving Day alone in my house eating up the salami and withered carrots that are the only things left in the refrigerator and marking student papers treating the subject of What I'm Thankful For. Too many of my students are ostentatiously thankful for the privilege of living in this great country of ours, and it occurs to me in the middle of one of these that *they* undoubtedly read the *Daily* and know which side I'm on, even if my more literate superiors have better things to do. The vast majority of the writers, however, express gratitude for The Family: Mommy and Daddy at the foot and head of the table respectively. The ones without both Mommy and Daddy don't write about The Family, I presume. Maybe they're not thankful. I never wrote about my meager family, not even when it was reconstituted with the approved leadership. Especially not then. But then I never wrote about this great country of ours, either. Ungrateful, my mother would say.

She's written me off, more or less, hasn't called in months, hasn't communicated in any form since the card on my birthday, *Love, Mom and B.* with a check. For ten dollars. I suppose any-thing more would have been covert disloyalty to Bob, at least in her mind. Anything more in the way of contact, too: my mother has a strong sense of priorities. First she devoted her life to me and now she's devoting her life to Bob. I hope he's enjoying it more than I did.

I really hadn't expected him, not in any form, and when he showed up it took me a while to understand what a reversal was underway. For one thing, he didn't seem to be at all my mother's type. Actually, men weren't my mother's type since my father the rat; they were, my mother insinuated into my earliest memories, overrated as company although awfully good at ordering people around. Ordering her around, she meant: that's what she did at Fred Barclay and Sons, took orders, with little spastic flutters to veil her efficiency. My mother always wore blouses with small, round, lace-edged collars or shirtwaist dresses with embroidery on the bodice; little feminine touches she called these, and lectured me on the importance of maintaining gender identity in an office situation. What she was doing, though, was emphasizing that she wasn't a man. Even the deferential flutters were in part to maintain the distance: they couldn't very well take liberties if she refused to be *jolly* with them. Or perhaps that was only my reading of the situation. I may well have got it altogether wrong, my mother's teaching, her life's work up to that point. She concentrated all her energy on educating me, but I always had the feeling, even after I had become brilliant, that in things that mattered I was a slow learner.

Anyway, after sixteen years of believing I was conspiring with my mother against me, or against men in all their brutish aspects, I was suddenly presented with Bob, a *fait accompli*. What I mean is my mother didn't play straight with me. Take the way we met him, for instance; only recently has it occurred to me that my mother couldn't have run into him for the first time in the bowling alley. After all what were we doing in the bowling alley in the first place? We'd never been there before, and I'd always understood it was frequented by people in nylon shirts with their names embroidered across the back, and therefore out of the question. (Any number of places and activities were out of the question for similar reasons; I can only imagine what kind of scope my mother would have given to her penchant for ruling things out had we lived in a town where there was more to do.) When the girls in our neighborhood put on their tight jeans and went off together to heave those impossibly heavy balls into the gutters until a suitable group of boys appeared to show them how to do it right, my mother only sniffed and remarked that if you were a certain kind of person, then that was the sort of thing you did. But one Friday night, when I was just settling down to a re-reading of *Green Dolphin Street*, she said brightly that there was no sense in my just sit-ting around letting the blues get to me, and hustled me out to the car before I could come up with a story about what I was doing that would prove I wasn't letting the blues get to me. Reading was usually tantamount to succumbing to the blues, in my mother's view of things. Perhaps this was why she wanted me to become a librarian: that was I would be doing something active with books, shelving them or cross-referencing them or something.

Anyway, there we were all of a sudden, actually in the bowling alley in those shoes you rent that are like no other shoes, with the size written in huge numbers across the back of the hells: me in my straight skirt that was too long for fashion, my mother in one of her shirtwaist dresses with the embroidery. I couldn't take the long, bent-kneed steps you're supposed to use to the get the ball sliding in the right direction, and my mother kept getting the ball caught in her skirt so that she'd end up swinging herself around in a circle emitting little girlish shrieks. We should have been wearing pants, but at the time neither of us owned a pair. My mother has since acquired a whole wardrobe of them, along with, I believe, one of those nylon shirts with her name embroidered across the back, but at the time she was maintaining that a lady always wore skirts an edict that worked only in conjunction with the assumption that a lady never went bowling.

The worst part was that there was a party of high school boys a couple of lanes down. It was bad enough that I could only shove the ball directly into the gutter, but my mother kept throwing her ball up in the air so that it came down with a tremendous booming that seemed likely to shatter the floor of the alley, and after every booming she would giggle hysterically and squeal something about getting the hang of this. The high school boys, all of whom I knew, of course, although none of them had ever spoken to me, were so entranced by our performance that they stopped playing and just stood there watching us and shouting things like "Spaz!" and "Grace!" My mother pretended she didn't notice, but I suspected she was even playing to them a little. "I just can't make it *work*!" she cried pettishly after she had run with little mincing steps over the line you're supposed to stand behind, setting off a red light above our pins, and I wondered for a horrible moment if somebody like Dave Cavanaugh, who was co-captain of the basketball team, was going to come over and give her directions. But then all of a sudden there was Bob standing over her showing her what holes to put her fingers in, and then, in the kind of move I'd been watching in a haze of erotic jealousy since I entered adolescence, he was standing behind her with his arms around her explaining something about wrist movements while my mother—*my mother*—like any Shari or Darlene or Joni pre-tended she didn't know what was happening while at the same time she was leaning back into him. And giggling.

So I stopped looking until I heard Dave Cavanaugh should something about feeling her up, and then I turned around to watch Bob detach himself and walk casually over to the boys and tell them that if they didn't behave they'd have to leave. It turned out that not only did he bowl; he owned the bowling alley. Not remotely my mother's type. After we'd used up the rest of the game we'd paid for, he took us into the snack bar and bought us each a drink called a Brown Cow, which was made of root beer and chocolate syrup. I waited for some sign of polite revulsion from my mother as she drank it, but she said it was delicious really. It was, too.

It should have been clear sooner that what we had here was a major shifting of allegiances. I was just confused. For a long time I assumed that my mother thought Bob was basically contemptible—he was certainly contemptible by the standards on which I'd been raised—and then I assumed that while he seemed contemptible by those standards he was actually, in subtle much momentous ways that I hadn't caught on to yet, admirable by those standards. It didn't really hit me that the standards had changed until the two of them were already married. That was when I finally realized that my mother didn't need me anymore. It was a bit of a shock: I'd put up with a lot over the years on the theory that she needed me. Now it appeared that what she needed was Bob. All those years of manipulating me were just a category mistake on her part, and what she really wanted was to *be* manipulated. I was finishing my junior year of high school at that point and had just discovered that the university would accept me without a high school diploma.

"Well, you can do that, I suppose," said my mother when I told her. I waited for her to go on to say that she thought I should aim to be well-rounded instead but she didn't seem much interested. For years she'd been telling me to be well-rounded. Not too good at anything; they might resent you. "You might as well," she conceded suddenly, catching me off balance. "Heaven knows you've never fit in around here."

"I'm not *likely* to fit in, wearing saddle oxfords and crew socks," I said. I'd never dared bring up the subject before: I'd been sure she wouldn't be able to take it. Now she just looked blank. "If you don't like those things, why don't you buy something else?" she said.

In a way, it was necessary to my pride to become brilliant after that incident. If I was going to stick out, it was going to be for something I chose—that was one part of it; and then too, I was determined to get as lopsided as possible, not remotely well-rounded, never again. I was trying to get back, of course, but she had already turned to Bob, who was mildly disgusted with me but wouldn't put the energy into being actively irritated. I resolved further to go to graduate school in New York, where my father lived. I hadn't seen him since I was four and I didn't remember much about him, but I figured that would get a rise out of my mother. And she did sound alarmed when I called to tell her about it, but she got over it more quickly than I'd anticipated. On reflection I'd say she was more worried about my father's turning into a topic of general conversation than anything else: he was the rate who had left her, after all, and it might have occurred to Bob, who on his own has no imagination, to take this as a precedent. The upshot of it all was that I found myself in New York, where I delayed calling my father for almost two years, or until I figured I had something so important to tell him that I was warranted in bothering him. He turned out to live in Mount Vernon, not New York at all, and to have a wife and three children—he said "three children," too, not "three other children." When I told him I was going to marry Frank, he said he was sure congratulations were in order and where was I living, and for a moment there I thought he was going to come down, but as it turned out he just wanted to know where to send the check. For twenty dollars, *Best Wishes From Arthur and Shirley*. I'd somehow thought he might understand that in marrying Frank I was going over to the other side, but naturally he wouldn't have understood what the sides were. And in fact I'm not sure they even existed at that point; if they did, more people than I had gotten realigned. I'd also nurtured the vague hope that he would offer to give me away, but I suppose I'd already been given.

By my mother too: she barely took the trouble to disapprove of Frank, which she could have done on principle without even meeting him, as Frank not only cultivated a Brooklyn accent but habitually used both big and dirty words. In fact, I suspect she was relieved that I was getting married at all, never mind to whom. "He's very *bright*," I told her with poignant hostility, but she didn't come back with any of her old saws about how it's better not to be too bright, you know how *they* are. It was clear at that point that she had written me off. It doesn't seem to have been for anything I did.

I'm only about halfway through the papers at ten o'clock, when the telephone finally rings. The voice is so low and fuzzed that at first I think it's Tom doing another one of his sub rosa routines. "I'm alone," I say to encourage him.

"I know you are," says the voice, which is husky and somehow more excited than it ought to be.

"Who is this?" I try not to sounds anxious in case it's Tom after all.

There is a long silence in which I can hear a rhythmic pulsing: some effect of the connection, I'm just deciding, when there is a gasp and I hear, "I'm fucking you, Eleanor." I hang up. Then I take the receiver off the hook and sit on my bed trying to think what to do next. I'm not sure what will happen if I call the police. They might say soothing things. They might ask me to repeat what the caller said, and then of course they might get off on that, hearing me say, "I'm fucking you, Eleanor." I'm not sure what to do. What I want to do is call Tom, but it could have been Tom on the other end, even if it didn't sound like him. It could have been anybody.

In the end I ring the operator, who gives me a number to dial during business hours. "You could call the police," the operator suggests. "How many incidents have there been?"

"One," I say, feeling craven.

"Perhaps he won't call again," says the operator, I think about mentioning the letters but decide they don't apply. They're written, not oral communications, not her area. "It was probably just a prank of some sort," says the operator.

"Thank you," I say. "You've been very helpful." I want to keep her on the line, but I can't think of anything else to say. After I've hung up I take the receiver off the hook and lie down on the bed with it. I'm still not so much frightened as confused about how to react to this experience. I don't know what to call it, how to describe what's been done to me. Again, I want to talk to somebody. But of course I was talking to somebody. That was precisely the problem.

In the morning the telephone rings again while I'm standing in front of my full-length mirror considering the effect of my new bell-bottoms with my Columbia sweatshirt. Even granting that casual dress is appropriate for a poster-painting session, I'm not sure I'm ready to move into the Now Generation after having spent so much time establishing myself as a member of the skirt-and-nylons set. "This is Tom," says Tom. "I'm in Schwindemann. They've got the heat off for the whole weekend and I'm freezing my tail off." It's impossible to mistake the satisfaction in his voice.

He said "tail," I note: unbuttoned language for Tom. I cuddle the receiver against my cheek and sit down on the bed. "That's terrible," I exclaim. They like to be admired and pitied at the same time: I learned that from observing the techniques of the Sharis and Judis and Earlines in my high school.

"It's a rotten deal," he agrees. "Some of us like to work even if it is a holiday. I mean, the fact that it's a holiday doesn't mean you just turn off your *mind*."

"I'm sure it does to some people," I feed him.

"Maybe it does" he concedes, "But I'm not one of those people."

"I know you're not," I say, marveling again at his ability

to absorb flattery. It's a real gift, one I have to envy because it derives from unshakeable self-confidence. He doesn't think it's flattery. He thinks it's true.

"Listen," he says, dropping his voice. I like back on the bed slowly so he won't hear it creak. "I was wondering if you'd come up and have lunch with me. On campus, you know?"

I don't have to be on time for the poster session, I reason, instantly reshuffling my priorities. "Sure," I say as casually as I can manage and begin revising my wardrobe plans. I end up wearing the bell-bottoms but with the powder-blue twin set my mother gave me for graduation. Mixed messages. Ladylike but incipiently swinging. Demure but knows where it's at. An intriguing mixture of the traditional and the contemporary. By the time I get to his office Tom is huddled inside his topcoat and seems inclined to blame me for the temperature, which is in the fifties, but he keeps me there for twenty minutes while he reads me a continuation of his Thought on the issue of student insubordination in the Basic program. Second Thoughts, he calls them. "The more I thought about it the more it just kind of dawned on me that these kids come into the classroom and what they see are women," he tells me. "I mean first it's their mothers and then it's their teachers, those are all women, and even in high school mostly they get women, especially in English."

"I'm a woman," I say.

"Yeah, and you teach Basic too," he says, accepting my remark as confirmation of his point. "Well, you begin to see how these guys must feel."

"A lot of the Basic students are girls," I say. "About half, actually."

"I didn't *mean* the girls," he says, and I don't pursue it.

We end up eating stale cellophane-wrapped sandwiches and cups of soup out of the vending machines in the basement of the Pub and rubbing calves under the formica table. Rubbing calves is an overstatement as we're both wearing pants, but there's definitely contact. I checked once just to make sure I wasn't' rubbing up against the pedestal of the table. While we rub calves we conduct a solemn conversation about wen the committee is likely to conclude its deliberations, which is pure hypocrisy on my part as I'm convinced that the committee is committed to perpetuating deliberations into eternity. After lunch Tom offers to drive me home, but I tell him I'm heading somewhere else. He doesn't seem particularly interested or particularly disappointed either. As I walk across campus toward Kiley's house I wonder what might have come of that and whether I'll ever get another chance.

Mary Ellen directs me to the basement, and I come down the stairs to see the think, intense young man named Kenny standing directly below me brandishing a paint brush. Herb Kiley is standing beside him, hands on hips, look uncharacteristically mussed and unusually attractive. Kiley is wearing a pair of very faded jeans and a pale blue tee-shirt, both speckled with red paint from the brush Kenny is waving. Kenny is also wearing jeans and a blue tee-shirt but both are newer and thus darker and less impressive, even though he has managed to smear a blob of red paint across his stomach like a wound. My immediate impression from the top of the basement stairs is that Youth Versus Age isn't the real issue, that Kenny is simply incensed at being outclassed. But as I watch I'm inclined to believe Kenny is unaware that he suffers by comparison. His long, bony face is ardent with indignation as he flings out his catchphrases, "our bodies on the line," "*old* guys," and one that's new to me, "liberal bullshit!" By dint of sheer volume he is prevailing. People seem to be waiting for him to run his course. Kiley hasn't said anything but he's simmering with frustration, running his fingers through his wiry hair until it stands straight up in little clumps all over his head giving him the appearance of an agitated terrier. He looks more appealing without his usual composure. I want to smooth him. Looking over the rest of the group I see Tyrone sprawled across some newspapers watching Kenny intently. He doesn't look contemptuous, more speculative.

In the end it's Linda who interrupts the tirade. "Kenny," she calls from the far corner where she's been sitting cross-legged working on a banner proclaiming US OUT OF VIETNAM, "I don't think we need to break up the group to settle this."

He freezes in mid-gesticulation and for a moment I'm

afraid he's going to attack her with the paintbrush. But he only says in a shaky voice," Ken. Not Ken*ny*. Can't you get that straight?"

"Ken," says Linda. "Sorry."

"You always do that," he says.

Kiley has found his opening. "I'd like to outline my objections to Kenny's, ah, Ken's choice of slogan if I may," he says. "then other people can answer them if they choose. And then we'll take a vote. Is that all right?"

A murmur, not entirely approving. I know what's bugging Kenny although I don't have much sympathy for him. Kiley is too smooth. He simply controls by habit. He's so matter-of-fact in his manipulation that sometimes you want to take over just to show him it's possible to do things differently. "What's the slogan?" I mutter to Linda, who is bent so far over her banner that the ends of her blonde hair are trailing in the paint.

She sits up and smiles at me. "Hell no, we won't go," she says. "I don't have anything against it myself, although I guess I'd feel a little silly yelling it."

I think about it. "Me too," I say. "They never bothered to invite me."

"But I suppose we could say that we wouldn't go even if they did," she says.

"I suppose so," I say. "Maybe we could yell Hell no, we wouldn't go even if you tried to make us. Although it loses some of its punch."

"It's too belligerent," Kiley is saying. "We're not actually confronting the Pentagon or a draft board and so defiance would serve no useful purpose and could only offend. Furthermore, the language will undoubtedly put of a number of people who might otherwise be inclined to listen to us."

"What language?" It's a female voice. I can't place it immediately.

"Very funny," says Kiley. "When in doubt I think it's wise to avoid profanity. You don't want to alienate potential allies, do you?"

"Hell no," says the voice, and suddenly all over the room people are laughing.

"Yeah, well you've got the principle. There's a more important reason, though," says Kiley.

"I think I've got that one figured out." The voice is relaxed, even amused, but it provokes absolute silence. I don't have to look around for the speaker. It's impossible to mistake Tyrone. "You're worried about who it's associated with, right?"

Kiley doesn't miss a beat. "As it happens, I am. It's that same question of allying yourself with extremist elements that we've disagreed on before. And I still think you've got to avoid extremism if you're going to build a mass movement."

I want to ask Linda who he's talking about, but it's too qui-et. I can see I'm going to have to spend more time in the National Affairs section of *Newsweek*. Tyrone is sitting up now, long legs crossed, back perfectly straight. Something is about to happen, I recognize, but I don't know what's at stake in this argument.

"Well now," he says, "I think we've got a case in point here of why I get so uncomfortable when people start talking about extremist elements. You see, I think there's a semantic difficulty here. You say extremist. I'd be more inclined to say black."

There is a little hissing sounds in the room, as if any number of people were drawing in their breath. But Kiley says easily, "Stokeley Carmichael is an extremist. I've been a member of SNCC for years, but I think they've gone right over the edge with this Black Power business. I can't condone it, and it's done nothing but hurt the Civil Rights movement."

Tyrone nods as if confirming a point. "White Power good enough for you, is it?"

"Right *on!*" cries Kenny, ecstatic with righteousness. "We've had enough of this racist hypocrisy." He looks around the room a little wildly.

People are stirring uneasily now. "We're talking about a slogan," Lee point out. "Can't we just decide whether or not we're going to use it without, you know, polarizing everything?"

"I think we should get this out into the open," shouts Kenny, and looks at Tyrone hopefully, but Tyrone is staring down at the newspaper on which he's sitting. "I mean, you can't just pretend we're all the same politically."

Or racially, I supply silently. Or rather, we're all the same racially except for Tyrone. Yet I don't fell as if I have all that much in common with either Kenny or Kiley. Looking at Tyrone sitting there, erect and aloof, I'm conscious again of the gap be-tween his experience and theirs. I know something about that gap. They don't even know it's there.

We vote not to use the slogan, though, and neither Kenny nor Tyrone shows up for the demonstration, which proves to be a lackluster event. There are never more than seven of us at any one time trudging around and around on the sidewalk in front of the Post Office, and as the Post Office and all the stores down-town are closed there are even fewer onlookers. No one shows up to interview us, so we're not given the chance to explain that we're acting in support of a much larger demonstration in Washington. One overweight man looks as if he's going to harass us, but he only stares hard at Linda's legs for a while and then walks away. We break up early at Kiley's suggestion.

At the composition committee meeting the following week Ralph suddenly announces that we're due to turn in an interim report to Norford right after Christmas break. "To let him know we're not just pissing around," he explains, twitching his eyebrows at me, and I smile in appreciation of how impossible it is that we could be just pissing around although in fact I'd rather assumed we were. I've noticed that language is getting looser on the committee these days and that there is less tendency to apologize to me for it. This may mean that I'm slowly metamor-phosing into one of the boys, although I doubt I'll get much beyond provisional boyhood since they need to leave me enough secondary sex characteristics to function as coffee-server, mi-nute-taker, and typist.

"What kind of report?" asks Tom, alert and bright-eyed at Ralph's right hand. Tom and I now have regular places at the end of the conference table flanking Ralph, as if we were his two good children. The arrangement allows us to play cautious footsie un-der the table and Ralph's generally benevolent gaze, although occasionally I've discovered I've mistaken my object and for half an hour or so have been playing footsie with Ralph. I don't suppose that's altogether bad for my career. He certainly hasn't complained. Occasionally I've wondered whether Tom hasn't also been playing footsie with Ralph, mistakenly or otherwise, but I haven't had the nerve to look.

"Oh, no big production." Ralph flaps a hand airily, "Not one of your fifty-page jobs." Tom emits a knowledgeable chuckle. "Say ten, fifteen pages. Just the meat."

"Don't you think Ralph," says Arnie in a voice full of ingenuous complicity, "we should maybe pick a team to draft this report on behalf of the whole committee?" I write *Team to draft* on my legal pad and sit back to wait until I'm tapped. Whenever we have to come up with a written product I'm on the team. I suppose you could call it being a team player, although I'm not exactly out in the field with the rest of them. I have a necessary support function. It's like being water boy.

This time seniority intervenes as well. No one really wants to take on a report when term papers and exams are coming up, so the job goes to the junior people, Tom and me. Tom is enthusiastic. "It's real challenge for us," he explains as we walk back to my office. "It show they feel we're up to the responsibility, which is pretty awesome when you get to thinking about it."

"Maybe we should confer about it now," I suggest, managing to jostle his shoulder with my own as I fumble with my key.

We end up at the Hyacinth Room again. He buys two rounds of drinks all by himself when I tell him I'm out of money, and drives me home in the chilly darkens while I huddle beside him on the front seat shivering ostentatiously and hoping he'll take the hint to put his arm around me. He doesn't, but after he has pulled up to the curb in front of my house he mutters, "I feel we've achieved a lot tonight, don't you?" and squeezes my knee. I go inside punchy with arousal. It's only much later that I realize we've done nothing yet that involves our faces. We've rubbed feet and calves and now we've escalated to knee-squeezing, but for all the sexual signals flying back and forth none of this activity is quite acknowledged.

The next two weeks are hectic and anticlimactic. Ted, absorbed in his Dostoevsky paper, has to be rescued from a class discussion in which it becomes clear that not only does he speak for the Underground Man but he has difficulty distinguishing the Underground Man's experiences from his own. This leads to an unnerving exchange in which one of the more adamantly ordinary students hints darkly that certain kinds of weirdos get A's in this course, and I find myself involved in an argument over whether it isn't more important to be well-rounded. Louise Feitelson takes up two consecutive office hours arguing with me about being yourself and getting a higher grade than B-minus for it. Neither of us mentions the fact but she has stopped wearing the nylon ankles socks. Instead she wears the little flesh-colored elastic foot-coverings that are supposed to be invisible but in her case slop out over the top of her orthopedic oxfords. At the next committee meeting Tom and I present a list of tentative points for the interim report and discover that no one believes these are the things we've been discussing. In the ensuing argument Arnie volunteers to give us a hand since we're a little out of our depth and Tom, eyes shining, thanks him. Afterwards, instead of going to the Hyacinth Room we go to Arnie's office where Arnie talks, Tom makes ardently supportive noises, and I, predictably, type. At the end of the session Arnie remarks that Francie will be holding dinner and Tom symmetrically counters that Patsy will be holding dinner too. Then they both drive off in their separate cars, leaving me to walk home. During the next meeting Tom plays footsie with me as usual, but I don't let him get above the ankle.

My Basic students are finally reading *Hamlet*, or are assigned to read Hamlet. It's not clear that they know it's a play or even in English. "Picture Hamlet standing here at the front of the stage all alone" I urge them. "You see, he says 'Now I am alone'?" They gaze at me with open hostility. "For the purpose of the drama he's talking to himself," I flounder on. "We call it a soliloquy." I put it on the board but nobody writes it down. They're not about to deal with new information this late in the semester. "Look, think of me just for a minute as Hamlet," I say. "I mean,

these words here in your books, they're supposed to be somebody talking. Hamlet talking. Like this." I close my eyes and
remember Sarah Bernhardt. "Now I am alone," I begin.

O, what a rogue and peasant slave am I!
Is it not monstrous that this player here,
But in a fiction, in a dream of passion –

"That's a definition," I say. I hadn't notice that before.
"That's what a fiction is, a dream of passion." They're shrugging
into their coats; the bell I due to ring any second. "I mean, *Hamlet*
itself is a dream of passion by that definition. Passion in the broad
sense of the word, I suppose," I say, and add, "That's rather good,
fiction as a dream of passion." But now I'm sounding like Polo-
nius, and anyway the bell is ringing and I'm talking to myself.
Soliloquy. I'm thinking, for the first time in a while, about my Lenoreans.

Tom shows up in my office shortly after my last World
Masterpieces class, where only a third of the students were in attendance to turn in their term papers, Ted among them. "It's
verbose," Ted muttered as he pressed a great wad of typed pages
into my hands, and then, turning away in embarrassment, "We'll
be back to start moving in about a week before classes start. By
that time I expect you'll have read it." I'm sneaking looks at the
paper now. It's long, not the sort of thing I'm used to grading.

"I'm not going to be around much after classes end," says
Tom. "I mean, I'm not giving finals or anything."

I am. The Basic program requires them. "Well, maybe I
should wish you a merry Christmas," I say, and blink. Luckily he
isn't looking at me; he's lounging in my doorway where he can
watch the hall, presumably for members of the Boys' Club. "And
a happy New Year," I say, feeling spiteful.

He takes a last look at the hall and focuses on me. "You're
going out of town?"

"I don't know yet," I say. I do know, of course. Where
would I go?

"I won't see you at the Warners' Christmas party?"

"I haven't been *invited* to the Warners' Christmas party,"
I say, wishing suddenly that he would just leave.

He raises both eyebrows at me. "Oh, it's not like that. Everybody's invited, the whole department. The invitations aren't out yet, but everybody knows about it. It's a regular thing, the Warners do it every year."

Why don't I know about it then? Where was I last year? Home, undoubtedly, on one of those nights when Frank just wasn't around. All I can think of to say is "Oh." I feel exposed.

He's leaning on my student chair and examining the fingernails of one hand. They're nice hands. He's got a nice body generally. It seems a pity.

"I'd kind of hoped I'd see you there," he says, buffing the fingernails against the sleeve of his suit jacket.

I swallow and fumble in my top desk drawer to give myself something to do. The first thing I pull out is a page of manuscript that begins, *Disrobe! She repeated, a faint moué of frustration downturning her perfect lips.* I put the page back in the drawer and close the drawer.

"If I'm in town I'll try to go to the Warners' party," I say.

He straightens up and looks directly into my eyes. If I weren't sitting down I'd probably fall over. "I hope you do," he says. I note that he's managed to time his exit so that he runs into Arnie right outside my door, but I'm not bitter about it. I'm hyperventilating, in fact, so I work on exhaling while I listen to them exchanging the kind of pleasantries that suggest they're punching each other in the upper arm. After a few minutes Arnie bounds in waving a number of typewritten pages at me.

"Well, Eleanor, here it is," he announces. "The final draft."

The episode with Tom has slowed me down. "You've made me a copy?" I ask stupidly.

He looks blank for a moment and then grins. "Oh Eleanor," he crows. "You really need this vacation, I can tell. No, I've made all the final changes in our last draft."

"I thought that *was* the last draft," I say.

"Well, I'd thought it was too, but then I decided to just, you know, look it over again and see if it need a little more, ah, polish. You know, stylistic changes. This is for Norford, after all." He hoists himself up on the corner of my desk and sits there for a moment swinging his legs and looking out my door. Then he twists around so he can bring his face up close to mine. "Frankly, Eleanor, you want to be sure you make the best possible impression on Norford."

"Yes," I say, thoroughly cowed.

"I haven't made all that many changes," he assures me, but even at this distance I can see the snarled threads of writing looping into the margins of the report I painstakingly typed last week. "All you have to do is make it all, you know, nice looking." It's probably to Arnie's credit that he can't ever admit he's telling me to type. "We probably ought to see that he gets it sometime today," he adds. I nod, although for normal purposes today is already over. I'll start now and put it in Norford's mail box whenever I finish. It's not as if I've got plans for the evening.

At the door he turns around again. "Say, Eleanor, you going to the Warners' Christmas party?"

"I don't know," I say. "If I'm in town I will."

"Hope you do," he says. "Ralph was asking too. Might be fun to get together when we can all, you know, unbend."

It might, I think after he's gone. Faculty parties ought to be a little more pleasant now that I'm on the committee and know a few more people. Now that I'm wanted, I mean, but it's hard to even think in those terms. It's hard to believe I'm wanted, even though generally speaking I'm only wanted for functional reasons. At least I have a place. It's a lot better than last year.

A hundred watts is too many, by about sixty watts, but I'm committed: after unscrewing the forty-watt bulb I dropped it into the wastebasket, where it exploded with a sonorous pop. Now the mirror is spectacularly lit and all the tiles and fixtures glitter like celebrity teeth, so that I have no recourse but to begin what *Vogue* has termed the uninhibited appraisal of my own features, "uninhibited" being the ambiguous term, the one that misled, since it made narcissism sound enjoyable if fundamentally still bad for you ("Don't be so self-conscious," my mother would snap, "everybody's looking at you"). I had actually managed to forget during the short, exhilarating period when I was getting up on faces what it was that had inhibited me. Now, leaning across the washbasin to confront my reflection ("confront" is another of *Vogue*'s operative terms), I remember—worse, see it all, my eyes sunk like chips of granite in a relief map of blotchy continents, my other features lost in the expanse of gravelly complexion, the vast reaches of uncharted Nyland, my personal topography. I am not pretty. The fact had escaped my attention recently, to the point where I'd planned to revel in the cakes and pencils and wands and brushes and pots of variously colored stuff that I carried home from the drugstore yesterday, but now, defied by the evidence, I am beginning to consider these things as necessary tools, means of plastering over the worst of the damage, and narcissism as less an indulgence than just another form of duty. It's a hell of a start to the evening in which I'd intended to regain my sexual identity.

With faces, as with houses, you begin with the foundation. Mine cost six dollars because *Vogue* cautioned against skimping on the essentials. In *Glamour* and *Mademoiselle* the models seem to favor less expensive and probably less drastic cosmetics, but I'm pinning my hopes on *Vogue* these days now that I'm past what *Vogue* chastely calls my first bloom, which must have come and gone without my noticing it, or anyone else's noticing it either. Frank maybe. Or he noticed something although he didn't want it showing, kept me scrubbed and natural, his word, and said he liked me quietly beautiful. Once he said secretly beautiful. I bought that, too, even though he never seemed to mind paint on other women, or perhaps he didn't know it was paint. I even managed to derive a perverse sort of satisfaction from being secretly beautiful, fading into the background with a sense of willed eclipse while others flamed and led him off in triumph. "I like to think of you as my own personal discovery," he confided in bed after one of these incidents, and I was still gulled enough to derive some comfort from the thought that my appeal was strictly private. I didn't realize until he left that my beauty was such a secret only I believed it existed.

I find I'm shaking the bottle of foundation while considering my options. The light is deceptive, obviously. Nancy Warner won't have her living room lit up like a movie set; there will be places to blush unseen, although blushing unseen seems to run counter to my motives in going to this party where I'd planned to *be* seen, damn it, maybe for the first time. Now I'm going to have to work on fading back into the periphery. All because of the testimony of this mirror, a powerful corrective to the image of myself I've been developing on the basis of the committee's chivalric banter, Tom's ambiguous attentions, the antiwar group's comraderie, Ted and Tyrone's diffident regard, the escalating admiration of my admirer, and the glances out of the corner of my eye as I sweep past the mirrors of the ladies' rooms in my life. Out of the corner of my eye I'm flushed and glinting, all impressionistically daubed and soft-edged, one line of cheek, of flying hair, and then into the first toilet stall because as usual I'm drinking too much coffee. But clearly I haven't been taking serious stock of myself in those stray glimpses. Clearly I'm not facing up to my face, so to speak, viewing it as a challenge to my decorative talents. I've washed and spackled and sanded and rolled enough walls in my time to understand the principle. What

I have here at six dollars for two ounces is primer, the base coat, preparation of the surface for the work still to come. I'm starting from scratch, which suggests that up to this moment I've *been* scratch, raw material, which of course would explain a lot.

Two hours later I decide this will have to do. The first time around, everything showed. Even the foundation streaked like unmixed paint and I had to resist the urge to splash gouts of Bella Contessa Bisque across the twinkling mirror, tiles, and fixtures of my bathroom: six dollars and what I had was brush marks. Every line and shadow that I laid down following the paint-by-number instructions in the magazines in the magazines simply sat there on the surface like the lineaments of a doll's face superimposed on my own to the point where I felt trapped inside, unable to work this alien set of features. I had to totter into the bedroom, sit on the bed and chant a trembling litany of "fuck it fuck it fuck it" before I could summon up the courage to try again. The second time I was sparing and left no edges. Better, I decide now, still unused to seeing my eyes eerily winged with smudgy color but reassuring myself that in shadow they'll look different, I'll look different. The black jersey dress is laid out on the bed-spread. Frank liked me in black, not because it made me look sophisticated but because it's the wife's color, right for blending in with the shadows at the edge of the frame. Tonight, however, I'm wearing it to be sophisticated, wives be damned. I even have a pair of rhinestone earrings and a sequined evening bag, both from Woolworth's, the sequins of the bag already flaking off like fish-scales. I have new spike-heeled pumps that pinch and will probably have run both my smoke-tone stockings by the end of the evening. Underneath, a black lace garter belt. Under that, my pink cotton day-of-the-week panties embroidered, correctly for once, *Saturday*. Innocence and experience, but of course that isn't why. I'd planned on buying black lace panties along with the gar-ter belt but found that somehow I couldn't carry them both up to the counter at Penney's. You can only go so far.

When I come downstairs finally I feel sneaky as if I were going somewhere I shouldn't, as if I were about to behave in a manner my mother would have dismissed succinctly as fast. When I reach the street I look back at the house. It looks small and dark and dilapidated. It lies behind me like a shed skin.

The air is clear and biting and redolent of frost. The wind picks up my hair until I draw my collar around my face, shoving my hands in my pockets and looking down at my new high heels clicking along the concrete. Cars pass, their headlights picking me out of the winter darkness. I hug the inner edge of the sidewalk trying to stay in shadow, pretending—the idea taking shape as my body slouches into character—that I'm a refugee drifting unobserved over a forbidden border, very casual as if I had every right to be here but avoiding close scrutiny. Spike heels tapping against the pavement as if nothing at all were the matter. Hunched shoulders, veiled eyes, bright mouth. With Frank sometimes I was a famous spy, passing as the wife of this amusing little man until we got to Constantinople. After that it's arrivederci, darling. It's been fun.

I let myself think of Tom now, not someone I can take seriously of course. I see myself telling him this, tapping him lightly on the chest with my folded fan. *No one I can take seriously darling, you do understand, really, deep down inside you do.* I have a faint Slavic accent. Tom, in tails, trails after me like a puppy. *For flirtation, yes,* I tell him, dark-rimmed eyes flashing suddenly. *But nothing serious. You must not ask for more.* I can't imagine dialogue for him.

He'll be there of course. Even if he hadn't said so I'd have known I could expect to see him. Tom can be counted on to show up wherever the Boys' Club congregates, fetching drinks, laughing convulsively at jokes, asking for professional advice. I won't seek him out. It will be enough for him to see me, high-heeled and taut-calved, tantalizingly slender because black after all is a slimming color, seemingly absorbed in conversation but faintly aloof, certainly self-contained, *a bit of an enigma that Eleanor, wouldn't you say?* From a cultured voice emerging above the mingled crowd noises—

Across the street a car has pulled over to the curb. Another car passes and then a woman's voice says distinctly, "It *is*, it's what's her name, you know the one who was married—" before another voice interrupts. I keep walking, straightened up now, my spy persona momentarily in abeyance. They seem to be disputing something inside the car.

I'm all the way to the next street light by the time they resolve whatever it is, and the car has to pull forward before the driver can shout, "Hey, Eleanor, want a ride to the party?" and ten, "Move over, you two," directed at the back seat. I obediently cross the street as the back door swings open. It takes me several seconds to pull my skirt back over my knees and close the door again. Then I realize I'm sitting next to Patsy Lippman.

"Hi Eleanor," says Patsy in her normal speaking voice, which is sort of a drone. "Gee that's a cute purse you've got there."

"Thank you," I say, trying to adjust my eyes to the darkness so I can offer a return compliment. "I got it at Woolworth's," I add, mainly to fill in the space, but then I remember you're not supposed to get things at Woolworth's. Tacky, my mother would say, for once echoing received opinion in my high school.

"Lots of nice *things* at Woolworth's," says Patsy gamely. "I mean, I get buttons there sometimes."

"That's a cute dress you have on," I offer now, having ascertained that she is at least wearing something underneath her coat.

"Why thank you," says Patsy. "I made it myself."

"Really," I say.

"I really did," says Patsy. "It was easy. I mean, it was Simplicity, that's the pattern, you know?

"Really," I say again.

"Really easy," she says. "Lots of nice things in that pattern book. Even doll clothes."

"*Doll* clothes!" I say, to keep my end up.

"I have all my dolls from when I was just a little girl, you know?" I nod, too vigorously. "I always did like to dress them up, like for parties?"

"You're kind of a doll your*self*, Patsy," Bill Brewster contributes, and Patsy giggles.

We have to park well down the street from the Warners' house, which is outlined in blinking Christmas lights. Patsy and Tom lead the way toward it arm in arm, but as we climb the steps to the porch Patsy reaches back and slips her mittened hand through the crook of my elbow so that we're suddenly a linked threesome on the model of the protagonists of *The Wizard of Oz.* "I have to pee," she murmurs confidentially in my ear. "Do you have to pee?"

I think about it. "A little." If I think about it I generally do.

"The nice bathroom's upstairs," she murmurs. "The other gets *used* a lot, know what I mean?"

I nod sagely although I'm not sure.

"What are you girls whispering about?" calls Tom from the other side of Patsy, the first words he's spoken since I got in the car. Patsy giggles. I don't answer.

Pete Warner collects our coats at the door and Patsy links her arm through mine again. I'm beginning to wonder if there is some significance to this buddiness, if she has some plan in luring me away upstairs with her, but on balance it seems more likely that Patsy is the sort of person who spontaneously takes to you. It's flattering in a way, but in the overall scheme of things this is an ill-omened attraction. I can't imagine vamping Tom with Patsy clamped to my side. In fact, around Patsy I can't imagine vamping Tom at all. He doesn't seem at all the kind of person I'd want to vamp. Not my style. My style—here the vision begins to reassert itself—is yearning but courtly, hand-kissing, bending from the waist, pleading but in a sinuous and white-tied way. I, on the other hand, am just a bit removed, not quite of this world or a least of this party.

"Eleanor and I are going to powder our noses," Patsy is telling Pete Warner. "*You* know," she says to Tom, "powder our noses?"

"Right," says Tom.

The bathroom door is locked so we lean against the wall across from it, Patsy letting go of me in the process. "I just love the Warners' house, don't you?" she asks rhetorically.

"Yes," I say.

"I just love parties," she essays after a minute. "I always have. I don't know what it is with me."

Popularity, I supply. "You look very nice," I say. She does:

she looks like a Kimi Kelly ten years down the road, still material for beauty pageants and the more wholesome variety of wet dream. I picture her in the company of my elegant, pleading stranger, who kisses her hand passionately. She giggles. He is charmed. It could be Tom after all, I realize. The secret is that he'll always be her admirer, not mine. My admirer is a totally unknown quantity.

"Thank you," says Patsy, and I see now that I've put her in a socially ticklish situation. She doesn't have much experience talking with people like me and she can't in all honesty say that I look very nice too; we're not in the same league. "Those are *unusual* earrings," she blurts out finally, and I feel rather sorry to have forced her into euphemisms.

"Aren't they," I concur, resolved not to tell her that they too came from Woolworth's and at that point the door opens and Jo Michaelson comes out.

Patsy squeezes my shoulder. "Me first?" she cries. "I *really* have to go."

I nod and she whisks in and shuts the door. Jo Michaelson looks after her as if she were some species of bug. "Friend of yours?" she inquires, and I'm reminded of Tom's reaction to my conversation with the janitor.

"That's Tom Lippman's wife," I say.

"About what you' expect," she says. "God, I hate these things, don't you?"

I shrug, listening for the first time to the noises from below, the well-bred tinkling of a jazz piano on the record player signaling that this is a wine and cheese sort of evening rather than a bourbon and potato chip sort of evening. Somebody laughs shrilly and Jo's nostrils flare.

"I figure I have to put in an appearance," she says, "but God, it's like martyrdom standing around making conversation with all the people I try to avoid the rest of the year. Why are you wearing so much black?"

"Mourning," I say as Patsy emerges from the bathroom. She and Jo eye each other warily. "Do you two know each other?" I chirp and slip into the bathroom myself, leaving them faced off.

After locking the door I sit down on the lid of the toilet. I'm feeling too tender to face people yet and wishing that I could have walked here all by myself. I hug my arms and suck in my cheeks and rock to some tune threading up from the party below. Elegance is the word to concentrate on, I tell myself. It gives me backbone. After a while I stand up and take a look at my face in the mirror. It looks more ravaged than when I set out, although maybe it's just the light here. My eyes, with their darkened rims and the crescents of smeared turquoise and purple swooping out from the lids, seem impossibly deep-set. I get out the pale pink lipstick I bought for the occasion and put on some more of it. The principle, if I follow it, is to get your lips to recede into the rest of your face so that your eyes become commensurately larger and more waif-like. My lips are so pale by now that I look, in some unfathomable wan way, tanned.

When I open the door Bill Brewster is leaning against the wall waiting his turn. I flash him the smile I've been practicing all week, mysterious, conspiratorial. My lips feel stiff. "Hooeee," he says, and then, "Is this the face that launched a thousand ships?" I tell him he has me confused with somebody else and start downstairs feeling better. The thing to do, I tell myself as I descend, is to have an immediate goal upon entering so I'm not just standing around feeling unwanted. A party, after all, is an aggregate of little communities, and when you go in you're not a member of any of them. My goal, it occurs to me, is a drink, a strong one. Not wine: that takes too long. With something dark and undiluted coursing through my veins I'll have the presence of mind to hold on to my notion of elegance no matter what happens, to remember that at root I am not of this gathering but of another time and place entirely. It's still unclear, of course, what time and place I'm of.

The party is well under way, which is to say less well-bred than it sounded upstairs. Already the jazz piano is being drowned out by a sporadic chorus from the Boys' Club, the burden of which is

> *It takes a Welsh miner*
> *To reach her vagina,*

With the rest trailing off into *la-di-da*'s until someone takes up the refrain again. Not many of the Boys' Club Wives are present, I notice. Lois Lafferty is jiggling the ice cubes in her glass and proclaiming, "That's a very *old* song, actually," in the intervals when no one is singing it, but she isn't getting much attention. As I edge past, Arnie, who is sitting cross-legged on the floor between Ralph and Petie Havermeyer, calls out "Hey Eleanor, listen to this," and begins singing it all by himself. I point at the kitchen and mime drinking while he furrows his brow in puzzlement until Ralph shouts something in his ear. Then he cries "Good *idea*," and gives me the thumbs-up sign. I throw Ralph one of my slow Sphinx-like smiles: bit of an enigma that Eleanor, actually.

Tom and Patsy are in the knot of people surrounding Nor-ford and his wife. Patsy is making little sprightly gestures with her hands and forearms while Norford radiates approval. When I catch his eye he nods perfunctorily and I'm seized by the familiar despair: why can't I be more like Patsy when Patsy is so evidently what is called for? Also a dedicated teacher in the Basic program, of course, also a fine little accumulator and collator of the Boys' random Thoughts. But it ought to be possible to be all these things simultaneously. Surely it's just obstinacy that keeps me from being any of them, as if I were bent only on denying these people everything they so manifestly want. I remember suddenly one of the books my mother left around for me at the onset of puberty. *Patterns for Personality*, it was called. It's not that I've ever lacked for patterns.

"Dolls," Patsy is saying. "From when I was just a little girl, you know?" Norford beams paternally.

I look around for Jo Michaelson but she isn't visible. It's very likely that she has already put in her appearance and gone home. I can't imagine who else I'm going to talk to. Elegance, I remind myself, clutching at the word as if it could summon a genie or transport me somewhere else altogether, but nothing happens. Drink, I think, and resume my progress toward the kitchen.

When I get there it's hard not to keep going, out the back door, into the night, home. My coat is upstairs, though, and anyway I haven't had a drink: I haven't given the party a chance yet.

There seems to be more scotch that anything else, so I start with that.

I've choked down most of a wine glass full and am pouring a more refined dose over two ice cubes when Ralph comes lumbering through the swinging doors from the living room. "Great party, huh?" he says. "What are you drinking, scotch?" I nod, too numbed by the first shot to say anything. "Hey, we've got some-thing in common, you and me." He fills his own glass, not even bothering with ice. I manage what I hope is a comradely smile as he raises his drink to me. "Two scotch drinkers," he affirms, and sits down heavily on the bottom tier of the stepstool by the sink. "Hey, you're all right, Eleanor."

"Thank you," I say. "Would you like me to put some water in your drink?"

"Water?" He squints at me. "Nah. This is scotch. You don't *put* things in scotch."

"Oh," I say. I was about to put some water in my own glass but now I content myself with sipping dubiously from the edge.

Ralph shifts his weight on the stepladder but doesn't get up. "I want to tell you something," he says, looking into his glass. "We're having this party on New Year's Eve, I expect you're heard."

I haven't but I nod anyway. I'm supposed to know these things; it's an index of how important they are that everybody is supposed to know them.

"Well, the reason we didn't invite you is nothing personal, that's what I want you to know," he says. "I mean, it might look funny that most of the guys and their, ah, wives are invited and you're not, but when you think about it it makes sense. It's that this is a party for couples, you see?"

I do see, of course; it's the official reason why nobody invites me to anything; but at the same time it occurs to me that he's going to have a hard time justifying it. I want to see him try. "No," I say judiciously.

"Hey, look at it this way. It's midnight on New Year's Eve. Everybody's kissing everybody. How would it be if there were single people there? I mean who would they *kiss?*"

I snort. "You just kiss your wives on New Year's Eve?"

He shrugs, impatient. "Look I kiss Francie Stutke and Arnie kisses Arlene. That's even. But put in a single woman it throws everything off. The wives wouldn't like it, you know?"

With a little thrill I realize that he's saying I'd be a sexual threat. "Well, I can see *that*," I admit.

"I thought you would," he says, relieved. "Anyway, I wanted you to know it's nothing against you, Eleanor, because we all think you're doing just great."

"Who?" I ask playfully.

"Who what?"

"Who all thinks I'm doing just great?"

"Well, all of us. All the guys on the committee, you know, we think you're fitting in really well." He tilts back his head and takes a long swallow of the scotch: almost half the glass, I note, wondering how he keeps from gaging. An acquired taste, they say. "And hey" he adds huskily, "You're *looking* good too."

"Thank you," I say, and then note that his hand has snaked out and is groping for a hold around my waist.

"Really good," he mutters. Then he stands up and pulls me toward him.

I try giggling but it comes out more like a gasp. He is pushing himself against me. I arch my back, trying to put my pelvis out of range. I can fell, just slightly, the shape of his penis against my stomach. "Hey," I say, trying to be offhand about it, "I need some more scotch."

"We think you're doing just fine," Ralph is murmuring. "A real asset to the team."

"That's nice to you," I assure him, pulling away. "I need another drink," I explain. "You need another drink?"

He lurches at me but I get on the other side of the drink table. "You scared of something, Eleanor?" he mumbles. "I thought you like me."

"I do," I cry gaily, making a show of scrabbling in the ice bucket for more ice cubes. All of a sudden he's pressed against my back with both arms encircling my waist. "Hey, let's go back and see how the party's doing," I suggest.

"It's doing just fine," he says.

"No, I mean Arnie and Bill and Petie and all those guys, they'll be wondering where you are—"

"I thought you liked *me*, Eleanor," he breathes in my ear. The hands are moving downward over my abdomen.

"I do," I cry, twisting away and putting the drink table between us again. I have a vision of it turning over in slow motion while I am crushed to the floor under Ralph in a great confusion of ice and broken glass and of course scotch.

"You're not *acting* like it—" he complains, but at the moment Arnie bursts through the swinging doors laden with glasses.

"Eleanor!" he cries. "Just the person I want to see. We need some drinks here, I've even got them written down on this napkin."

"Of *course*," I carol back at him. "Here, Ralph, you just go in and Arnie and I will take care of this."

Ralph is back on the bottom step of the stepstool with a napkin in his lap. "I'll watch," he says.

Arnie and I pour things into the various glasses and then put the glasses on a tray, which I carry out while Arnie holds open the swinging doors and sings "Ta-*da!*" As soon as I can put the tray down I push through the bodies until I'm in the entrance hall by the door. I stop there, in the cooler air, trying to piece together what happened. The scotch has gone to my head and other places as well: I'm sweating so hard that I feel as though I'm melting down. Maybe Ralph won't remember this, I reassure myself. But if he remembers anything it will be that I insulted him: that's what my behavior amounts to, being unattached and spike heeled and made up and saying no. I climb the stairs with my head buzzing, disentangle my coat from a pile on the bed in the master bedroom, and resisting the temptation of the bathroom hurry back downstairs and out the door. On the porch I remember my sequined evening bag, still on the drink table in the kitchen, and resolve to do without it. Nothing much in it, some change, a comb, the foundation, mascara, and pale pink lipstick. Nothing I'll need.

My feet hurt all the way home. You pay for vanity, I remind myself, stoic in the moonlight. In all sorts of ways you pay: would any of this have happened if I haven't been trying to reclaim my sexual identity? At the moment it seems an absurd thing to want, a sexual identity, a willful baring of the throat to the knife. It's not, after all, as if I could choose the object of my de-sires. Desire makes me available, that's all, and I'm either available or not. Wanting Tom, it stands to reason I'd get Ralph. For one thing, Ralph has seniority.

When I get home I kick off the spike heeled pumps and leave them by the door. In the process I snag one of my smoke-tone stockings; I can feel the run moving up my leg as I limp up the stairs. The phone begins to ring before I reach the landing. I pick up the receiver without turning on any lights; it feels safer that way. I recognize the rhythmic swishing sound immediately, before the whisper begins: "Eleanor, do you know what I'm doing now?"

"Who are you?" I cry. The rhythm accelerates. There is a little moan and a click as the line goes dead. "Do I know you?" I cry, jiggling the disconnect button, but there's only a dial tone. I drop the receiver on the floor. The house is very quiet. Slowly I unzip the black jersey dress and slide out of it; carefully I turn down the bed and get into it, still wearing my slip, bra, panties, garter belt, and stockings. A recorded voice begins to tell me to please hang up. I listen to the recording until the voice is supplanted by a steady pattern of beeps, and then I fall asleep.

Christmas nets me a card with twenty dollars enclosed from my mother and a set of six place mats from Jo Michaelson, who is in Hawaii with one of her mysterious friends. My gift to myself is a slog in the fresh snow to Penney's, where I buy galoshes and, on impulse, a black nylon slip, which I have sent to my mother. It won't get there on time but it ought to worry her. I stop at the public library on the way back and check out *Persuasion*, *Villette*, and *Jane Eyre* as holiday indulgences. Given the choice I'd rather reread than read. You run less risk that way. Frank said that was one of my major shortcomings in that it was symptomatic of a basic lack of intellectual courage, but ten Frank only reread things he was writing articles about, and even then he always pretended to be surprised by twists in the plot (*Audience expectations are thwarted, however, when...*). He'd say these are the wrong kinds of books too, girl books. Unlike what we normally term literature, or boy books, they tend to portray small, despised heroines who inexplicably triumph: *Reader, I married him.* The triumph of course is what makes them unworthy of consideration. In real life he may marry you but there's no guarantee   he   won't   take off again.

New Year's Eve is harder to deal with. All my upbringing converges on it because it's the most social night of the year, the point where you're proven a pariah if you don't have a date or at least a party to go to. I figure I can remind myself of Ralph's party if I get despondent, everybody kissing everybody else but restricted to couples so that things stay even. My mother would say that was sour grapes. It's sour grapes by definition whenever you don't care if you don't go to something. My mother had no tolerance for not caring. You're supposed to feel left out.

I've never spent a New Year's Eve by myself before. Not altogether by myself, at least: being abandoned by Frank while everybody around me was blowing whistles and copping feels doesn't count, and neither does my mother's compensatory ritual of cocoa and popcorn in front of the television set after she had once again established that I hadn't been invited anywhere. Despite the fact that I still haven't been invited anywhere, I'm a little elated at the prospect of an evening stretched out before me equally free of anxiety and Guy Lombardo. It seems auspicious somehow that I should be ushering in the new year accompanied by nothing more demanding than a new assortment of sticky liqueurs.

But once I'm settled in the study with my first slug of apricot brandy oozing gummily around the ice cubes in my wine glass and the radio tuned in to an announcer frantic with the responsibility of cheering up an audience left at home on the ultimate date night, I realize that I'm waiting for something, I'm not sure what. The annunciatory peal of the doorbell, young man in rented tux with orchid. A knock, poly-knuckled and insinuating as castanets, my white-tied stranger in tails and tap shoes to take me clicky-clacking off into the orchestrated darkness. The slow rasp of the kitchen window sliding open, a shadowy intruder intruding feet first. The ringing of the telephone. I'm waiting for my admirer to call. Surely he'll call tonight of all nights, if only to come in my ear to the strains of Auld Lang Syne; surely he won't be otherwise engaged, won't stand me up. After the indignities he's heaped on me it's the least he can do to give me a ring.

Other than that, there is nothing awaiting me this evening but a radio countdown of the year's top 100 hits and the typing paper stacked on my desk top, expectant and unsullied. After two or three more sample bottles of sticky liqueur I should be in the mood to sully it, that and the hitherto intact Lenoreans, whose technical virginity is beginning to bother me in the same way Janet's used to, and for the same kinds of reasons: the series of triumphs that constituted Janet's holding out served to emphasize that Janet had something to hold out against and that I, by contrast, didn't. "Animals," she explained once, with satisfaction, allowing me to touch reverently the purpling finger-mark just above her nipple, sympathetic participation in a near thing. "They keep hoping just this once they can get you to give it away for nothing."

"Give what?" I persisted on this occasion, although of course I was familiar with the decorous phrases the girls in the dorm cherished along with their circle pins: hold it dear, give it away, save it for the man you love.

But she only snorted and shrugged into her nightgown. "*You* would," she said, and went off to the bathroom in search of more shockable confidantes. She was right, too. In her terms I was dying to give it away. In my own terms it didn't feel like giving: I simply wanted; it didn't feel at all altruistic. Getting, I would have said, or, at certain frenzied moments, taking. Another aberration on my part; you weren't supposed to want. Sex was slipping or being caught off guard or giving in. Ideally you swapped it for something you did want, a fiancé traditionally, although a steady was considered a reasonable deal and more than one senior settled for a date to the homecoming dance—inflation was setting in even then. I stumbled among these arabesques of exchange graceless and uncomprehending. I couldn't give it away. Alternatively, I wasn't getting any.

My Lenoreans aren't giving it away either, which keeps them smug but means in essence that *they* aren't getting any, an unworkable premise for pornography. I'm hoping they'll loosen up for New Year's Eve, a propitious time for fresh starts, breakthroughs and penetration. Given the general atmosphere of licentiousness I should be stimulated to spray a fair number of inviolate pages with erotic description. More ominously, I may be recalling the pervasive mythology of my undergraduate years. If I don't get in tonight, it's likely I never will.

I'm into the crème de menthe, which tastes like toothpaste, and the countdown has hit number eighteen ("Hang On Sloopy," a big hit for the McCoys) when I finally decide it's now or never. Same setup. Satin-draped queen, elevated, nipples protruding through the slick fabric like grapes. Burlap-clad adventurer, depressed, tongue flickering over simian lips. Courtiers in attendance. A lot of ogling all around. Some posturing: bulges on both sides. Fore play. But this isn't what I'm after. What I'm after, I reflect muzzily, is contact, mutually pleasurable contact with the emphasis on mutuality, none of this ramming banging poking prodding sticking drilling screwing violating penetrating invading wounding business; just, you know, intercourse. Surely this is possible, even granting the unfortunate precedents.

"All right," she breathed, and reached for him.

A great shout rang through the enclosure as they met, grappled, fell writhing to the ground where they continued to twitch like galvanized frogs as the currents of desire coursed through them.

Yes, well, observed the courtiers, it's going to look funny from outside, a question of point of view really. Objectivity and distance obviously aren't doing a thing for you, what you need is more permeability and fewer edges, more suppleness and less rigidity, a more inherently ambiguous accepting inclusive

Yes he told her yes I will yes yes yes

It's been known to work, they said.

Yes it was yielding it was bliss he was overtaken submerged his will resistless back arching with the indefatigable strokes—

Yes the shudders rippling up her body as she posted rhythmic above him slick muscles gripping as he cried and clawed to be absorbed into the palpitating dense enclosing surrounding

Yes indeed what you might call the suffocated as opposed to the skewered mode of coition but the question, as always, is: is it credible? Was it ever credible even when he was probing and drilling, she heaving and fainting? Or, why do descriptions of fucking presume a fucker and a fuckee?

"I want you more than life itself," he murmured into her shell-like ear.

"Prove it," she said.

He proved it. It was indescribable. It felt terrific. The courtiers were disappointed. "Clichéd," they called out. "Euphemistic. Vague. We couldn't see."

Languidly she raised herself on one elbow and stared out over the massed bodies of her subjects. "Fuck off," she said. Turning to her sinewy paramour she inquired gently, "Was it good for you?"

All I can think of at first is my back, which seems to have twisted into some witchlike configuration and hardened while I slept—I must have been sleeping, sprawled across my desk, my cheek gouged with the outline of my pen, eyes burning under bloated lids, the ice long melted and a pale green residue of crème de menthe tinting the water in my wine glass. I feel like a leftover from the orgy where, typically, I didn't come. I want to kick something. It's two-thirty in the morning. The phone is ringing.

It's hard getting out of the chair: my body seems to have thickened. I missed the New Year. My admirer didn't rouse me in time for Guy Lombardo. It's too late now. But I pick up the receiver anyway, sitting gingerly on the very edge of the bed. "Hello," I say, trying for some reason to keep the irritation out of my voice. Force of habit. Training.

"Hey, Eleanor. I didn't wake you up, did I?"

"Who is this?" I demand, although I was brought up not to put direct questions to the receiver. It's not anyone I could have anticipated, certainly not my panting voiceless stranger.

"Aw, Eleanor." Voices in the background, many voices. Party still going on. "You don't have to *be* like that—"

"Frank," I say.

"Hey, you're not in the middle of something—"

"It's two-thirty in the morning, Frank," I say.

"Shit, it's three-thirty here. I mean, it's New Year's Eve, Eleanor, it's not like you've got to get up and *teach* or something—"

"It's two-thirty and that's late no matter what night it is," I say, feeling stodgy. Frank has that effect on me.

"Shit, I woke you up, didn't I. I'm an asshole, I should've *known*—"

Trust Frank to know I wouldn't be doing anything in particular on New Year's Eve. Once a wallflower always a wallflower. "I'm going to bed now," I say. "Go back to your potting friend."

There is a short silence in which I can hear a tinkly piano.

Academic party: that piano is universal. Then Frank says," My what?"

"Your potting friend," I say, biting the words off crisply. "You know, the one who's into the non-intellective? The one you live with. Or is she perhaps a *weaving* friend now—"

"Oh," he says. "Oh, I thought you knew about that. Ah Lynda. Ah, that's all over."

"Oh," I say, feeling deflated.

"It wasn't working out," he says.

"I didn't know that," I say.

"I thought you did," he says. The pause hangs between us, fuzzy and full of party noises.

"I'm sorry," I say.

"Right," he says. "Hey, how'd you like to come out for a few days?"

"What?" I find I have to go back over this to get the sense straight.

"Yeah, you've still got tomorrow and the weekend, you could get a plane easy, nobody flies right after the holidays."

"Come to Baltimore?" I'm still not sure I've got it.

"Yeah, I've got a great place. You'd really like it. On the water."

"When," I say.

"Oh, let's see." Background voices now. A giggle. "Well hey, tomorrow maybe? I could reimburse you for the ticket, no problem, or if you can't handle that I could wire you the money—"

It's the offer to pay that convinces me. Scares me, too. "Frank," I say, "I can't come to Baltimore. I've got things to do."

"Well yeah," he says. "But you could come for the weekend."

"I'm staying here," I say. "I'm busy."

"Bullshit," he says. "You've never been busy in your life."

"Happy New Year," I say, but he's hung up. I put the receiver back on the cradle with a sense that I've done something final and rather important. Granting the ambiguity, granting him the last word, even so, I did reject him. Perhaps it wasn't an *unmitigated* rejection, but the worm turned there. Or flexed a little, at least. Feeling stiff now, I ease down on to my back, which hurts, and reflect that I didn't miss the New Year after all. It's all the new year now. If I can locate a single source of frustration it's that my admirer didn't call but I can cope with that; it's the same old story; they're all fickle when you come down to it, even the heavy breathers.

I spend the weekend pairing up Lenoreans with sinewy, rough-fingered sailors. One by one, which runs me though a lot of typing paper. Each story is different; each involves a unique and mutually satisfying position through which ecstasy is not only achieved but sustained. Most of the positions are anatomically impossible. Most of those that are possible don't feel all that good. I've basically gone back to the conventions of mainstream pornographic representation, *Beaver Country* with clitori. The end result will be one of those mass marriages like at the close of a Shakespearean comedy, society rejuvenated, everybody plugged into everybody else. It's going very well.

Ted and Tyrone show up on Sunday laden with cardboard boxes and parts of hi-fi's, and I listen to them bumping around below me while I insert the last appendages into the last orifices. Then I go downstairs and get out the six-pack of beer I've brought for the occasion of their arrival. They have the hi-fi too loud to hear my knock, do finally I open the door and shout down the stairs, "Isn't that Dylan?"

After a while Ted comes to the foot of the stairs and peers up at me. "Am I disturbing you?" I call. He looks puzzled, then smiles radiantly and beckons. I go down the stairs carrying the six-pack before me like a talisman. They haven't turned on the overhead light. In fact, they don't seem to have any of the lights turned on. As I round the corner into the apartment proper I see that instead there are two squat candles, the kind that go under chafing dishes, guttering in saucers at either end of the counter separating the kitchenette from the living area. In the shadows everything looks as bare as before except for the bank of hi-fi equipment under the casement window. After a moment I make out Tyrone sitting cross-legged in one of the butterfly chairs, head tilted back, eyes closed. Ted waves me to the other butterfly chair and lowers himself a bit shakily to the linoleum. The music is very loud, electric guitar, drums, organ. "Eleanor," says Tyrone without opening his eyes.

"I brought you a beer," I tell him.

He reaches out his hand like a blind man. "Opener."

I didn't bring one. I look at Ted, who is looking at one of the candles. "Upstairs," I say. Neither of them moves.

"You want to smoke, Eleanor?" Tyrone says at last.

I think about this. I know he doesn't mean Marlboros, of course. That much I learned at Columbia, where graduate student parties generally involved a cluster of people at one corner of the room or back in the bedroom where they put the coats, and the point was not to notice. That was being cool if you weren't actually smoking. We weren't smoking because Frank had done it once and couldn't see the point. He'd done it authentically too, in the company of some jazz musicians he'd been introduced to at the Village Vanguard, and if there was no point under those conditions what was the percentage in getting stoned around a bunch of white kids who didn't even dig the right kind of music? Now I look up again to see that Tyrone is bending over me holding out a thin cylinder that glows at the tip. "Pot," I say, hoping to suggest easy familiarity without coming out and saying I know what to do with it.

"Dope," intones Tyrone. I'm not sure whether he's correcting me or offering an alternative. Ted, I realize, is watching me narrowly from the floor.

"Ah," I say, which doesn't resolve anything. Tyrone remains poised above me hand extended, the cigarette pinched delicately between thumb and forefinger. The problem is that I know you're supposed to smoke it but I don't know the technique. Frank said the way you go at it reveals everything about you, whether you're hip or lame: those are the categories. It's like virginity, there's no glamour in inexperience. At least not in my case: Frank said what's the matter, you a virgin or something, and I said oh no, no, wondering if my body would betray me, if I'd bleed or something, but as it turned out there had been that Tampax. I think if you're extremely beautiful you can get away with not knowing how to do things. I finally take a hasty drag and pass it back to Tyrone, who puts it to his own lips. I watch closely, wondering if it's amusement lifting the corners of his mouth or only the effort of drawing in and holding that much smoke. At any rate I have the principle now: you hold your breath. When he extends the cigarette to me again I take it without hesitation from between his fingers, the contact sending a little tingle up my arm, and pull on it so hard that the tip glows orange-red.

Two things happen immediately. The first is that my eyes fill up and overflow before I can even shut them. The second is that my need to cough becomes so intense and enveloping that I'm afraid I'll go into spasm if I do anything further with my lungs. I breathe out as slowly as I can, wondering if I'll be able to stop coughing if I allow myself to start. When my eyes begin to clear I sneak a glance at Tyrone. He's back in the butterfly chair but now he's bobbing his head to the unheard-of rhythm of Dylan singing rock and watching me with what looks like approval. "Good stuff, huh?" he says.

I nod, not trusting myself to speak, and get up from the butterfly chair. Ted gives me a beatific smile as I leave.

But I come back the next night, after I've typed my punctuation examples onto ditto masters, and the night after that wen I've finished marking the diagnostic writing samples from my three new Basic classes. I've come near to memorizing the new Dylan album: Ted and Tyrone and I now join in on choruses, *Something is happening and you don't know what it i-i-is, Do you, MIStah Jones?* It all helps, especially now that I'm in new trouble with the composition committee.

It began during the first meeting after vacation, when I found myself serving coffee in an atmosphere of disapproval that permeated the conference room like swamp gas. "Black, two sugars," I chirped, setting a Styrofoam cup in front of Bill Brewster.

"No sugar," he snapped without looking at me.

"But you always take two sugars," I said, adverting to the intelligently conceived mnemonic devices (*B.B. Black Two*) that had got me through college with Highest Honors.

"I don't *always* do anything," said Bill, and insisted on a fresh cup, unsugared, although I could tell he didn't much like the way it tasted. That was the meeting when Ralph announced that Norford's secretary Dale would be joining us from now on so we could have reliable notes on our proceedings, "reliable" just slightly stressed. I looked at Tom and he looked at his fingers. He could play footsie with Dale I decided.

I should have anticipated that Ralph would get back at me in the most direct way possible, but with my newfound interests in Dylan and pot and with the completion of my pornographic manuscript (I sent it out under the *nom de plume* of Gabrielle Stephanie De Vere) I hadn't really thought much about any of the Boys' Club. I start thinking about them again with some reluctance. They're not that interesting, even if they do have my future in their hands.

At the next meeting Arnie passes around a mimeographed sheet, beautifully typed—Dale's IBM Executive beats Arnie's Remington upright hands down. *Accumulate/Collate, it says. Analyze/Prioritize. Propose/Dispose.* "Wait a minute, Arnie," I say. Dale, now seated at Ralph's right, my old place, lifts her pencil from her memo pad and looks resigned. "Stop me if I'm wrong," I say, "but isn't this what we've been doing all fall semester?"

Kitty-corner from me now, Tom is frowning at the table top. Beside me Dale is studying her nails. Ralph sighs heavily, gathering in our attention, but it's Arnie who answers. "That's the *point*, Eleanor," he says. "I mean, we kind of decided that since it worked so terrifically last fall we'd go back and do it again this semester."

"Do it all again? I press. "Do all the accumulating and collating and analyzing and prioritizing and proposing and *dis*—"

Arnie looks relieved that I've got it. "Granted it'll take a little while," he says, "but we've really got it down now. Even if we have to continue into the summer we know we've got the *procedure*—"

"Into the summer?" I squeak.

"Um," says Ralph. Everyone looks at him. He looks pained. "Dale will be helping," he points out. Dale smiles prettily at her stiletto-tipped pinky. "And I'd just like to say it's great having her on the team," he adds.

"Hey, right, welcome aboard, Dale," calls Arnie. He beams at Ralph. "She fits in so beautifully that I just forgot she was new," he explains. Ralph grants him a magisterial nod. Arnie turns back to me. "Not that she can do it all," he tells me.

After we've adjourned, the accumulating and collating duties assigned now to Dale and me, "as a team," Arnie explains, "or sort of a sub-team, you know, of the main team?" I catch up with Tom in the stairwell. "Look," I say, "what about our interim report?"

He doesn't stop, so I have to climb along beside him. "What about it?"

He doesn't stop, so I have to climb along beside him. "What about it?"

"I thought we'd finished that stage" I puff. "I thought we were going on to the next stage." It occurs to me that I don't have any idea what that is. Maybe they don't either.

We've reached the third floor landing and he swings around to face me. "It's an *interim* report, Eleanor," he says. "Don't you know what interim means?"

"I don't see what that has to do with it," I say, but he only shrugs in exasperation and pushes through the door into our corridor. "And I do know what interim means," I all after him. It's just as well not to foster any obvious misunderstandings.

That afternoon Ted shows up in my kitchen while I'm standing at the sink looking out at the apple tree and making what he and Tyrone call my ferret face, which involves positioning my upper teeth over my lower lip and wrinkling my nose. "I'm inviting you to dinner," he says. "Tyrone's cooking. I'm helping."

"That's terrific," I say. As far as I can tell they've only eaten potato chips since they've moved in. "I'd love to come."

"We're having hamburger stew," says Ted. I start in on my ferret face again and make myself stop.

The hamburger stew is beige and has almost no flavor because the only seasoning either of them possesses is salt, but we pass a joint around between mouthfuls and I've contributed beer and three of the place mats that Jo gave me for Christmas, so the overall feeling is festive. We sit around a rickety card table that Tyrone salvaged from somewhere, resting our elbows because Tyrone says if you can't put your elbows on the table in your own place what's the point of having your own place, and giggling into the jelly glasses Ted's mother pressed on him when she finally accepted that he was moving out of the dorm. Ted's father has not accepted this and is not speaking to Ted. Neither parent, I gather, knows about Tyrone.

"A toast!" Ted cries suddenly. In the flickering light provided by two more stubby candles from Tyrone's apparently unlimited supply his face has the unearthly purity of Renaissance *putti*. Tyrone, beside him, is looking carved, all cheekbones and eyelids and modeled lips, and he has a sort of luster, as if he's been oiled recently. We raise our glasses, unexpectedly self-conscious. I've never been in on a toast before, I realize, and I'm supposed to be the knowledgeable one. Ted looks at me and then at Tyrone, his eyes shiny. "To us," he proposed, and we clink glasses, Ted and me, Ted and Tyrone, Tyrone and me. "To us," I murmur with each of my clinks, not really loud enough for them to hear over the music. I like saying us. Usually it's just me.

But while Ted and I do the dishes I wonder whether this three-way bond is interfering with other potential combinations. The fact that there are two of them is exerting a kind of control, I'm beginning to realize. There's a sort of triangulation of sexual tensions here that has effectively kept things from developing. There are times when Ted looks up at me from under his smoky lashes and decorum vanishes, or when I look up to meet Tyrone's appraising gaze and we both smile, a little ironically, in acknowledgment that we could go on—as my neighbors in the dorm used to say, usually with little admonishing clucks—all the way. The problem is that there are always three people present, that when we're congregated the dominant mood is always jovial comraderie, one for all and all for one. I wish there could be something else as well. Comraderie plus lust. I realize, of course, that it's not supposed to work out that way. You go for one or the other; I learned that in the dorm.

But as I turn away from the sink I find that I'm saying conversationally, "Did I ever tell you about my admirer."

It doesn't even come out as a question. I know I haven't told them. The only person I've ever told is the woman at the phone company. Somehow the subject has always been too personal to mention to anyone else. "I mean, that's what he calls himself," I say. "That's how he signs his letters, Your Admirer. I know it's a he because he writes about wet dreams."

"*Really*," says Ted.

"No shit," says Tyrone.

I pour us all another jelly glass of beer and tell them the whole story, more or less. Less my reactions, mostly, because I'm not sure what those are, and because when I am sure, they're too embarrassing. They listen raptly, interrupting only to ask for more details. When I get to the part about the typefaces and my discovery of the similarity between one of the letters and Tom Lippman's Thoughts for the committee Ted breathes, "Oh wow, Professor Lippman, he's supposed to be charismatic."

"Ted's big on charisma" says Tyrone, and when I look at him I see that he's scowling at the joint between his fingers.

"Well, that's what they say about him," insists Ted. I tell him in my Miss Brooks voice that he'll get over it, and Tyrone and I exchange what I construe as a rueful grimace at the promiscuity of Ted's hero worship. "Anyway," I say, "Professor Lippman may not have anything to do with this. What makes it tricky is that there are at least three typewriters involved."

"Let's see the letters," Tyrone says, so I go upstairs to my study, where I've stored everything since the beginning of the break, and bring down the whole collection. Both of them immediately spread everything out on the floor and squat down to pore over it. After a moment Tyrone gets up and switches on the overhead light. I go back to the butterfly chair, where I sit blinking into the beer at the bottom of my jelly glass while they arrange and rearrange the evidence, and remind myself that I brought up the subject of my admirer in order to arouse their admiration, as it were. They don't seem particularly aroused. They seem a lot like the Hardy Boys at the moment, and I'm not sure they even remember I'm here.

Finally Ted stands up and wipes his palms vigorously

against his thighs. "*Four* typewriters," he announces, "and one of them is definitely the same as the one Professor Lippman used, so we'll start there."

"Where?" His purposefulness is disorienting.

"Professor Lippman's office. I'll just ask if I can use his typewriter for a minute. I'll say I found an error on my paper and I need to retype a page right away."

"Then we'll work down your hall," adds Tyrone. "Trying to get a sample from all the typewriters, you know." He shrugs. "We've got to start somewhere."

"Also, when he calls again," says Ted, "see if you can let us know so we can listen in on our extension."

"Pound on the door," says Tyrone. "Three loud knocks. You should repeat them a few times so we're sure—"

"Wait a minute," I say. "I'm supposed to tell him to hold on while I run downstairs?"

"Tell him you have to get undressed," says Ted, and I'm cheered that at least my sexuality enters into this somewhere.

But my admirer doesn't call or write, and as the days slip by and the trail gets colder Ted and Tyrone withdraw into the basement leaving me with my radio and my beer, twitching whenever the telephone rings. They do establish that the one letter was written in Tom's office, through a procedure that according to Ted also establishes Tom as an absolute *ass*hole, but my satisfaction at these discoveries is limited by the fact that I'm getting so little of their company. I'm taking second place to their homework, I suppose—after all, they're both top students—but I also suppose that they've made a conscious decision to keep me upstairs. Sitting in the living room with my first set of Basic papers, a total of ninety-two on the subject of My Favorite Place on Campus (the Pub wins hands down, with the only competition coming from a protected area in the stadium under the bleachers), I can hear clearly the wailing organ of the Dylan record. *Something is happening and you don't know what it i-i-is*, Dylan sings, and I read, *Under the bleachers one can kinda "snuggle up" etc. with ones boy friend."* I'm beginning to feel left out again.

We're almost four weeks into the semester and I've fallen back into my reclusive habits to the extent of resuming work on

"Wordsworth and the Neoclassical Tradition Once Again," when Paul calls. "Eleanor," he snaps. "Paul Fisher here," and I have a moment of panic before I remember who he is. "I suppose you've heard they've convicted Miller," he continues. I say I haven't, which seems to lower me in his estimation. "By and large the local media haven't picked it up yet" he tells me with just a trace of smugness. "Anyway, now that the peace offensive is over and there's been this conviction we figure it's about time to reconvene the group."

"Peace offensive," I say, wishing I hadn't let my *Newsweek* subscription lapse.

But he takes this as an English teacher's sneer and comes back, a little less confidently, with "Contradiction in terms, isn't it?"

"It is," I say.

"I thought it was," he says.

A number of people are already gathered in Kiley's living room when we get there the following afternoon, among them Kenny, who addresses Tyrone as "Brother," albeit in a dropped-voice manner so that it comes out a "Bruff." Not to be outdone, Kiley claps first me and then Ted on the back and cries "*Good* to see you!" Tyrone arches his eyebrows at me before he detaches himself from Kenny, who is trying to mutter something in his ear, and lopes across the room to a spot on the floor between Linda and Lee where he remains for the duration of the meeting. I'm not sure whether I'm supposed to follow him or only arch my eyebrows back, so I end up sticking with Ted, who is busy asking Kiley questions about the escalation of the war during the last week. If I weren't so demoralized by my lack of information I probably would have noticed that Tyrone has chosen to occupy a sort of demilitarized zone in the Kiley living room. As it is, I find that when the shooting starts I'm caught on one side and furthermore that it's the fascist pig side, as it were.

Kenny draws the lines, as usual. "I just want to know," he growls, "why it's always Professor Kiley that calls these meetings and why we have them in his house."

Everyone looks at Kiley, who takes a sip of coffee before

he says," You could have decided it was time and called the meeting yourself. You didn't."

It's perfectly straightforward but it isn't the whole story. I find myself pitying Kenny, who says now, "It just always happens that way, right?"

"We certainly don't have to have it at my house," says Kiley, but all I can think of is that nobody else has a centrally located address, a large, furnished living room, supplies of china and silver a coffeemaker, a Mary Ellen. "You're welcome to make changes," he says, palms out, nothing up his sleeves, philosophy professor proving we've made him our leader by an exercise of free will. Only it doesn't feel as though we've made any choices. Everybody looks embarrassed. "We could have it at Eleanor's house, for instance," he says.

Everyone looks at me. I nod. I could get Styrofoam cups, I suppose. Paper plates. Plastic spoons. I don't know where I'd get coffee. Given the precedent I can hardly serve instant. "It's okay with me," I say, "only I'm a little out of the way."

Kenny glowers at me. "How far?"

"Near the IGA," I say. "At the south end of town>"

"Too far," pronounces Charlie. "Anybody have something closer in?" We all look at each other.

"Well I'll tell you one thing," Kenny cries, desperate now. "A lot of people aren't coming because they think it's too tight. They say we're Kiley's group and they don't want to tag along behind Kiley."

Kiley shrugs. "That's an insult to everybody here," he says. "I can't be responsible for other people's sloppy thinking." His gaze sweeps the room, seeking out challenges. "Well then, do we want to have our next meeting at Eleanor's?" he continues. "Because we ought to be getting to the business of what to do about Miller's conviction, don't you think?"

We note to have the next meeting at Kiley's and go on to talk about new strategies for overcoming public apathy, but nobody seems particularly enthusiastic, and after about an hour of polite discussion the gathering breaks up. Kiley claps me on the back again as I'm leaving. "I'll give you a call sometime this week about doing some more, ah, publicity," he says, and I feel as if I've been singled out as a collaborator.

The telephone rings around ten-thirty that night. There is a long pause and then the rhythmic swishing begins.

"Just a minute," I say. "I mean, I'm really interested in, ah, talking with you but I've got something going on. Can you hold on?" As I slide down the hall in Frank's old sweat socks I think about how "Can you hold on?" isn't figurative language.

In the basement the hi-fi is throbbing. Smokey Robinson and the Miracles, *Ooooo, baby baby*. I knock on the basement door three times, wait, knock three times again. Nothing happens. "Hey!" I call. Not too loudly or he'll hear me upstairs. I ball up my fist and pound. "Hey!" I call again. *Oooo, baby baby*, sing Smokey Robinson and the Miracles. No answer. Could they have gone out, with the hi-fi still going? I turn the knob slowly and push. They're using the bolt on the other side.

"Hey!" I call again, but I know it's no good. They probably can't even hear me. I go back upstairs and pick up the receiver. My admirer has hung up. It's absurd to feel disappointed, but I do.

There is nothing from him either in my mail box or under my office door on Monday, Valentine's Day. The bastard has no sense of occasion. There is, however, a large manila envelope containing twenty or so typewritten pages and a cover letter, typed neatly on departmental stationery, from Dale. *We are to do this as a team, that is share the responsibilities and I have certainly done my share of them*, she has written. *Now you should fix these up Eleanor*. Most of the enclosure is made up of Arnie's continued Thoughts, transcribed verbatim. Dale has even more trouble with his handwriting than I do.

I'm marveling at the suggestion that the composition committee *reconsider several aspics [sp?] of its situation* when Lois Lafferty appears in my doorway. "Not a Valentine?" she inquires, hugging herself. She is wearing a fringed paisley shawl today, and it hangs artfully over where her waist might be, obscuring outlines while suggesting that there would still be concavities if you lifted enough layers of material. "No such luck," she concludes. "More Bonehead?"

"Committee work," I mutter.

She titters. "Yes, I hear you and Dale are trying to decide who's secretary."

"Dale is *a* secretary," I say. "I'm *the* secretary." It sounds like a ridiculous distinction, even to me.

"And that makes all the difference," she observes. "Or should I say oh, the difference to *you*?"

"Lay off Wordsworth," I growl, surprising myself.

She gives me her closed-mouthed camel smile. "Yes, Tom was saying he was your, ah, man. Wordsworth, I mean. Not Tom. Daring of you, we thought, seeing as nowadays most people think Wordsworth is *shit*—"

"Language!" roars Ralph Hamilton, looming up in the doorway behind her.

Lois falls off one of her high heels and has to grab at the door frame. "Why Ralph," she squeaks as she steadies herself, "you *scared* me—"

"Um," says Ralph, looking past her. "You in there, Eleanor"

"Right here," I call to him. "I was just looking over the, ah, material for the meeting."

"Good girl," he says abstractedly. I'm grateful. "I came to talk to Eleanor," he tells the air above Lois's head.

Lois pulls the shawl closer around herself and looks up at him in appeal. He stares over her, not quite at me but in the direction of my desk. "If you could just excuse us for a few minutes," he says, still not looking at her. She melts away. Shaking his head, he lumbers into my office and lowers himself into the student chair. "Can't stand that in a woman," he says. "Obscenity. Never could. Don't know what gets into her."

I know better than to register triumph so I keep my eyes fixed on Dale's beautifully typewritten page. "She probably had a hard day," I volunteer. He snorts. "Although I sometimes think she's kind of *down* on me," I add hesitantly. "I don't know what I could have done to offend her."

I keep my eyes lowered. I can tell he's checking me out. Graceful martyrdom, I tell myself. Nice girl. Not like some. "It's not you," he says.

I risk looking at him. My Snow White look, grateful

innocence, wide eyes. Nurturer of dwarfs. He gives me a tight smile. "She's been out to get you ever since Frank dropped her," he says.

I lower my eyes to the papers on my desk again but he's already got my reaction. No defenses: I was a sitting duck. Now I can feel the blush spreading again, all over my chest, neck, face. Don't cry, I tell myself.

"Aw hell, it's not important," he says after what seems like house. "Just some committee stuff. I'll talk to you about it some other time." Breathing heavily he hoists himself out of my chair and wanders to the doorway. "When you're a little calmer," he adds, and disappears. I count to ten, then get up very slowly and put on my coat. No crying, I tell myself as I walk down the hall. Somebody might see.

Jo Michaelson takes one look at me and shoves me into the corner of her couch without even letting me take off my coat. "I've got an afghan here somewhere," she says, pawing around in her file cabinet. "You remember afghans. And this." She flourishes a half-empty bottle of scotch. I let out a piercing wail. "Not scotch," she says and puts it back. "How do you feel about sherry, then?" I nod, snuffling. "Anything else you don't want, you just scream, okay?" she says. "Now tell me about it."

I give her about five minutes of disconnected key words punctuated by nose-blowings while she nods and smokes. I also get through two paper cups filled so full with sherry that most of the second one goes on my collar. When I've finally petered out, she lights another Lucky Strike, hands it to me, and lights one for herself. We sit smoking in companionable silence. It occurs to me that I might be enjoying this just a little.

She finally says, "I guess I thought you knew." I shake my head. "You didn't, huh? Shit, I guess I should have told you."

I can't imagine her telling me. How do you tell somebody something like that?

"It was mostly last winter, end of the first semester, beginning of the second," she says. "I mean, it wasn't a secret, you know? They were going to parties together. I guess I figured, everyone figured, you had an understanding. Know what I mean?"

It occurs to me that I ought to ease the humiliation out very slowly, nothing too violent. Some low-key moaning for starters.

"Then he dropped her. I mean, everyone knew that, too. He *said* he dropped her, you can just imagine Frank shutting up about something like that. I mean, I don't even like the woman and I felt like slugging him. Of course, I didn't know about you or I probably would have."

That warms me a little. To my knowledge, no one has ever before offered to slug anyone for my sake. "Do me a favor," I say. "Don't tell anyone I didn't know." She nods briskly and refills my paper cup. I'm already cheering up. It's not as if it were yesterday that Frank humiliated me, after all. It's been a year now; I just didn't know the details. In an odd way, knowing the details helps. Or some of the details: I'm beginning to wonder who else Frank auditioned before he finally settled on his graduate student. I'm not wondering actively enough yet to ask Jo, but I know I'll ask her one of these days. When I'm feeling strong enough, or maybe drunk enough. I might even tell her how I rejected Frank on New Year's Eve, although I'm not altogether sure she'll believe me. I'm still a novice at public ridicule.

That old hand at public ridicule Ralph Hamilton comes by my office again the next day to see how I'm taking things. I deflect him by explaining with great animation that Dale has done such a terrific job of accumulating and collating that I wouldn't want to change anything. "She's a terrific addition," I tell him. I want to say "to the team," but I can't get it out. Ralph gives me a cozily contemptuous smile before he leaves.

Kiley calls me at home that evening. "I've been thinking we ought to do some publicity on the group," he says. "Given the climate of opinion these days, I think we could attract some new members."

Given Kenny's charges, we'd better, I think. "And you want me to accumulate and collate some notices," I say.

"To what?"

"Fix them up so they look nice and everybody can have a copy," I say.

"Hey, that sounds like a good idea," he says. "Let me just

read you what I have here." As he reads I reflect that Mary Ellen probably types better than I do but that she doesn't have access to the English Department mimeograph machine. Politics is the art of compromise.

I do all the mimeographing Wednesday night, alone, although Dale offers to come in and help. "You've done your share," I remind her while she squints suspiciously at me through the little thicket of false eyelashes she's developed since the last meeting. I run off Kiley's notice on colored paper. Yellow and blue: I decide not to use pink. Color is more effective, also of course more expensive.

For the first time ever I don't arrive in the conference room early. When I come in Tom, Petie Havermeyer, and Ralph are already seated and flipping through the mimeographed sheets I've put in their mail boxes. Dale is pouring coffee into Styrofoam cups. "Eleanor," she says as I'm sitting down, "I want to *talk* to you."

"Light cream no sugar," I tell her. "And Tom likes it black, no sugar. Don't you, Tom?"

"Um," says Tom. Dale turns around and stares at him. He looks at Ralph but Ralph seems absorbed in his reading. "Yes," he says uneasily. Obviously no one has clued him in on how we're treating me this week.

She points to her own stack of mimeographed papers. "About that," she says.

"Terrific job," I say. "Didn't you think, Tom?"

"Um," says Tom.

"I mean, it's like night and day," I say. "Do you realize that last semester I was typing those things?"

"You were *supposed*—" Dale begins, but Tom gives her one of his winning smiles and she stops and lowers her eyes demurely. That's how it works when you're used to sexual cross-currents; your eyelids swing shut of their own accord; you don't have to think about it. Although I suppose the false eyelashes augment the effect a bit. They look heavy.

"Terrific," says Tom. Ralph is looking at me. I can feel his eyes on me, sagging aggrieved eyes with yellowish whites. I don't look back at him. I assume he's concluding I'm a good sport. That's what you're supposed to be if you're not the one they're paying attention to; it dovetails nicely with their condescension. My mother always wanted me to be a good sport, but I was the wrong personality type, too sullen.

Dale puts a Styrofoam cup of coffee by my elbow now and I say "*Thank* you," all graciousness, as if I were used to being served, and take a sip. When I look up again Arnie is standing at his place across the table from me, his soft face twisted with the effort of registering both fury and incredulity.

I compose my own face into what I hope is an expression of bland solicitude. He's clutching his stack of mimeographed sheets in a hand that trembles a little. "Eleanor," he says, "what *is* this?"

"Isn't it terrific?" I say. "We were all just saying how terrific it looks."

"Uh," he says, momentarily thrown, but he recovers and charges on. "Eleanor, you've got 'aspics' here, right in my title. And again in the first paragraph. Aspics. That's like tomato jello."

I give Dale a complicitous smile. "Tomato jello," I say. "Arnie, you're a *stitch*. Isn't he a stitch, Dale?"

Dale is examining her nails. "A stitch and a half," I say recklessly. "You guys see what he's got here? 'Re the Teaching of Composition In Our Basic Program: Several Aspics.' Aspics. Can you *imagine*? Instead of aspects, you see? He thought he'd sneak that right by us but Dale was too quick for him."

"That's not what I *wrote*," Arnie thunders and then stops dead. "Dale?" he says.

"You see, she's got a little question mark here," I say. "In brackets. Sharp girl." I shake my head. "Aspics," I say. "You're a stitch, Arnie. Isn't he a stitch, Tom?"

Tom directs a martyred look at Ralph, but Ralph is watching Dale, who is still examining her nails. "A real joker," says Tom at last.

Arnie looks first at me and then at Dale. Ralph reaches over and pats Dale's hand. "I wasn't joking," says Arnie, and Tom shrinks into his chair. "Anyway, you don't know anything about it."

"Um," says Ralph, collecting our attention. "Um, very funny, Arnie," he says. "Also, your handwriting is kind of hard to read. You know?"

"Eleanor never had any trouble," says Arnie with apparent sincerity.

"That's because we worked *together*," I remind him brightly. "Maybe you and Dale should work together."

Dale looks up from her nails. "I don't think Professor Norford would want me to take off so much time from the main office," she says. Everyone nods hurriedly. She bestows an Annette Funicello smile on Ralph and then turns to Arnie. "I honestly thought it was aspics," she says. "That's what it looked like. You really should be more careful the way you write."

"I have to get my thoughts down while they're still, like, warm," says Arnie balefully. "Eleanor knows."

"But I don't type nearly as well," I point out. "I mean, we were agreeing this is like night and day." Ralph beams at Dale.

At this point Bill Brewster bursts into the conference room. "Jeeze what a balls-up," he shouts. "You see what Eleanor did here, right on the first page?"

We disperse earlier than usual and in a generally nasty mood, although I've maintained my girlish good humor. Tom catches up to me outside the door. "Hey, you feel like a drink or something?" he proposes huskily.

I look at my watch and shake my head. "Gee, Tom, you know I'd *love* to but I've got something on just now."

"Rain check then?" he presses. I smile enigmatically. It won't last, of course. He's too accomplished a toady to be out for very long. But I feel awfully good just the same.

The week goes by rather smoothly, all things considered. Now that I'm committed to a policy of hypocrisy I'm having much less trouble dealing with people. I greet committee members especially with demonstrations of unfettered joy that I associate with large dogs, and they treat me like a large dog more or less, good old Eleanor, what a good sport. The one time I cross the path of Lois Lafferty I assure her that we must have lunch together *real soon*, and she skitters backwards into the janitor's cart. At Thursday's meeting of the composition committee I radiate enthusiasm while the boys pick at each other and scrupulously refrain from picking on Dale, and afterwards both Arnie and Bill Brewster corner me and suggest a drink, which I refuse, regretfully. On Friday, however, a number of things go wrong all at once.

When I check my mail box during the hiatus between my second and third Basic classes there are three things waiting for me, any one of which has the potential to disrupt the tone of the whole week: a fat manila envelope from Corona Publishing bearing my neatly typed address label (*Miss Gabrielle S. De Vere, c/o Nyland*), a plain white envelope with only *Elinor* typed across the front, and an inter-office envelope from F.R. Norford. The envelope for *Elinor* is probably the least dangerous, I decide, which just goes to show how far I've come this year. Then the memo from Norford. Then the envelope from Corona, the envelope with my pornographic manuscript in it.

Arnie waylays me as soon as I get out of the elevator. "Hey, heavy correspondence there," he observes. They can all spot a manuscript no matter what you've got it under, particularly if it's just been rejected from somewhere. Walking along beside me he cranes his neck until he can get a glimpse of the return address. "Corona," he says, and lets out a whistle.

"I'm, ah, reading it for them," I say.

He looks worried. "How come? I mean, why you?"

"Wordsworth," I say. "It's about Wordsworth."

He rears back to look at me, forcing me to stop in the middle of the corridor. "I thought Corona was dirty books," he says in a conspiratorial whisper.

"And Dorothy," I say. "*You* know."

His lips come together in a little sphincter-like pucker. "Oh I think that's going too far," he says. "Some of these people go too far, don't you know? Anyway, couldn't they get sued? For libel or something?"

"It's fiction," I tell him. He looks puzzled. "A dream of passion," I say.

He considers this. Finally he says, "Well fiction is one thing. But passion is something else again, don't you think?" Then he brightens. "Say," he says, "lucky thing I ran into you. I was wondering if I could give you this." He squats down, snaps open his brief case, and pulls out a number of crumpled yellow pages. With a sinking feeling I recognize the tiny, pale, barely differentiated scratches that he calls his handwriting. "I had, you know, like a brainstorm last night, you wouldn't believe it," he says. "I was almost asleep and suddenly it started *coming* to me. Luckily I keep a pad and pencil by my bed."

"Lucky for you," I say. "Uh, aren't you going to give it to Dale to, ah, put into shape so everyone can see it?"

"Well, I was going to do that," he says, snapping shut the brief case, "but I tell you nothing against Dale but she's had *problems* with my work. She can't quite get her mind around how ideas kind of come to me so I have to get them on the wing, so to speak. You know?"

"Kind of shoot them down when they're in range," I say, to show I understand.

He nods emphatically. "Exactly, Eleanor. I've always thought we spoke the same language. Anyway, she said she'd really appreciate it if from now on I kind of typed things up myself, kind of roughed them out if you know what I mean, and I said okay I'd do that, but you know me." He beams. "Two fingers. I mean, it'd take *hours*. But then it just dawned on me, you know how things kind of *hit* you? And I thought wait a minute, there's Eleanor, she's always been what you'd call sympatico, why am I doing this? And so I went looking for you."

"And here I am," I say. I can read the writing on the wall, even Arnie's. "Maybe you could give me the part you typed yourself, too," I say. "Just to start me off."

He snaps open his briefcase again. "I'm kind of embarrassed to have you look at my typing," he confides. "I mean, you're so much better and all." He passes me a sheet of yellow legal paper on which is typed,

*Analysis and prioritizing when you get right down to it
only take so far: nitty-gritty=people=inchrge of
WHOLE ballof wax.
So big question is Who/???*

"It didn't take you long to decide you wanted my help" I observe.

"It took *forever*," he says, and I'm actually a little sorry for him.

As soon as I'm closeted in my office I tear open the envelope from my admirer. Inside is a single sheet of typing paper with a single-spaced paragraph on it. The typing, as always, is impeccable.

Dear Elinor,

It is with a twinge of sadness that I write you for the last time. I would not have thought it would end thus but I am finally convinced your heart is elsewhere and I must bid you "Farewell."

> *Best Wishes,*
> *Your Admirer*

Well, there's a story there, I decide, and I'll probably never know what it is. The admission is frustrating and a little saddening too. Twinged with sadness, as it were. I've gotten used to having an admirer, and it may be a long time before I have another one. I lay the letter aside and open the inter-office envelope.

Dear Eleanor:

Professor Norford is concerned about the amount of supplies that have disappeared since the duplication equipment has been utilized by you. Please advise.

Thank you very much for your attention.

> *Sincerely yours,*
> *D.V. Knapp (Miss)*

So much for my policy of hypocrisy, I tell myself, my late successes dissolving and evaporating as I contemplate my future. So much for subversive activities too. I'll probably be arrested for theft. Somehow the prospect of being hauled in and charged feels only humiliating, not at all political. I can't imagine involving Kiley, for example, or anyone else in the group for that matter. Even if Kiley did suggest that I liberate the departmental supplies—and it's hard now to be sure that the whole thing was his idea—I'm the one who performed the act, the criminal. I can hear Kiley on the subject now: free to accept or reject, free to choose, free to fall. Maybe they'll fire me. Maybe they won't let me even finish out the semester. The prospect, which I've invoked to make my degradation complete, cheers me up a bit.

It would certainly clear my schedule, I tell myself, picking up the manila envelope from Corona and turning it over in my hands. If I were in disgrace I could opt out of my afternoon Basic class. I could forego the big meeting at Kiley's this evening and sit home drinking beer and making plans to leave town. I could get a map. I could arrange to rent a car. I could balance my checkbook and see how much I've got for the getaway. All these ideas are so uplifting that I rip open the envelope with something like equanimity. It's my manuscript, of course, with a letter attached. There are worse things than rejection, I think, and then it hits me, where would I go? And the fragile mood collapses. That's always been the sticking point: where would I go? Meaning, what would I do?

The Corona letterhead is plain to the point of austerity, nothing playful here, nothing even commercial. Dedicated is the word that suggests itself. If you hadn't heard of them you might assume they specialized in something more abstractly elevating, archives or analytic philosophy or psalms. The letter gets right to the point.

Dear Miss De Vere:

I regret to inform you that your manuscript, "The Lenorean Queen," has been judged unsuitable for publication by Aureola Books. Our editorial board felt this story lacked "the feminine touch." We suggest that you consult Aureola's recent release, "Till I Faint," by Miss Olivia LaBarr.

Thank you very much for your submission. Do think of us again if you have another manuscript that might be "right" for the Aureola audience.

Best wishes,
Aurora Madden-Pryce
Aureola Books

I lack "the feminine touch." In quotation marks. What she's saying is I don't have it at all, don't have a clue about female sexuality; I'm probably not even a girl. It's too much to contend with in one sitting, and the worst part is that I can't cancel my third Basic class without calling up Dale, so after a few minutes of numb torpor I gather up my books and trudge off for still another session with the coon. It would be the colon again. My life is packed with fortuitous symbolism. When I get home I open the basement door and call down that I'm feeling sick and not going to Kiley's meeting. Ted comes up a few minutes later to ask if I'm going to be all right and I say, truthfully, that I'm just a little nauseous. "Oh how exis*ten*tial!" he exclaims, and I reflect that Ted may be the only person on whom I've ever had an intellectual influence. After they leave I cry for a while in a way I remember from my child-hood, great shuddering sobs of rage and despair and impotence. When I'm finished I go to bed. I'm there when the telephone rings.

It's a little breathy voice. "Is Tyrone there?"

"He's out at the moment," I say. In times of crisis I revert to the clerical manner my mother instilled in me. "May I give him a message"

"Ah," says the voice. "Well, yes, if you could ask him to call Kathy."

"Kathy," I say. "I'll give him the message."

"Thank you," says the voice. Faint with jealousy I write it down. Kathy. Kathi? Cathi? Somebody has a love life, at least, whereas I don't even have an admirer anymore. Although the whole thing is rather strange, I find myself thinking. It's not as if he's gone off me, more as if he thinks I've gone off him. Inasmuch as I was ever on him, oh so to speak. The more I think about it the stranger it becomes, and eventually I get out of bed again and go downstairs to the breakfast nook where I've left all the papers I brought home from school: letter from my admirer, memo from Dale, manuscript and letter from Corona. And Arnie's newly shot-down ideas, I realize when I've spread everything out on the table. I supposed I'll have to figure out a way to type these early next week. It will be tricky because I no longer have Arnie's typewriter in my office and I don't want to use Dale's.

When Ted and Tyrone get back I'm still in the breakfast nook. I've been sitting with my elbows on the table staring out into the dark back yard and thinking of very little. After they thump around in the basement for a bit they knock at the cellar door, and I call to them to come in and help themselves to bee. They're revved up, full of the meeting and internal politics.

"Well, we're going to have another demonstration," Ted says. "Kiley didn't think it was a good idea, but he got voted down."

"No kidding," I say. It's difficult to give this information my full attention. It feels distant and rather arbitrary.

"Yeah, he said we needed an occasion, something specific to protest, like Miller's arrest. But Tyrone said the war was specific enough and anyway it was hard to keep meeting as a group if we weren't going to *do* things."

"Tyrone shrugs and looks down at his beer, but I can tell he's pleased.

"Oh, by the way," I say, "you're supposed to call Kathy. I'm telling you now so I won't forget."

He snaps his fingers. "I knew there was something," he says. We listen to him clattering down the stairs, and then Ted raises the beer can to his lips. I watch his Adam's apple bobbing as he swallows. Finally I say, "You're chugging." That's what they call it in the fraternities according to several papers I've had on the subject (How I Spend My Leisure Time).

He sets down the empty can. His face is very pink. "Mind if I have another?"

"Okay by me," I say, and he gets up slowly as Tyrone burst in wearing his jacket and a hat I've never seen before, a sort of helmet in leather with ear flaps. Very sharp, I think grudgingly. Lucky Kathy.

"Sorry to drink and run, folks," he says, picking up his beer as he swings by.

"You coming back?" Ted is leaning against the refrigerator holding an unopened can, but he doesn't seem at all relaxed.

Tyrone spins around. "I'm coming back," He says. "I'm not saying when. Don't wait *up* for me, okay?" Ted doesn't say anything. "Okay?" he says, louder this time.

"Okay," Ted says in a strangled voice. It occurs to me that this is somehow familiar. To cover my embarrassment I begin gathering together my papers again. The front door slams. Manuscript and letter from Corona back in the manila envelope, memo from Dale underneath, where no one will see it, letter from my admirer on top—

"Got an opener, Eleanor?" I gesture toward the counter, unwilling to look away from the two new pieces of evidence my admirer's letter and the address label on the envelope from Corona. The address label that I typed myself. It's not just a superficial resemblance either. There's a break in the top bar of the capital E. In *Department of English*. In *Dear Elinor*.

"Ted," I say, "I've just noticed something amazing."

But when I look up, tears are running down his face. He's standing in the middle of the kitchen with the can of beer in one hand and the opener in the other as if it were beyond his capacities to do anything further. His eyes are impossibly blue.

"Sit down" I say.

He does, heavily. I reach across the table, take the beer can and the opener away from him, and open the beer. "Here," I say when he doesn't seem inclined to take it back. He looks at it dazedly, so I get up and get another can out of the refrigerator for myself. When I sit down again he's drinking the beer down in spasmodic gulps. Chugging. When he's finished he gasps like someone coming up for air.

"We're so different," he says.

Like night and day, I think but clearly this isn't what he means. "How so?"

"Oh," he makes a choppy gesture, palm up. "Tyrone, you know. I mean, he swings both ways."

"Swings both ways," I say. I know what that means, God knows, but right now all I can think of is a song lyric, Herman's Hermits, very syncopated and chipper,

This door swings both ways,
It goes in and out—

"And I don't!" he cries. "I mean, I've never been able to get it on with a chick. Never!"

"A chick," I say. There's a part of me that wants to point out that by most definitions I'm a chick, but this is hardly the time to identify myself with the enemy. Ted desperately needs a friend. Which means I've got to act as if I knew all this, all the time. It's another thing I'm supposed to have known. If I were shocked he'd be destroyed. It would be even worse if he ever suspected I'd been entertaining chick-like feelings toward both of them.

"You shouldn't be drinking on an empty stomach," I say. "For that matter, neither should I. I'm going to make us some eggs." He tries to smile at me.

It's after midnight when he finally goes wavering off downstairs and by that time my eyesight isn't entirely trustworthy, but when I spread out the papers to compare typefaces again it certainly seems as though the capital E in Arnie's typewritten notes also have a break in the top bar. "Arnie's reconditioned upright," I mutter into the silence. It was in my office for a long time. But I can't quite get at the conclusions that would seem to follow, and after a while I give up and go to bed.

I spend the weekend stripping and rewaxing all the linoleum, exhausting my supply of the strong remover in the process. I keep the radio on at full volume in case either Ted or Tyrone is considering coming up the stairs to discuss the situation further. It's not that I'm unsympathetic, but I need time to brood over my own lacerations now that I'm once again unreservedly single, without prospects, without admirers. I have only so much nurture in me.

The more I brood, the less I believe I have to lose, and by the time Monday rolls around I'm in a trigger-happy mood, convinced that if I'm going to be shot down it makes sense to take a lot of people with me. I give a pop quiz on the reading to all three Basic classes and not one person passes, which is a record of sorts and may earn me the lowest teachings ratings in the history of the department. As soon as it's time for my office hour I shut my door, dial New York information, and get the number for Corona Publishing.

After some confusion at the switchboard I'm put through to a rather pleasant male voice. "Robert Morris here," it says, articulating very precisely.

In reaction I find I've dropped my own voice to a growl. "I want Aurora Madden-Pryce," I say.

There is a pause. Then the voice says, "Whom shall I say is calling?" Another *whom* person.

"Gabrielle Stephanie De Vere," I growl. I'm aware the growl doesn't really go with the name.

"Oh," he says brightly. "Well. Well, I suppose I'd have to say *I'm* Aurora Madden-Pryce."

"No you're not," I say in my regular voice. "Aurora Madden-Pryce wears pink mohair suits and drinks stingers."

"Oh," he says again. "Oh, well, in a sense you're right, of course, but, ah *that* Aurora Madden-Pryce is no longer with us."

This almost throws me but I recover quickly. "Here today, gone tomorrow," I observe, trying for sinister inflections. "Easy come, easy go. There's just no keeping those porn ladies."

"I'm sorry, I—"

"And that would explain a lot," I say.

"Pardon?"

I clear my throat. "Where do you get your feminine sexuality anyway, D.H. Lawrence?"

A long silence. Then: "I have always been under the impression that Mr. Lawrence had remarkable *insight*." Bullseye.

"He had his finger up his ass," I growl.

"Really!" Mr. Morris is either shocked or charmed. "Well, ah, Miss De Vere, perhaps you have alternative notions of what women, ah—"

"In my book," I say. "*The Lenorean Queen*. You didn't even read it all the way through."

"Oh," he says. "Well, that would be the decision of the editorial board—"

"You don't *have* an editorial board," I say. It just comes

out, but I know as soon as I say it that it's true.

"Well, perhaps not in the technical sense," he agrees.

"Doesn't it strike you as strange that you're in charge of this whole operation and you're not even a woman?" I ask.

"Well, it's a small operation" he says.

The fit is on me. "I'll bet you wrote the first book yourself, *Till I Faint* by Miss Olivia LaBarr."

"What did you think of it?" he asks eagerly.

"I haven't read it," I say. "I'll read it if you'll read my manuscript. With some intelligence this time."

He sighs. "I could do that, I suppose. But you would read *Till I Faint*?"

"I think I could make the time," I say.

The moment I hang up the telephone rings again. "Yes," I say. Clipped, competent, a suggestion of whips flicking.

"Eleanor!"

"Yes!" I snap back.

"Professor Norford want to know when you're going to respond to his letter. We need to know what you've used, *item*ized—"

"You tell Professor Norford," I say ominously, and stop. I don't really have a message that answers to the situation. I do have the tone, though, and her attention. "You tell him," I say, "that if he's concerned about the committee's use of supplies he can take it up with Professor Hamilton. You can also tell him that from now on he can ask you to account for supplies since I wouldn't dream of doing any more work for the committee if it results in my being *blamed*—"

"It's not the committee work we're concerned about," she says.

"I find that particularly offensive," I say. "You can tell him that too." It occurs to me that anything else that happens in this conversation can only weaken my position so I hang up. The telephone starts ringing again as I'm buttoning my coat, but I ignore it.

Lois Lafferty is waiting for the elevator as I round the corner. "Lois!" I cry joyfully. "Hell hath no fury, right?" Her eyebrows come together, but as I continue to bear down on her she darts through the door into the stairwell. I consider chasing her down the stairs shouting similar maxims—the stairwell has a nice echo—but just then the elevator comes and I take this as a sign that I'm supposed to descend decorously. She's nowhere in sight when I get out on the first floor, but I do spot Linda standing bundled up in her coat and muffler in a little knot of graduate students. I wave at her and she detaches herself and comes over. "I need to tell you something," I say, and she nods and leads the way out to the steps, where we're less likely to be overheard. "Has anybody talked to you about the mimeograph supplies?" I ask her. She shakes her head. "Well, there's no reason for anybody to know you're involved," I say. "Or Lee. Dale's on to me, but I'm not admitting anything. I'd appreciate it if you just, you know, didn't know what she was talking about."

She grins. "Who, me?" she says. "Mimeograph supplies? Why that's private property. That's practically sacred." She looks around and adds in a lower voice, "And they can't prove you did anything either, if you don't admit it. Frankly, I think you're just wonderful to have taken the risk when everyone else was chickenshit."

It hadn't occurred to me that chickenshit entered into it one way or another. "Really?"

"Oh sure," she says. "You think philosophy doesn't have a mimeograph? Or poly sci?"

"Oh," I say. I hadn't thought about it.

"They talk big," she says. "Look, I want to tell you something." She pulls her coat around herself and looks at her feet for a moment. Then she straightens up and peers down into my face. "I had you wrong," she says. "I mean, I want you to know you've been absolutely terrific about this. I can't imagine anyone behaving better. And the worst part was I started out believing you were a bitch on wheels."

"What?" I say.

She shrugs. "Well, that was what Frank told me. Of course, that was what he *would* say, but I didn't really know him very well back then."

Linda, I think. Lynda. And that's another thing I'm

supposed to know already.

She's warming to her subject. "I probably could have figured out that anything he said about you was bound to be wrong," she says. "I mean I was just incredibly naïve. I actually respected him, can you believe it?" She shakes her head. "And he's such an *ass*hole," she says.

"Well, not entirely," I say. "I mean, he has his good points."

But she keeps on shaking her head. "A total asshole. I mean, one day I just thought, hoo boy Lynda, you've got to get *out* of here, you know? Like, I'd actually been thinking about spending my *life* with the creep."

Me too, I think. At the very least, putting down Frank in such global terms ought to be my prerogative. "I have to go now," I say. "Thank you, for, ah, telling me you don't think I'm a bitch on wheels." She nods in a friendly way. I wonder as I go down the stairs if that was really what Frank thought. Maybe there's something to it. Maybe I am a bitch on wheels. But selectively, I think.

I don't get any further messages from Norford or Dale, which suggests that Lynda was right and they can't really do anything if I don't make any admissions, but before I go into the conference room Thursday afternoon I spend half an hour in the third floor ladies' room rehearsing expressions of embattled innocence. If Norford is coming after me I won't be able to get anybody to take my side, but at least I can play dumb and they won't be able to pin anything on me. At the moment that's all I really care about. A while ago I would have been in danger of cracking, but that was back when I worried about whether they like me.

I wave Arnie's notes, which I've typed, badly, on Jo's machine, at Arnie as I walk in the door, a propitiatory gesture since he's huddled with Ralph at the end of the conference table chortling in the jowly manner peculiar to senior faculty. On the other side of Ralph, Dale is leaning back in her chair gazing up through stiff lashes at Tom, who is saying earnestly, "You know who you remind me of? I mean, it's just uncanny." Rifts are healed, harmony reigns, I observe. Not auspicious for me.

As I slide into my chair Arnie punches Ralph in the upper arm and straightens up. "Hey, gang," he cries, his cheeks wobbling with excitement, "this is it! I mean Ralph's got something important to say to us. Don't you, Ralph"

Ralph twinkles at him and then more generally around the table. He even favors me with a benevolent smirk. "Well, yes," he says. "A few of us just happened to be talking this weekend—"

"Just happened to be talking!" splutters Arnie. He and Bill Brewster snort happily at each other.

"Between *taking* us, you mean!" cries Tom, in with the in crowd once again. "These guys," he tells Dale. "I don't think I can go on playing with them, they're cleaning me out every time." I look at Petie Havermeyer. He's looking at his hands. Well here's somebody else who doesn't play poker with the boys, I think, ready to give him a comradely smile if he looks at me. He doesn't, though.

"Oh you *guys*," coos Dale.

Ralph raises his voice to carry over the general hilarity. "As I was saying, we were talking and we decided the committee has pretty much accomplished what it set out to do. That is, I think we know what we're looking for now. So we're ready to move."

"Get some really *good* guys," says Arnie.

"What?" I say.

Ralph turns to me. "Advertise," he says patiently. "Write up job descriptions for the people we want to hire."

I must look blank because Tom says kindly, as if to a retarded child, "Specialists."

"A senior and a junior man, to start out with," says Ralph.

"*Good* guys," says Arnie again.

I always seem to be the slow one. Here I was expecting an attack and instead they've stopped even seeing me. "To take over the Basic program," I say.

"Except we won't be calling it that, you know," Arnie explains. "They'll want to figure out another name."

"Why?" I ask.

"Because that's what we've *been* calling it, Eleanor" says

Bill Brewster, and I subside into silence for the rest of the meeting.

It doesn't last very long. Ralph, Arnie, and Tom are deputed to draft a proposal to take to the Dean. "I take it we won't be meeting as a group anymore," I say to Ralph while Dale is gathering up the styrofoam cups and legal pads.

He looks astonished. "We can't just stop meeting in the middle of the term," he says, and I don't have the courage to pursue the question.

Tom climbs the stairs to the third floor with me. "Isn't it terrific?" he enthuses. "It really gives you a feeling of satisfaction to know you've done the job you set out to do, doesn't it?"

"What about me?" I ask him.

"What?" He really doesn't follow at all.

"What about me? That's my job one of the really good guys is going to be taking. What am I supposed to do?"

We're on the third floor landing by this time, and when he turns toward me I can see it's just dawning on him that I'm going to be embarrassing. I move in front of the door to block his exit.

"Well, ah," he says, "I mean, I thought you were on one-year contract."

"Renewable," I say. "I also plan to be alive next year. It would be nice if I could support myself."

"You were planning to stay here, then?"

"I wasn't planning to take a job at Hopkins" I say. "I was on that damned committee, you know. Which should indicate I have some interest in the future of the Basic program."

"Well, yes," he says, "but I figured you were interested. I mean, it's the principle of the things, right? Wresting the Basic program out of the hands of the schoolmarms."

"Tom," I say very quietly, "who are the schoolmarms?"

"Well it's just a figure of speech," he says.

"Bullshit," I say. "You can fuck yourself." I leave him standing there, turned to stone for all I know or care.

Attendance is up again in the peace group. Kiley's living room is packed when we walk in, and there is even something resembling a racial mix, two gigantic black football players and an Indian woman who is doing a doctorate in sociology among all those blonds. "The whole world is here," I say to Paul.

"The whole world is *watching*," he corrects me.

The other surprise is that the leadership issue has been resolved, or at any rate the mantle has passed from the shoulders of the old guys, although on balance Kenny doesn't seem much happier. "The big news is that the three days at the end of this month have been designated International Days of Protest," Tyrone announces after everyone has quieted down and he keeps the floor despite Kiley's refractory "Designated by whom?" It's clear we're seeing ourselves somewhat differently these days and that Tyrone is our new ideological prop and stay. When the meeting breaks up Ted and I go out to the Studebaker and wait for him.

The trees along Kiley's street are bare and I can smell frost, but there's still the sense of potency that I've always had when spring is due, and I'm restless in my sweater and jeans and boots, itching to make sweeping gestures and statements. Ted is excited too, but in a way that jars my own mood. He's smiling but keeping his mouth closed as if he were holding in his exhilaration determined not to share it with me. And what could I share? What could I say to enter into that tense, clutching happiness? *Quite a guy.* It's not enough, I want to tell him. *Quite a guy, that guy of yours.* It's not enough, I wanted to tell the Sharis and Ear-lines and Jonis of my high school, but they were too busy identifying with those guys of theirs: being the girl who went with the student body president, the captain of the football team; the leader's girl, the girl leader. It doesn't guarantee anything, I want to tell him, I wanted to tell all of them. Sour grapes, my mother would say.

When Tyrone finally gets in the car all he does is drop us off at the curb in front of the house. "Got to take care of business," he explains, soul brother tonight. You're among friends, I want to say, but I don't dare. I'm afraid it doesn't matter. We stand there as he drives off, then Ted gives me a little chin-up smile. It's who he is," he says. "I mean, that's the way he is. That's all. I can handle it."

For whatever my man is, I am his, I think. Ted as Billie Holiday? He's walking ahead of me, hands shoved into the pockets of his windbreaker, and I admire in a detached way the width of his shoulders, the narrowness of his hips, the strained jauntiness of his step as he bounces onto the porch. Ted as aesthetic artifact. But he hardly compels assent: only Billie could bring off that model of cringing femininity, making self-abnegation into a triumph of assertion, and then only in art, not in real life. A pas-sage from Janet's letter comes suddenly into my mind: *if he left you you just have to say he was an asshole and it was all for the best.* Glib, I thought when I read it. Hackneyed, intrusive. For the first time it strikes me as kind. Not that Ted is ready for this sort of advice or any advice at all, certainly not from me. Nurturing, yes. Counsel, no. I'm not sure why I'm offering either.

He comes in with me and settles down in the breakfast nook while I hang up my jacket and find him a beer. There's something about sexual martyrdom: you assume it gives you privileges. And of course I'm probably the only other person to know about all this, which presumably gives me privileges too, creates a unique bond between us. I don't feel especially privileged right now, and this rather shocks me. I find I'm thinking of alternative ways to spend the evening.

He takes a gulp from the beer bottle ad sets it down carefully. Monitoring himself, I see. "Well Eleanor," he says, "and what's been happening in your life lately?"

"I'm quitting," I say. As a declaration of intent it's too emphatic, especially if you consider that technically I don't even have a job after this semester, but it expresses perfectly my state of mind at this moment.

Out of the depths of his misery he gives me the beginnings of a pained smile and then checks it and looks merely puzzled. "Quitting what?"

"Quitting working here, in this department, at this university." I'm articulating very precisely, which gives me a sense of commitment to what I'm saying. I hadn't known what I was going to say until the words were out.

"You're kidding," he says.

"Why would I be kidding? I'm not doing anything here. I've had it. I'm leaving."

"But what will we do without you?" he wails.

I shrug, although the question has thrown me. I didn't know I was leaving. I didn't know I was needed, either. "You'll manage," I mutter. It occurs to me that I wouldn't be at all pleased if it turned out he couldn't manage.

After I send him downstairs to bed I sit up drafting my letter of resignation from the committee. I'm aiming for something terse and caustic but what comes out is a long howl of humiliation at having been employed as a go-between in the business of procuring two really good guys. In the end I decide that I have to choose between laying out my grounds for complaint and retiring with some semblance of dignity so I settle for a short sentence to the effect that my other work is demanding my full attention. Not everybody would opt for dignity, but then not everybody has done without it for as long as I have.

I go in even earlier than usual on Monday morning to type it on Dale's typewriter in the main office. I've decided on Dale's typewriter because it's accessible when Dale isn't and because it's an IBM Executive with variable spacing and I've always wanted to use one of those. The variable spacing turns out to make correction almost impossible and I have to begin again six different times before I achieve a perfect version of my one-sentence letter, but the final effect is fairly impressive and suggests that I've had my secretary type it. I put the original in Norford's mailbox and carbons, in order of increasing smudginess, in the boxes belonging to Ralph, Arnie, and Tom. Jo Michaelson wanders into the mail room scattering Lucky Strike ashes over the floor while I'm doing this and stands watching me and blowing smoke out of her nose until I'm finished. Then she says, "I've got a great story to tell you. How about lunch tomorrow?"

"I can't wait," I say, and she wanders out again, ignoring Petie Havermeyer, who flattens himself against the door frame and looks after her cigarette with twitchy-nosed disgust. I ignore him too, even though it's clear he wants to say something devastating about ladies and Lucky Strikes and in public. If I want to hear that sort of remark I'll call my mother.

I'm almost to the outside door when I hear "Miss Nyland! Oh, Miss Nyland!" and when I turn around there is Louise Feitelson running down the hall toward me. It takes me a moment to realize that it's Louis Feitelson, in fact, and in hesitating I lose my chance to escape or at least to get the conversation to a more re-moved spot. She catches up to me outside the door to the main office. Through the door I can see Dale removing the dust cover of her IBM Executive.

"I just wanted to *thank* you," explains Louise shrilly. She's standing too close to me, and the effect is that I first lean and then step back while she first leans and then steps forward. I have to stop this movement consciously, otherwise I'll end up flattened against a wall. "For the A-minus," she adds in what seems like an even louder voice. "It really brought my grade point up."

"I grade on effort," I say, also loudly. "Too," I add as an afterthought. I hadn't really counted on having everybody know I gave Louise and A-minus. Or having anybody know for that matter.

"I'm not saying I didn't *deserve* it," Louise continues, inching forward. I see now why I didn't recognize her at first. The glasses are gone. Not replaced, gone. Her eyes look exposed and a little obscene. Her hair is different, too, bulgier on top.

"Have you considered eye makeup," I say. It just comes out. Louise has that effect on me.

She gives a little neighing giggle, new to me. "I'm going to start as soon as I get used to my contacts. My roommate's going to show me." She hunches up her shoulders self-consciously and adds "Nylons too."

"Ah," I say.

"No ankle socks," she says. "Like, nylons make your legs look better, don't you think?"

I rear back and look down at her legs. They still look bumpy. "Much," I say.

"You see, I'd been thinking about what you said about change, how it might be for the better" she says, blinking at me with desperate sincerity. "I mean, I'd never thought of it that way—"

"You worked hard for it, you deserved an A-minus," I interrupt in my Miss Brooks voice. I'd rather not admit to the grade, but I'll claim it rather than taking responsibility for this transmutation. Not only do I actually feel nostalgic for the old Louis, who at least had the innocence of her frumpiness, but I resent having the burdens of creation thrust upon me. I'm not really interested in the role of creator. If I'm going to do *The Rainmaker* I want to be Katharine Hepburn, not Burt Lancaster.

"Well, thanks," she cries. "Say, maybe we could have *coffee* sometime—"

"I have to get to class," I say quickly.

"Well gee, then, thanks again."

"You're welcome," I say, and realize that Ralph has just gone into the mail rom. "Got to run," I say. She nods cheerfully, still standing in front of me so that I have to dart around her to get out the door. She'll do all right, I decide as I scuttle off down the sidewalk. The ones that don't notice they're in your way nearly always do.

I snap at all three of my Basic classes for being unprepared, although I don't quite have the nerve to give them another pop quiz. I comfort myself by reflecting that last Monday's pop quiz did accomplish something even if it didn't alert them to the possibility of another pop quiz. It established me as a hardass. I heard about this last week, or rather overheard it in the Pub, and today as I snap at them I keep the word *hardass* in mind as a kind of mental talisman. It's even an identity of sorts. I repeat it to my-self while I'm walking back to Schwindemann, invoking it as protection against my office hour, when Ralph, Arnie, or Tom—or, the worst-case scenario, all three at once—can reason-ably be expected to drop by and demand an explanation for my letter of resignation from the committee.

Once I'm behind my desk, however, I'm at loose ends un-til someone shows up, so I get out a sheet of typing paper and write *Hardass* across the top of it by way of a reminder. After a few more minutes of psychological flexing I get bored and write below it,

"You talking about me, boys?"

The bunkhouse fell silent as one by one they raised their eyes to her lush figure, silhouetted in the doorway against the vivid fuschias, purples, and tangerines of the Wyoming sunset. In her blue Levi trousers, stretched almost beyond recognition by the curves of hip and buttock and enticingly ample thig, she was at once a woman so desirable that something in them rose to salute her and an embodiment of authority, one whom they could not but obey.

"Well?" Although her face was in shadow each of them was aware of the lip curling in contempt. Or was it contempt? The tallest and leanest and biggest of them, him they called Phoenix, narrowed his eyes and leaned forward.

"Hard. . . ass." She drew out the word, as if considering it seriously. "No." And now the smile was frank and open, if mocking. "Not hard. Firm, perhaps." Collectively they widened their eyes.

"Or perhaps you'd rather judge for yourselves." They looked at one another in wonder, sinewy Phoenix, big-biceped Fred, young Tom of the olive eyes. For now she was fumbling with the silver buck-les of her tooled Mexican belt, and now the belt hung open and her hand was moving down the path of her zipper

"Um," says somebody from the door, and I whisk the paper off my desk and into my lap. It's the janitor, looking so em-barrassed that for a moment I forget he can't have seen what I was writing. "Empty your wastebasket," he says, not looking at me.

"There's nothing in it," I say, still in my hardass mode.

Unnecessarily brusque, probably, but it feels too good to stop all at once. I think of all the drafts of my Lenorean novel, all the mistyped committee notes, all the aborted tries at wanting and being wanted that have gone into that wastebasket. My own peculiar grievance file. Over and done with now, I think. "I'm out of strong remover," I say.

He nods, almost as if acknowledging my new authority. "Have it for you tomorrow," he says, and vanishes.

There is a note in my mail box the next morning impeccably typed and perfectly centered on departmental letterhead:

Dear Miss Nyland,
 Please make an appointment with my secretary
to speak with me at your earliest convenience.
Yours,
F.R. Norford

He's slipping, I conclude. Am I supposed to make an appointment with him at my earliest convenience or to speak with him at my earliest convenience? But I'm intrigued enough by the notion that my convenience enters into the scheme of things to look into the main office, where Dale is brooding over the coffee urn. She looks subdued, I think, and then realize that she isn't wearing her false eyelashes. I wave the note at her.

"Norford wants me to see him at my earliest convenience" I say. "It's convenient for me now."

She straightens up. "I'll see if he's in."

I know it's one of those conventions, like *at your earliest convenience*, but I'm feeling sensitive about phrasing these days. "You know if he's in or not," I say. "He has to go right by your desk."

"I'll see if he's in," she says, and disappears into the inner office. After a moment she comes out again. "He'll see you," she says.

Norford's desk is as clear and as glossy as before, although it has gathered more pictures, one of a middle-aged woman who isn't smiling and two more of the English Springer

Spaniel. I lower myself gingerly into the imitation leather visitor's chair. Today he has several pieces of typing paper lined up in front of him. One of them is definitely my letter of resignation from the committee. He gives me a frosty smile as I yank my skirt over my knees.

"Miss, um, Mrs. Nyland. It's been a while."

"Yes," I say.

"When we last talked," he says, enunciating beautifully, "I suggested that you inform us of your intentions for next year. You sais at the time you weren't clear what they were."

"Yes," I say.

"Yes," he echoes. "Well. May I, um, ask if you're clear at this point?"

It isn't at all what I expected. "No," I say finally. "I'm not clear. I mean, not totally."

"Ah," he says. "Well. Perhaps it might help if I told you what we have in mind. I am in a position at this point to offer you a continuation of your present contract to extend over a three-year period. Do you follow me so far?"

"Yes," I say.

"As ah, um, a lecturer in this department, in the Basic program. I which, I've heard, you're doing an excellent job."

"Thank you," I say automatically.

We both stare in embarrassed silence at the pictures on his desk. He concentrates on the English Springer Spaniel while I examine the face of Mrs. Norford. I assume it's Mrs. Norford. Finally he pulls himself together and gives me a teeth-baring smile that makes me think of small mammals at bay. "Well, Eleanor," he says, "what about it?"

"Can I have a week?" I ask.

His brows come together, but he only draws in his breath and lets it out very slowly. After he's finished this he says, "Well, the department is trying to, ah, firm up its plans for the coming year, you understand, so I'll only emphasize that we'd like to know as soon as possible. As soon as it's possible for *you*, of course, Miss, ah, Mrs. Nyland."

More reason to get going right away on those really good

guys, I think, but I can't quite bring myself to mention them. I struggle out of the chair and hold out my hand. "I'll let you know as soon as I can," I say. He shakes it, too, although I can see he has to make an effort.

Jo takes me to the faculty club again. After our drinks arrive she leans across the tablecloth, sprinkling it with ashes, and whispers throatily, "Ralph and his boys went to the Dean last week."

"I'm on the committee," I remind her. "Was."

She cocks her head like a parrot. "Was?"

"I resigned last week," I say. I'm going to elaborate, but at that moment she explodes into her drink and has to bury her face in her napkin. I'm not sure if it's a sneeze or hysterics, so I keep an eye on her until I'm reasonably convinced that she's laughing. She's lost a lot of gin in the process.

When she finally emerges from the napkin she has lipstick on her front teeth. I keep motioning toward my own mouth to let her know, but all she does is shake her head and cackle. Finally she asks, "Anybody ever tell you you're a survivor, Eleanor?" but the waiter arrives before I can remember if anybody has. "Well," she says after he has taken our order, "So you want the rest of the story?"

"Please," I say, sipping carefully at my Manhattan. After watching Jo I'm pretty sure I don't want any of it getting up my nose.

"I wish I'd been there," she says. "It seems Ralph and the boys decided Basic was better off headed by two expensive men than by two cheap women. Really *good* guys, they said. With degrees in the field. It's a field now, did you know?" I nod. "Maybe I can publish in it. So anyway there they were, bright as little buttons, with this proposal they'd cooked up and typed up and mimeographed and passed around and Norford *loved* it. But of course they hadn't much thought about the Dean."

"The Dean didn't love it," I say.

She shakes her head happily. "The Dean doesn't love Norford much. Norford thinks he's going to be the next Dean. For that matter, Ralph thinks he's going to be the next Norford. I mentioned that, didn't I?" I nod again. "So when the Dean hit the ceiling Norford covered by hitting the ceiling too. Ralph's in bad odor. So are his boys. Not his girl, evidently."

She looks too innocent. "I'm not his girl," I say.

"I was speaking analogically. His boys, his girl, you see?"

"It doesn't *work* analogically," I say, and then remember Dale's diminished eyelashes.

"So Norford's going to offer you a job. He has to, really. It's you and me at this late date."

"He did offer me a job," I say. "This morning." She looks as though she has inhaled more of her martini so I wait to see what will happen, but she only raises her eyebrows at me. "I said I'd tell him within a week whether I wanted it," I say.

She snorts again, nearly tipping over the martini glass. "You didn't even know you had him by the short hairs."

I think about where the short hairs might be located. "It *felt* like I had him by the short hairs," I say. "But that wasn't why, you know. I'm really not sure I want the job."

The minute I say this is hits me that Jo is the last person I ought to be telling, but she only asks, "What else would you do?"

"I don't know. What would you do? I mean if you hadn't decided to do this?"

She sits back in her chair and begins picking her teeth with the ornamental toothpick that came with her olive. "I don't know that I did decide to do this," she says at last. "At least, I don't remember anything as definite as a decision. The problem with academic work is that in ways it's just a continuation of being a student. You go in. You never get out."

"Out," I echo, and wonder where that is.

Friday's meeting of the antiwar group is held in one of the Pub conference rooms, where we all sit on metal folding chairs prearranged in an egalitarian double circle on the shiny hardwood floor. Perhaps because of the change in ambience I'm conscious of divisions within the group the moment I walk through the door. On the far side of the circle Lynda, Lee, and Kenny have convened what seems to be a caucus of people with hair. Lynda spots me and waves at the same time that Kiley, flanked by Charlie and Paul, announces "And here's Eleanor!" so that I have to stop suddenly to wonder with side I'm on. The problem is that I don't feel as if I'm on anyone's side, or rather that there's no side that really includes me. I end up waving around the circle and going to sit with a little knot of foreign students, who ignore me.

I'm puzzled at first that Tyrone stays by the door, where he's lounging with one of the black football players and getting hurt looks from Ted. I discover fairly soon that it's showdown time, and that Tyrone is staying behind to pick up the pieces. The trouble begins when Kiley stands up to speak and is shouted down by a claque located near to Kenny but not obviously including him. Political ventriloquism, I decide, and wish Kiley wouldn't insist on getting up again.

"It's the lowest level of rabble-rousing," he shouts now over the cries of "Sit down!" "Mario Savio stuff, don't trust anybody over thirty. That's absurd! Don't you think, Ted?" Ted can't hope to speak above the noise, but he nods soberly. "Charlie?" Charlie, an old hand at this sort of thing, mimes disgust. "Will?" Will, on the far side of the circle from me, shrugs like a standup comedian.

"Don't trust *me*," he calls. "I'm forty-eight." A ripple of laughter and things begin to calm down. Inasmuch as oratory can carry the day, Kiley's got all the technique.

"Eleanor?"

I didn't ask to be part of this. Now I pull my head down into my shoulders as if that would tamp down the resentment I feel at Kiley's bland solicitation. "I'm not thirty," I mutter.

"Louder!" calls somebody across the circle.

"I'm not thirty," I say, louder. "I'm not. I came here as a wife and I stayed here as a teacher. Those are both *old* things to be." The noises are dying down. I'm not over thirty," I call, very clearly. "I'm not thirty. I'm twenty-six."

"Well, that's hardly the point." Kiley is clearly put out. I'm not playing to his cues. "It's not literally thirty, that's not what we mean, it's an attitude, a state of mind—"

"It wasn't literally schoolmarms either," I say before I realize that no one will have any idea what I'm talking about. "Oh hell," I say, "I wish you all wouldn't assume I'm so damned mature. It's an insult really." Better not to go on, I think. What I mean is sexless.

"Age isn't the issue," Kiley begins.

"Age is the issue for the draft!" Kenny counters, and they're off again. I stop paying attention after a few minutes. It's a power struggle. Its consequences are crucial to the future of the group. It doesn't seem to have a lot to do with me.

A letter for Miss Gabrielle S. De Vere c/o Nyland is in my mail box when I stop in after my second Basic class on Monday morning. As I don't have time to cloister myself in my office, I take it with me to my third Basic class where I break down and open it at the lectern while I'm waiting for the bell to ring. The first paragraph is so promising that I go on reading after the period has officially begun, while the students fizz and sputter around me. After I've reached the postscript I dismiss the class and read the whole thing again.

Dear Miss De Vere:

I am delighted to inform you that your manuscript, "The Lenorean Queen," has been judged suitable for publication by Aureola Books. Our editorial board judged the work especially "right" for the Aureola audience inasmuch as it reaches a conclusion in which a wide range of characters employ various means to an uplifting resolution.

"As it were" I murmur to the empty room. I've never seen a group of Basic students move faster. Obviously they felt they should clear out before I came to my senses. If that's what Aureola wants I can do it again, I tell myself, elated by the unaccustomed sense of expertise, my Wild West fantasy for starters. Already I'm getting the cast in order, the hardass boss-woman, him they call Phoenix. And there are more where those came from. Romantic porn, probing the abyss with the Eternal Feminine. Pastoral Porn: *Melt With Ruth*. And all of it quality, class porn, the work of a near-Ph.D. I turn back to the letter.

Please sign the enclosed contract and return it to us at your earliest convenience.

Very sincerely yours,
Robert Morris

P.S. I enjoyed our telephone conversation and would welcome any contributions of an editorial nature that you would care to make. Perhaps we might get together, should you ever decide to leave the groves of academe. You might even consider taking a more active role now that Miss Madden-Pryce has gone on to pastures new, as it were. Do think about it.

P.P.S. Have you had a chance yet to read "Till I Faint"? I would be most interested in your comments.

P.P.P.S. By the way, are you really an English teacher? (!)

"Till I Faint" will have to wait, I think, a faint moué downturning my perfect lips. Make him beg for it. And no, I decide, I'm not an English teacher, not really. Something of an editorial nature really seems more appropriate to my hardassed typed. After all, I seem to have bullied Mr. Morris into coming up with a job for me, and at a remove of over a thousand miles. Imagine how exciting it will be for him if I'm around to bully him on a regular basis.

I take the contract home with me and read it after dinner in the study while I drink Pepsi and envision leaning across the bar of the chic Manhattan nightspot I frequent. I'm telling my escort, in black turtleneck, refreshingly understated after all that white tie, that I'm a pornographer. "A what?" he inquires. "But you look so young." I'm working on a Brigitte Bardot pout in pale apricot lipstick when the telephone rings.

I'm convinced the phone can hold no surprises for me but once again I'm wrong. It's my mother. "Hello dear," she twitters. "I didn't disturb you, did I?"

"Mother," I shriek with all the vivacity she instilled into me in eleven years of conversation drills. "How *nice* to hear from you." All it takes is the sound of her voice and I revert.

"It's nice to hear you too, dear," she returns. "Lovely

weather here. How's the weather there?"

"Chilly," I say, and feel responsible. "But spring is on its way," I add to indicate optimism. I don't want her to think I'm *down* about it.

"Listen," she says abruptly, for the first time in our shared history violating the procedure, which is to maunder on about the weather for at least another five minutes. "Um, I suppose you're the one who sent me the slip from Penney's," she says.

Somebody else in this town sending you underwear? I think. "I'm afraid so," I say.

She ignores the sarcasm, or perhaps she doesn't regard it as sarcasm. "I mean, it was nice of you, dear," she explains wistfully. "Bob was just, um, curious."

"No kidding," I say, but I'm intrigued by this information, implying as it does that their relationship has its complications. "You don't have to tell him," I suggest. "For all he knows you have an admirer in Middle America." She startles me by giggling. "Is that what he thinks?" I ask.

"Well, I told him it was probably nothing at all," she says. "Probably a mistake of some sort."

"You didn't point out that it was likely to be from me?" Obviously she didn't, although I would have expected even Bob to have picked that up.

She sighs. "Oh, I believe he thinks you're still in New York, dear." I sit down on the bed, provoking a great creaking of springs. "You see I've always thought it would be fun to *visit* you in New York one of these days," she adds.

Whether or not I'm there, I think. I wasn't aware my mother was capable of so much duplicity. Or any duplicity. I'm rather impressed. "You could visit me here," I say, and then wonder what's come over me.

She gives a little ladylike snort that makes the receiver buzz. "Oh, I don't see much point in that," she says. "Where you are sounds a lot like here. I certainly wouldn't want to go visiting somewhere you could mistake for Salina."

This is news to me as she's always maintained that all places are fundamentally the same. I'd assumed that anywhere she hung her hat was Salina. "There are similarities," I admit. "Actually, I'm going back to New York in a couple of months. To work. For good, maybe."

Silence, except for the crackling of the connection. No direct questions, I remember. "Ah, Frank and I have um," I say. "Separated. We're getting a divorce. He isn't here anymore."

More silence. She has to work up a response, I figure. This isn't one of those situations you can handle by remarking on how nice it is.

"Well, I'd never really seen you as the wife type," she says at last. "If you know what I mean." I don't, I realize. I don't know if that's a compliment or an insult. She certainly didn't raise me to be a wife, but then that was pre-Bob. Presumably she's the wife type now. "I mean, I always thought you were the type to be a big success," she says. "At something. I'm not sure what, though."

"Really?" This is so astonishing to me that I flop back against the pillows, causing the springs to shudder resonantly. Ever since I can remember she's had me down as the classic type, the librarian type, the type that fades into the background with the easy attenuation of the born nonentity. I can't imagine how we get from there to the big success. I'd thought that for somebody who was my type, success was not only impossible but in bad taste.

"I'll let you know when I find out what it is that I'm a success at," I tell her guardedly. I don't know how much she can handle at one time.

Ultimately it's the idea that I'm the successful type that persuades e to throw the dinner party. I'm an old hand at dinners, after all, I remind myself a little frantically as I write out my shopping list on one of the index cards I was using for my Wordsworth notes. We're having the pot roast that went down so well with Frank's committee, cooked with garlic, basil, bay leaf, plum tomatoes and a whole lot of red wine, along with noodles, a spinach salad and a caramel custard. "You do all this from scratch?" marvels Tyrone, who has volunteered to drive me to the IGA and help me carry things, and I sigh in a way that he might interpret as jaded and offer to show him how it's done.

"If you're really interested," I add, but as it turns out he is, which is probably a good thing given the hamburger stew. On Saturday he shows up in my kitchen wearing of all things an apron and hangs around sipping at the red wine and opening cans for me while I chop and dredge and sauté, accompanying myself with a running commentary. "A good cook always cleans up after herself," I tell him, and then realize that this is another priggish axiom I've inherited from my mother, even to the intonations.

All he says is "Makes sense," and wipes off my knife blade. What's intriguing is that he's genuinely interested in cooking and doesn't seem at all worried about crossing gender boundaries. His interest dignifies what I'm doing now; it's almost as if he's taking notes. I'd never thought of cooking as a body of knowledge before, something I can teach.

By this time we've both had a lot of red wine. "What happens if you don't brown the meat?" he asks.

"You get a pink gravy," I tell him. "Very unappetizing." We make retching noises and stagger around the kitchen for a while, and then I show him how to tear up the spinach. "Bite-size pieces," I explain. "Bigger bites."

"I didn't even know you could eat it raw," he confesses.

"I didn't either until I went to New York," I say.

"Huh," he says and tears away in silence for a while before observing, "New York's the kind of place that *changes* you, isn't it?" I glance at him quickly but he seems perfectly serious.

Around five o'clock I go upstairs and rummage around in my closet for something suitable. There isn't anything, of course, so I end up wearing a professorial skirt and blouse with the rhinestone earrings and high-heeled pumps from the Christmas party. Jo Michaelson rings the doorbell as I'm teetering downstairs.

"I brought gin," she says, showing me. "Also tonic. And a lime." She holds it up. "For gin and tonic, you understand? Seasonal drink." Her lipstick tonight is sort of maroon. It makes her look as though she's bleeding from the mouth.

"It's supposed to get below freezing again," I tell her.

"Spoilsport," she says, but I'm grateful. I hadn't given

much thought to the question of drinks, and Tyrone and I con-
sumed a lot of the red wine.

"I'll make us some right now" I say. "How do you mix it,
about half and half?"

She opens her mouth and then closes it again. I wait while
she considers. "About that," she says finally. I hang her coat in the
hall closet and then carry the bottles into the kitchen.

Lynda and Lee arrive next, bearing wine, the kind that
comes in a basket-covered bottle you can use later to hold candles. Ted and Tyrone emerge from the basement to a burst of
music, Dylan again. "We thought we might contribute some
sound," murmurs Ted. They also contribute a bouquet of carna-
tions wrapped up in florists' paper. It's the first time anyone has
ever brought me flowers. I put them in an old beer bottle. By the
time I've made two more gin and tonics Jo has settled herself in
the big overstuffed chair that dominates the living room, the one
I think of as Frank's chair. "There's an occasion?" she asks suspiciously. I keep an eye on her drink: she's going to need a refill
pretty soon.

"Not really," I say, at the same time that Tyrone is saying
"Eleanor's under thirty."

"Twenty-six," I say.

"I'm twenty-seven," says Lynda, looking surprised. We
carefully avoid each other's eyes as we note the implication:
Frank ditched me for an older woman. For some reason it makes
me feel better to think about it that way.

"Well, I'm not telling anyone how old I am, but I'm definitely one of those people you can't trust," says Jo, holding out
her glass to me. Obediently I take it into the kitchen. As I'm pouring the gin I hear Ted's earnest voice raised in protest.

"I'd be ashamed to think that way," He's saying. "I mean,
it's incredibly *pueri*le." Jo just cackles. Lynda intervenes to ask
something about the International Days of Protest.

"International," Jo is murmuring as I come back in with
her drink. "Now that rings bells."

"Oh, we don't mean it that way," Ted assures her.

"I do," she says. I give her the glass and she takes a large
swallow before putting it down on the arm of the chair. Tyrone is

looking at her speculatively.

"You might think about coming to a meeting just to see what's going on," he says to her. "I mean, with Eleanor leaving we're going to have a leadership vacuum. We could use somebody with experience."

Leadership, I think, but Jo snickers as she turns to me. "Doing a lot of mimeographing, are you, Eleanor?"

It's one of her sybilline remarks. "How did you know?"

She raises her eyebrows. "Leadership. For women."

"I'm not asking you to do that," insists Tyrone.

She drops her eyes and starts fumbling in her purse for a cigarette. He shoves one of my ashtrays across the carpet toward her. "I'm not an organization type anyway," she mutters. "I talk back."

"We could use a little more of that," says Tyrone. Ted shoots him an appalled glance.

By the time we're ready to sit down to dinner everyone is in a fairly unbuttoned frame of mind. I burn my fingers trying to pick the bay leaf out of the gravy and then slop more gravy on my schoolmarm skirt carrying the pot roast to the breakfast nook table, extended for the evening with Tyrone's collapsible card table. Tyrone teaches Jo something called Give me some skin, man, which involves slapping someone's palm while looking knowledgeable about it, and we all practice giving each other some skin until our palms are red. Ted explains while I'm tossing the salad what a teach-in is and why that's what we're calling our demonstration next weekend, and Jo nods and blows smoke at him.

We go back into the living room to finish the wine, and it's then that Jo says to me, "So you're really leaving."

"I put the letter in Norford's box yesterday," I say.

She grins. "Wish I'd been there to see him get it. Where are you going?"

"New York," I say. "I've got a lead on a job in publishing. Not in a very, ah, major company."

Tyrone raises his eyebrows at me over the rim of his wine glass. "You'll keep in touch?" I nod vigorously. It hadn't occurred to me before that I should keep in touch. I hadn't thought there was anybody to keep in touch with. "I mean, I'll be headed that way fairly soon, I suppose," he says. Ted looks stricken. "I'm an actor," he says to Ted. "Really. I mean I'm trying to be. Actors have to get to New York sooner or later."

Lee, cross-legged on the carpet, looks at him with interest. "You planning on leaving the group?"

He shrugs. "Who stays with the group? The only people who are going to be here forever are the professors." Jo snorts. "Anyway, I don't think the revolution's going to start on this campus."

"Don't put it that way," cries Ted.

"I didn't hear a thing," says Jo, waving her cigarette in his direction. "Revolution? No revolutions here. Nobody here but us moderates."

"Anyway, there are a lot of very important things happening on this campus," Ted continues, looking as if he's trying not to cry. "Actions against ROTC and the military recruiters—"

Tyrone leans over and pats him on the shoulder. "You'll make a great professor," he says.

The party doesn't break up until almost one, when Jo stands up and says "Great evening," to me and "I'll think about it," to Tyrone. Lee and Lynda leave at the same time, and Tyrone and Ted disappear into the basement a few minutes later. I'm surveying the wreckage in the kitchen when Tyrone peers around the door again.

"Why didn't you ever mention you were only twenty-six?" he asks.

"Too intimate," I say. I can see he's filing it away to think over. Now he steps into the kitchen and closes the door behind him. "That friend of yours, Jo. She's wonderful. I hope she decides to come to the meeting next week. Can you imagine what just having her there would do to all that talk about old guys and young guys?"

I lean back against the counter and smile at him. He can be in my revolution anytime he wants.

"But what I really came up to ask was if you needed help with the dishes," he says now.

"Are you kidding?" I wave my arms at the mess. "Next week maybe. I'm going to bed. You go back down there and try to make that sweet boy feel better."

He looks at me intently and then smiles. "He is sweet," he says.

Alone in the kitchen, I stand over the stove dipping left-over noodles one by one into the leftover gravy and then eating them until it occurs to me that what I want to do now is call Janet. It should be all right. She works late. As I go upstairs I can hear Smokey Robinson and the Miracles moaning in the basement, Ted and Tyrone's music for doing unspeakable things to each other.

"Oh, it's you," says Janet when she finally answers. "Don't you know it's three fucking thirty in the morning?"

"I thought you'd be working," I say. "I'll call you back at a better time—"

"I *am* working," she snaps. "I just asked if you knew it was three fucking thirty in the morning."

"It's only two-thirty here," I say.

"Here. Podunk."

"Yes," I say.

"How's the porn coming?"

"Oh, it's done," I say. "One book is, at least. All these women stop fooling around with each other and come to terms with the universe."

"You're kidding" she says.

"No. They like it. The porn people, I mean."

"Maybe I'd like the first part, before they stop fooling around with each other."

"You might," I say. "Anyway, that's why I called. They like it. So I'm coming to New York, to work. I was wondering if I could stay with you for a while until I get my own place."

There is a long fuzzy silence before she says, "Okay. But no funny business."

"I'm not interested in you," I explain with dignity. "Mainly I'm interested in Mick Jagger, at least when he's in town. But I'll settle for Dylan."

Something like a hoot comes across the wires, and then she says, "You and half the city. As long as you don't mind waiting in line."

"Oh I don't mind," I say. "At least I'll know what I'm waiting for."

"Aren't you a little old to be a groupie?" She sounds put out. Injured vanity, no doubt. Even if you don't want any funny business you don't feel great about being supplanted. I know all about that.

"No," I say, "I'm exactly the right age, which is quite a bit younger than you, you'll remember."

She chooses to ignore this. "You're writing about women who come to terms with the universe?"

"Through the love of a good man," I say. "Good men. One per good woman."

"You believe that stuff?"

"Oh course not," I say. "This is fiction. A dream of passion."

"Not *my* dream," she says. "Fuck it."

"Fuck yourself," I say.

The screech is so loud that I have to hold the receiver away from my ear. "You mother should hear you, Ellie," she cries. "Jesus, a lady never talks back—"

"Fuck that," I say, inspired.

"Fuck *you!*" she shrieks back. "Come to the big city, baby, I'd love to see you."

"Fuck the big city!" I cry.

"Fuck Podunk!"

"Fuck pornography!"

"Fuck Mick Jagger!"

"Damn right," I say. "Or someone like him." After I've hung up I lie on the bed listening to the faint orgasmic groans of Smokey Robinson and the Miracles below me. They depress me enough that I turn on the radio and miraculously catch the tail of my song,

> *No satisfaction,*
> *No satisfaction,*
> *I can't GET NO—*

Of course, I think, and sit bolt upright on the bed. No satisfaction. Striving. Mick Jagger as romantic hero. As Faust. I can teach it now. It all seems unbearably portentous and then, just as suddenly, unbearably pretentious, and I collapse on the bed again muttering "Fuck that" in varying accents, ubiquitous rock-star Cockney, Eva Gabor refugee, Texas ranch-hand. It might be a good idea to work out an all-purpose Western accent, come to think of it. In New York they already think I talk funny.

If I had a Western accent of course I'd have to dress to type. The hardass boss-woman type, maybe. Rawhide mini-skirt. With fringe. Lots of different belts. Whips.

I work out variations on this costume until I fall asleep.

ABOUT THE AUTHOR

This is where the author biography text goes.

CPSIA information can be obtained
at www.ICGtesting.com
Printed in the USA
FFHW010932311018
49038912-53337FF